Basavaraj Naikar

Trends and Techniques

Basavaraj Naikar

Worldwide Circulation through Authorspress Global Network
First Published 2008
by
GNOSIS
E-35/103, Jawahar Park
Laxmi Nagar, Delhi-110 092
e-mail: authorspress@yahoo.com

An Imprint of Authorspress

Basavaraj Naikar: Trends and Techniques
ISBN 81-89012-55-X

Printed in India at Tarun Offset, Delhi.

Basavaraj Naikar
Trends and Techniques

Edited by
JAYDEEP SARANGI

GNOSIS
Publishers of Educational Books

Preface

> Out of the dark it whirls back
> Into a darkly mysterious house
> Is it the earth within?
> Does it keep us waking, give brief respite?
>
> ('Dawn', *A Rain of Rites*, Jayanta Mahapatra)

Basavaraj Naikar (1949—) is a beguilingly simple creative writer, translator and bilingual critic. He has written both in Kannada and English. He teaches at the Department of English at Karnatak University, Dharwad, Karnataka, India.

Naikar's publications in Kannada include *Paduvana Nadina Premavira, Huchchuhole, Kollada Neralu, Jogibhavi, Nigudha Saudha, Asangata, Kannada Asangata Natakagalu, Vatsalya, Samrachanavada, Beowulf, Gilgamesh Mahakavya* and *Bharatiya English Sahitya Charitre.* His English publications include *Sarvajna: The Poet Omniscient of Karnataka, Musings of Sarvajna, Critical Articles on Nirad C. Chaudhuri, Shakespeare's Last Plays: A Study in Epic Affirmation, The Folk-Theatre of North-Karnataka, Sandalwood, Sparrows, Kanakadasa, Fall of Kalyana, Sangya Balya: Betrayal, Indian English Literature* (7 vols.), *Indian Response to Shakespeare, Critical Response to Indian English Literature, Indian Literature in English Translation* and *Perspectives on Commonwealth Literature.*

His *The Thief of Nagarahalli and Other Stories* was shortlisted for the Commonwealth Fiction Prize for the Best First Book from Eurasia in the year 2000. *The Thief of Nagarahalli and Other Stories* records and celebrates engaging whispers of hearts, immaculate. It explores the mystery of love, the mystical element embedded in man-woman relationship and the mythical past of the land. When we read his sories, "world melts into a song". *The Sun Behind the Cloud*, a historical novel, and *The Rebellious Rani of Belavedi and Other Stories* were published in 2001 and well received by the critics. One finds no tangible story in *The Sun Behind the Cloud* but some well-knit episodes of a family life through the verbal appearance of mental organisation. Possession of human language is associated with a specific type of mental organisation, not simply a higher degree of intelligence. There is no better way to explore the essential and distinctive properties of human intelligence than through the detailed investigation of the structure of this unique human possession. The novel is about time— what the bondage of time does to people. The 'gypsy waves' of Time illumine the experience of our lived moments. He seemingly depicts this with an ardent voice. Naikar keeps this aspect of confinement of the masculine supremacy as a thematic matrix.

Basavaraj Naikar, a sensitive critic of literature, reviews Indian literary works regularly for *World Literature Today* (Oklahama, USA). His research interests include Shakespeare studies, Indian English Literature, Anglo-Indian Literature, Commonwealth Literature and Translation Studies. He has an intense bond with music and philosophy. Inward-looking and at the same time deeply rooted in cultural and interpersonal realities, his short stories speak to us in their own engaging simple language. For him, life is a human journey, a journey that dignifies the reader and enriches all who follow the way.

There are actually two forces in operation whenever language is used: centripetal force and centrifugal force. Centripetal force (term/idea from physics) tends to push things toward a central point; centrifugal force tends to push things away from a central point and out in all directions. Bakhtin says that monologic language (*monologia*) operates according to centripetal force: the speaker of monologic language is trying to push all the elements of language, all of its various rhetorical modes (the journalistic, the religious, the political, the economic, the academic, the personal) into one single form or utterance, coming from one central point. The centripetal force of monologia is trying to get rid of differences among languages (or rhetorical modes) in order to present one unified language. Language, for Bakhtin, is also always material.

Basavaraj Naikar has a passion for language, and he uses it effectively to deal with the Indian characters and situations. He succeeds in projecting Indian sociological experiences through their talk and character thought. The value of a society can have an effect on its language. Marriage is one of the recurring images in Naikar. He projects various facets of love and marriage in writings. To him love is a prime source of inspiration and ecstasy. In reality, it is followed by frustration and disillusionment. Woman no longer remains a figure of fairy but due to her own whims and caprices becomes a creature of flesh and blood with all sensuous feelings. Love is pure and love in marriage is a desired wish. Love in common man's eye remains an object of physical possession and experience. Marriage should not make us retreat to the ideas of 'sin': "The same thing /Over and over again." ('Marriage', Nissim Ezekiel)

Naikar is not cynical of marriage but he brings out the mystery in marriage, i.e., the bond keeps the wife and husband united; but all their indifferences and frustration move as undercurrents throughout their life. At times, Naikar portrays a man with a weak will, wavering and inoculate. Modern man's predicament is well presented in his short storis and novels.

His works explore some of the most discerning critical responses related to postcolonialism, raising some seminal issues as to how races are linked with nations, and how the imprisoned space liberates the post-colonial textual space in the horizontality of events chained in the discourse of resistance. The hyphenated space in any literature of subjugation or marginalisation marked by a systematic process of cultural domination through the imposition of global code on local experience seems to be the key issue in any postcolonial text. Roots of characters in Naikar's works are profoundly lying in the Indian mythology. The Western world cannot divert his philosophical journey. Like Raja Rao, for him, writing is a *sadhana*. All these factors have created Basavaraj Naikar as the modern *Sidhha* to India and the cultural ambassador of Indian philosophy to the Western world.

I record my indebtedness to Basavaraj Naikar who never failed to reply my letters/e-mails of enquiry. I am deeply beholden to him for his profound love, care and encouragement for my project. With regular e-mails and exchange of letters with the writer I've come to know that Love is a human phenomenon and we divinise it by loving it. This anthology is rich with two articles from his pen.

I express my gratitude to all scholar contributors who sent their articles and kept inquiring for the development of this project. The anthology could not have been in the hands of the readers without the most useful comments and timely suggestions received from all of my academic friends and scholars interested in Basavaraj Naikar. I am unaware of copyright problems of the published articles. I have used the articles submitted to me. The views expressed by the authors in this book are their own. They don't necessarily reflect my views. I must acknowledge with gratitude the distinguished critics, Professor Meenakshi Mukherjee, Professor G.S Balarama Gupta, Dr Christopher Rollason and Dr Subhendu Mund for their valuable suggestions. I'm indebted to the Ramesh Mohan Library, CIEFL, SCILET, Madurai and the library at the Indian Institute of Advanced Study at Shimla. I shall be failing in my sense of duty if I do not appreciate the relentless support and encouragement of my friends, colleagues and family members during the project. My five–year-old daughter, Titas, helped me steering through the raging seas and violent storms, manoeuvring the wrecks and sinks, navigating from the squalls and swells. I must mention Surabika, my little angel, for taking me into the fresh garden of simplicity and innocence. I am thankful to my wife , whose cooperation over the years has been supportive of my academic works. My parents are my powerhouse. I express my sincerity and unflinching devotion to them.

I register my thanks to Sejuti, Dishari, Jayakumar, Archana, Ajanta, Samudra, Udhaya and Saurav for silently inspiring me through a lullaby of memory. I also thank the Managing Director, Authorspress, New Delhi, for the confidence evinced in me and for seeing the book through the press.

Hope this edited anthology of research articles will be of great help to the students, researchers and the teachers of Indian Writing in English. The lamp looks shining outwardly. It is also true that the lamp that illuminates the structure gives substance to the self.

The present endeavour will be considered to be successful if it is able to act as a catalyst for generating new research projects on Basavaraj Naikar; by miracle of creation with close examination of craft.

Jaydeep Sarangi
Jhargram

List of Contributors

Alka Singh, Department of English, Vasanta College for Women, Rajghat, Varanasi, U.P.

Aroonima Sinha, Lecturer in English, C.M. College, Darbhanga, Bihar.

Basavaraj Naikar, Professor & Chairman, Department of English, Karnatak University, Dharwad -580 003, Karnataka.

Bhagabat Nayak, Department of English, Kandarpur College, Cuttack - 754117, Orissa.

Christopher Rollason, 16 rue de Belchamps, F-57000, Metz, France.

Jaydeep Sarangi, Head, Department of English, Seva Bharati Mahavidyalaya, PO-Kapgari-721505, Paschim Medinipur, West Bengal.

Jibesh Bhattacharya, Ananda Mohan College (Calcutta University), Kolkatta, West Bengal.

M.C. Prakash, Departmnt Of English, VVS First Grade College for Women, 2nd Block, 3rd Stage, Basaweshwaranagar, Bangalore – 560079, Karnataka.

Kh. Kunjo Singh, Associate Professor, Department of English, Manipur University, Imphal, Manipur.

Mallikarjun Patil, Reader in English Karnatak University, Dharwad-580 003, Karnataka.

P. Obula Reddy, Professor of English, Sri Krisnadevaraya University, Anantpur , Andhra Pradesh.

Pashupati Jha, Professor & Chairman, Department of Humanities, Indian Institute of Technology, Roorkee.

S.B. ***Singh,*** Professor & Head, Department of English, T.M. Bhagalpur University, Bhagalpur, 812007, Bihar.

S. G. ***Vaidya,*** Sr. Lecturer in English, B. E. S. Degree College, Byadgi- 581 106.

S. ***John Peter Joseph,*** Reader in English, St. Xavier's Autonomous College, Palayamkottai, Tamil Nadu.

T. ***Ravichandran,*** Associate Professor of English, School of Humanities and Social Sciences, Indian Institute of Technology, Kanpur, U.P.

Contents

1

Conflicting Images: Naikar's *The Thief of Nagarahalli and Other Stories*

— Alka Singh

Basavaraj Naikar, a bilingual writer, in Kannada as well as English, has various critical works and translations to his credit. He has edited *Vatsalya* in Kannada and *Sparrows* and *Sandalwood* in English. He reviews Indian books for *World Literature Today* (Oklahoma, USA). His first collection of short stories in English, *The Thief of Nagarahalli and Other Stories* was short listed for the Commonwealth Fiction Prize for the Best First Book from Eurasia in 2000. The various stories oscillate between the elemental and the social, not losing sight of the mythical dimension of life. Drawing inspiration from writers like Mulk Raj Anand, Raja Rao and Chaman Nahal he makes an attempt in writing in the native brand of English and asserts, "Our imagery and style should be redolent of our cultural ethos."[1] In an attempt to be distanced from the Anglo-mania the writer has kept himself aloof from any 'isms' including feminism. The chunks of Indian life presented are a fresh venture to delve into a cultural past and the present covering a vide range of topics wherein each story captures moments of Eternity.

The story, as a genre, has survived through times immemorial, for there is definitely something in the *homosapiens* that pines for a story with a gigantic curiosity as to 'what happened next?' The insatiable desire, to know the unknown is inherent and that's why the story appeals to one and all.

Naikar's *The Thief of Nagarahalli and Other Stories* displays a wide range of situations, desires and passions, lust, thievery, fear, professional rivalry, corruption, poverty, black-mailing, religiously mandated conditions of purity for a woman, the greatest female 'good' being invested in chastity, purity, virginity, virtue and honour, and sexual passion. Worse still this passion is mirrored in all its faces: incest, rape, adultery burdening the woman to ultimately accept the guilt for the crimes committed against them. Under the deviously disguised traditions, religion and cultural values the fear and machinations of women reveal the crisis behind the stories. The stories revealing some ugly escapade of youth or a looseness of temperament as portrayed through the various characters is a collection of thought for years which may have been slow but sure surge of the social revolution.

To define one's value and discover identity is a traditional understanding and a glaring truth of all life and literature. This paper attempts to explore the stream of protest against an idealist civilisation that exalts the spirit and degrades the body, its needs and basic amenities of survival. Ironically, the kaleidoscopic vision of this civilised existence is seen as fragile and barren when divorced from the passionate self. Naikar's stories are of the sojourn of the protagonists into their own unconscious along with the realisation that the experience of the chaos within is crucial to the achievement of the self-hood. It's a discovery of the whole and authentic self wherein the world is transformed and all life-denying characteristics stripped away. There is a subtle attempt to acquaint the female protagonist with herself, to discover what she can relish rather than what she has been taught to like, for one cannot taste with anybody else's tongue. She sees no futility in trying to repress herself for the sake of acquiring the status of an angel in the heaven or house. The treasures revealed in consequence are wholeness and community, overcoming the alienation and rejoining herself with the world.

The second story "All for Gold" dealing with sexual passion sets the tone for some of the other stories in the book. Sangappa, a charming youth and a rich man too, falls in love with a respectable married woman Ganga. Various attempts, manipulations along with bribing the old woman of the village Paramma were chalked out to find a release for the overpowering painful desire of Sangappa. The long years of conditioning in Ganga initially leave her in a state of shock on hearing of the illegitimate desires of the rich young man. It appears to be an "insult to her integrity and family honour."[2] Paramma, for her need and greed of the gold necklace from Sangappa, not to be defeated easily. She persuasively continues: "You must enjoy life before the flower of your youth fades. I am a woman like you and can understand your heart and its secret desires"(44). Ganga vehemently protests but ultimately succumbs out of fear for her reputation on seeing the secretly planted turban of Sangappa in her house. For the pure Ganga, her reputation seems more important than her chastity and Paramma's words echo: "My dear Ganga, you must enjoy life when it is possible in youth. Can 1 have such enjoyment at this old age? You fool you do not know the pleasures of life"(45).

Years of conditioning, of chastity, of virtue seemed to be washed away in a wave of fear—a fear of a superfluous reputation, which though abstract seem to be so very important. It does not take time to reconcile to her new situation. Ganga broods for a short while over her consent, the dilemma, the conspiracy but ultimately decides to face the situation after rationalising things for herself: "Sinning once in secrecy would not be a great problem, she thought. She would be free from all those machinations for good.... She also felt that anticipatory thrill and fear of uniting with a man other than her husband, she felt vibrations all through her body"(46). Ganga eventually considers this as a God-sent opportunity and is "excited at the amorous prospects" (47). Ganga's acknowledgement that "I never knew there is so much pleasure in loving you" (48) involves a willingness to lose control of the self. This surrender is not the woman's to the man but the person's to the body, an act of pure faith, and freedom in humility. The loss of the conscious self is a relief from alienation and solitude.

The two seem to enter an "ethereal world as it were and forgot all about the mundane world... They forgot the 1-Thou relationship between themselves as they were welded into each other in paradisal union" (49- 50). Ganga's husband has undertaken to give the primary fulfilment through marriage and thereafter tries to perpetuate the belief that she need not undertake a heroic journey. None the less the passion portrayed in its raw intensity is an attempt on the part of the narrator to show the transcendence achieved by Ganga and Sangappa. Although Ganga has initially decided to spend just one night yet later she willingly falls into a repetitive performance of the act for she is strengthened by a clearer sense of the necessarily independent nature of the lifeforce. Knowingly the two lovers, oblivious of anything else lose their 'selves' to form one entity. The love that Sangappa inspires in Ganga is aborted in its premature state but none the less even in her solitude at her parents' place she enjoys the spiritual numbness that follows the experience of intense emotion. The "fall" into life ultimately leads to death but at the same time this very fall occasions "growth and the acquisition of wisdom for both individuals and cultures; it also offers love and community, which the condition of stasis and purity does not."[3]

In "Mother's Husband" the narrator appears to distance himself from the pleasant experiences of Chandrasani with Adivesha and prefers to let the experience itself speak aloud of the enthralling moments of pure passion. The story is reminiscent of the incest of Oedipus and Jocasta culminating in shame, guilt and ultimately suicide. Somehow the Freudian complex looms large in the background, the most intimate moment presented between Chandrasani and Adivesha testify to the celebratory aspect of passion which transcends all barriers: "Adivesha was entranced by Chandrasani's marvellous features. Although she had tasted many men, she had never felt so attracted to any of them. Her body began to pulsate without her knowing" (93). The act itself appears to be joyous and autonomous for their "limbs indulged in a sweet but silent dialogue with sharply sensitive automatic responses to the stimuli" (94). Like Lear (father-daughter split), Hamlet (son and father) and Oedipus (son and mother), both Chandrasani and Adivesha surface as great embodiments of human tragedy. The power of the tragic story rests in the sense of inevitability that pervades the story and probably it is the gods that make fate inevitable.

Kamalata (Chandrasani's original name), on discovering that she has married a cobbler, becomes restless, ashamed and curses herself for yielding to her passions. The attempt to undo this one mistake leads her to another graver one, to prostitution with plenty of money and a high standard of living. It is not only professional relationship that she establishes with Adivesha, for "their souls were disconnected from their bodies as it were and soared in the sky like two balloons" (95). The satisfaction that Chandrasani derives that one night makes her speculate: "she never felt as much love for anyone as she felt for this young man" (96). The tragic moment of enlightenment in her dream of having slept with her own son leading to the birth of a child leaves her choking with suffocation, "Oh, did I get a son and a grandson at the same time?"(97) The betrayal of the inner vision leads her eventually to a tragic self-destruction.

Literary works of varied kind show how women use stereotypically feminine behaviour as a survival tactic. The story "She Wanted a Child" exposes the conflict between social expectations and a woman's actual situation. The culture requires Manjula to be chaste, passive, productive, innocent—to be a "good woman"—but her situation demands strength, aggressiveness, security and a stabilising force to sustain herself in the family. The fear of being forsaken makes her tell a blunt lie to her husband but this is not a result of innate wickedness but a realistic survival tactic. The traditional woman is under the constant scrutiny of her husband, so her disguise ought to be subtle but in Manjula's case her foolish glaring lie finds coverage in her God-sent appointment as a clerk in a post-office in Dharwad.

Manjula, having lived according to the requirement of her husband till now, finds herself in a world of chaos, into the void. Her husband, by placing her beyond the security of definition by a man, has ironically been the agent of a fortunate fall into freedom. Her two irreconcilable halves find solace in Sekhar, a colleague. Her boredom coupled with a "sudden surge of emotion" (115) for Shekhar tempts her to indulge in a trip to Hubli with him. She speculates, "Shekhar was more cultured than her husband and longed to be loved by him" (117). This moment of freedom and wholeness that she experiences in the hotel room with Shekhar includes a new sensation of pleasure in her physical and sexual self. Nevertheless, to sustain her status in her husband's house, she needs a child. The desire drives her to steal a child from the hospital. She confesses that the act was committed only to placate her husband, mother-in-law and society. She fights the fragmentation of herself and knows that she'd survive through the situation. The fight to assert herself is essential though survival is not all that easy, it is painful too.

"Coffin in the House" exposes men's dehumanisation of women and the monstrousness of victimisation, which automatically stems from the myth of female inferiority. The story is complicated further by the human tendency not to understand the ramifications of a single experience. Tennyson's dictum "man to command and woman to obey" clarifies that conventional marriages are not based on equality but on a master-servant relationship. Girija's marriage too in "Her Husband Went to America" was based on this. Girija from birth had been bombarded with social images, rewards and punishments, to develop qualities that are feminine and to restrict herself to a 'woman's place'. Despite her loneliness, she dares not transcend those virtues inculcated in her. Her self-restraint even on discovering her husband's second marriage is a reconciliation, which she achieves by consciously hiding her true self behind conventional female role. The 'place' as well as the image that a woman holds in patriarchy is a natural outcome of masculinist desires, needs and values, which is both a convenience and a necessity. For Girija, the serviceability factor that determines that her life is not for herself but to be lived for others' needs enables her to decide in favour of the ascribed role.

Falsification of all types governs various areas of our lives. The truth regarding the societies distorted vision of the world is partially represented through "Fulfilment". Society obscures facts regarding class and caste system although everyone is extremely status-conscious still and very often pretend that the existing differences have disappeared. Bharati, the central protagonist of the story, is faced with a whole raft of obstacles to self-actualisation and fulfilment. The social framework based on dualistic set of values bind a woman's lives by repression and oppression and it is this that confines Bharati to the needle and the hearth. The unidentified discontentment that arise within her despite the "wealth and plenitude of luxurious things" (179) makes her restless. The isolation is enveloping her from all quarters. She seeks momentary relief in the theatre only to be captivated life-long. In venturing beyond the threshold she undertakes a psychological journey to escape from the captivity of her conditioning. It is an aspect of the protagonist's own psyche that has to be overcome in order to gain a free, whole and joyful life: "Her heart was longing for something she could not easily identify.... There was no one to love or to be loved by" (179). The restlessness of her youth is a strong driving force in her isolation and so she tries to find an outlet in her limited space. A legal visit to the theatre under the protection of her father seems the obvious choice; she puts in extra effort to adorn herself in order to be 'pickable'. The fantasy of the marriage myth so strongly inculcated in women—a mystical tale of love, romance and marriage exercises incredible power over how they live their lives. Ironically the marriage myth unconsciously operates upon the consciousness of the women although in reality it may be totally absent. The myth and the forever romance works subtly on the mind of Bharati and thus she finds herself attracted to the handsome actor who enacted Basaveswara, "Bharati was not only enjoying the sight of the actor who played the role of Basaveswara, but was thinking who this actor might be and what his name might be and whether he was married or not" (181). She appears to be most affected by a marriage in the play between the untouchable bridegroom and a brahmin bride: "Bharati was also feeling a turmoil of emotions in her heart. The simple observation of the scenes of the play had induced her speculating seriously about the caste system of the society in which she lived. A sort of love, liking, admiration, longing, serious thinking and deep passion—all these feelings were simultaneously operating in the pores of her tender limbs"(182).

Years of passivity in the house has taught Bharati probably one traditional lesson of her life and that is she cannot be happy by her own efforts but rather through the intervention of a powerful protector who alone can make her secure. It was this that makes her search outside for those hidden moments of happiness. Her years of cherished dreams of being loved, and appreciated, sharing her husband's life, supporting, encouraging and working in a manner to please him and consequently seeking 'fulfilment' in the heaven of her world make her break through the essentially 'feminine qualities' to take the initiative to approach Chandrashekhar. Nevertheless, Chandrashekhar hesitates seeing her richness and social status: "Chandrashekhar stood staring at her dispassionately. Bharati stared at him longingly" (184-85). A second thought and discussion with friends propels him too despite his limitations, which he discloses, to Bharati: "You are a Brahmin lady whereas I am a poor untouchable. You belong to a fabulously rich family and I am only a poor actor and musician" (186). The obsession of Bharati's gets the better of her, transcending all barriers, caught in her passionate moments and so begs Chandrashekhar to accept her. Ultimately logic and reason lose their value and he succumbs to her tears: "He felt that it was his duty to protect the woman who had surrendered herself to him" (187). The male 'sex-role conditioning' comes to Bharati's rescue for he explicitly states that he has planned to 'help' her since it is inevitable for her to stay without him: "The softer, weaker and more dependent the woman is, the stronger and more powerful the man appears; the more a servant the woman the more a master the man. And the more the woman withdraws into home and gentility, the more the arenas of government and industry are left to the iron grasp of warriors and warrior values."[4]

Despite the fact that Bharati is socially stronger, her projected feminine weakness makes her surrender herself to the man who out of a brave magnanimous attitude decides to accept her. Ironically she is all that a man desires in a woman and yet in no instance we get a glimpse of his desire for her. It is an acceptance out of 'her' need and to assert his masculine attitudes. His desire for her, which according to situation may have been unattainable, is veiled by chivalry. Her elopement followed by marriage leads her to "consummate the experience she had longed for so many years" (190).

Bharati is content to receive the 'positive goods' in life after her connubial ceremony, in return for a complete surrender of the beautiful self, passivity of nature and for her services rendered. For the illusion of security, love and satiation the realisation dawns that she has battered her soul. The sorrow that she causes her father and the family name troubles her. Very soon pain and isolation once again envelop her when her husband is implicated in a murder. The 'good' woman in her without any complaint and grudge, bears the twelve years of misery and isolation and once again seeks solace in her handsome son Viswanath, named after her father.

The myth of living happily ever after is coupled with the pain that it often brings. The love, romance and marriage dream that pervades her in youth drive her to her fate and all else is subsumed under the title "ever after". It appears that the whole existence of a woman is wrapped up in a quest for a mate and on acquiring one all else is decided, and what really follows this appears to be irrelevant because the 'all important' has been done with. There appears to be viable alternative for all other aspect of our lives, public as well as private are governed by a wifely estate. The life that she indulges in, despite her victory, project her in a hopelessly lost state—she forgoes her identity, her self-concept and her sense of autonomy and direction. The serviceability factor worked itself to portray that her life is not meant to be lived for herself but the need of her husband and her child to beautifully fit into the cultural image defined for her.

References

1. Basavaraj Naikar, *The Thief of Nagarahalli and Other Stories.* Calcutta: Writers Workshop, Lake Gardens, 1999, Preface, p.1.
2. Basavaraj Naikar. p. 38.

3. Carol Pearson and Katherine Pope, *The Female Hero*, New York and London: R.R, Bowker Company, 1981, p. 142.
4. Sheila Ruth, *Issues in Feminism*, London, Toronto: Mayfield Publishing Company, Mountain View, California, 1990, p. 85.

2

M.M. Kalburgi's *Fall of Kalyana*: A Study in the Revolutionary Perspectives

— *Kh. Kunjo Singh*

Dr. M. M. Kalburgi's *Fall of Kalyana* (originally written in Kannada as *Kettittu Kalyana*) translated into English by Basavaraj Naikar bears the mark of success. Authored by a great Kannada scholar and translated by the masterly hand of a tactful, sensitive and adept Professor of English the play may be studied in the perspectives of revolutions in (various aspects of) the socio-cultural, politico-economic and religio-philosophical/ideological firmament of the twelfth century Karnataka launched by Basaveswara.

Passing through the experience of agrahara-culture, temple-culture and palace-culture Basava grew from static to dynamic level. He progressed from *karma* to *dharma,* from the physical to the spiritual and from the spiritual to the social and ultimately suffered in the hands of static force. The main concern of the play is Basaveswara's social philosophy of dynamism without neglecting his spiritual philosophy.

Basaveswara's reaction to the traditional static environment creating a dynamic socialism to be ultimately destroyed by the static situation forms the theme of the play. The play presents Basava's rejection of Vedic Brahmanism just to promote the concepts of *kayaka, dasoha, istalinga, jangama,* social equality, gender equality, etc. in the right perspective making him relevant to modern times. Basava's principles of a unique and unparallelled total revolution may be studied more elaborately under the following sub-themes:.

Religious Revolution

One important perspective of the play *Fall of Kalyana* is religious revolution launched by Basaveswara. He discards *Vedic* religious system of wearing sacred thread, which distinguishes a person to be a brahmin instead of a human being. Giving the reason for his rejection of the sacred thread he argues:

> *Basava*: No, no I don't want this sacred thread which makes me a brahmin instead of a human being. I would like to follow the path of *dharma*. I don't want this sacred thread, which pushes me into the swamp of *karma*. I don't want it. (Sc. 1, p.1)

To Basava, the sacred thread is a tool of brahmanisation which is the basis of caste system. Brahmanisation of a person brings caste discrimination. Caste. Because under this system the lowest of the four classes, i.e., the *shudras* are termed as untouchables by ignoring their human dignity. Rejecting the priest's glorification of the brahmins by wearing sacred thread and reservation of it for only brahmins and males Basava aptly argues:

> *Basava*: What? Are *brahmins* holy and *sudras* unholy? Who say so? Am I holy whereas my younger sister Nagalamba unholy? This is the reason why I say that the sacred thread is not merely a string but a symbol of contempt for life. (Sc. 1, p. 2)

Opposing his own father Madiraja's idea of the priests being big people learned in the *Vedas* and the *Agamas* and thereby leading the society according to the ethical codes, Basava expresses his views:

> *Basava*: Father, these people cannot lead the society, but on
>
> the contrary, drag it backwards. They may be big people, but. Truth happens to be even greater than these people and their ethical codes. My soul longs for that Truth. I cannot forsake the Truth.
>
> (Sc. 1, p. 3)

Reacting to his mother's idea of one's being a part and parcel of society and its customs, Basava argues:

> *Basava*: Society? What is society? Who formed the discriminating society? I don't want to corrupt my personality by being part of this society. I will cross the boundary of agrahara-culture and defy society.
>
> (Sc. 1, p. 3)

While receiving a summon for an explanation in the meeting of the brahmins in the agrahara hall for his desecration of the holy thread Basava outrightly rejects the summon and fearlessly argues:

> *Basava*: I will not come there. How can the wolves sit in judgment on a lamb? (Sc. 2, p. 5)

Challenging the announcement of the decision of the brahmins to excommunicate his family from the Brahmapuri of Bagewadi for his not wearing sacred thread as a mark of adopting *Vedic* tradition of brahmanism, Basava bravely remarks:

> *Basava*: You excommunicate us from Brahmapuri? This is indeed maladministration in the name of religion. I can live without the help or co-operation of brahmins. If you have courage in you, you may excommunicate us. (Sc. 3, p. 8)

Attempting at a correction of the concept of God and His presence as prevalent within the community of Kudala-Sangama which he has suddenly joined after leaving his parents and home at Bagewadi, Basava in a very learned way explains:

> *Basava*: (Entering suddenly) No, no Lord Siva does not dwell in the vicious and the evil. He dwells only in the virtuous and the devout. God is embodied in the devotees. (Sc. 4, p. 9)

Reacting to the ill-treatment meted out to his son Basava for disobeying the brahmanic religious codes Madarasa consoles his wife, who is anxious of his son's safety elsewhere, by rebuking the Brahmins in the following words:

> *Madarasa*: Don't cry, darling. These Brahmins are ruined by their mechanical reading. These agraharas and monasteries have been destroying the process of thinking from the very beginning. They have been torturing the real thinkers. These fellows are veritable bats and owls which have never seen light. (Sc. 5, p. 10)

When Basava's father Madarasa dies, the neighbouring brahmins do not like to extend a help in the cremation of the dead body since the deceased family has been excommunicated. But they decided, ultimately, to cremate the corpse if Basava apologises to the brahmins and resist himself and his sister from touching their dead father. The Brahmins say that Basava has to suffer this because of his antagonism towards society. But contrary to their expectation Basava challengingly remarks:

> *Basava*: Society, what society? Who has made these cruel laws and regulations? I want neither your society nor your funeral rites, Don't touch my father.
> (Sc. 8, p. 15)

Thus, Basava emphasizes the social welfare through a dynamic religious revolution.

Social Revolution

Another important perspective of the play *Fall of Kalyana* is Basaveswara's social revolution. In order to bring justice in society, which is the artificial creation of man, Basava, on the eve of his departure along with his sister, gives away all his properties to the servants. But the servants are hesitant to accept the properties. To remove the hesitance of the servants Basava shows his generous and self-sacrificial ideal by saying:

> *Basava*: . . . This property has grown on account of your sweat. I am giving it back to you. You release me from the debt I owe you. Later you distribute the land, the house, the open site and the cattle among yourselves. Now, come on, you take this money. You take this gold and silver, you sweeper, take these ornaments; you take these utensils.
>
> (Sc. 9, p. 17)

Basava stands against the *agrahara* society which looks down upon non-brahmins and other communities thereby making artificial social differences. Defying such a society, for a new harmonious and peaceful society, Basava boldly says:

> *Baṣava*: When I am rejecting your society, what do you mean by excommunicating me? I don't want your water or fire or even your sacred thread. Take it back. (Sc. 1, p. 3)

To Basava, wearing of sacred thread means division of society into brahmins and non-brahmins; whereas the wearing of icon called *istalinga* means a class-less and harmonious society. Emphasizing the worship of *istalinga* for social unification Basava rightly remarks:

> *Basava*: . . . . .Whereas the sacred thread divides society, the Siva string unifies it, ... The sacred thread classifies people on the basis of their birth, the *istalinga* does it on the basis of merit. (Sc. 11, p. 21)

While discussing the nature of society with his guru Isanyaguru, Basava rejects the view of the *Vedic* philosophers who preached only the individual welfare but not bothered about the social welfare. In order to bring harmony the two divisions of society, the exploiters and the exploited should be united. Emphasizing social equality he says:

> *Basava*: The divided society should be united like the confluence of two rivers i.e. Krisna and Malaprabha. (Sc. 16, p. 33)

Supporting his own idea of the need for removing caste system and untouchability for establishing social equality he tells a *jangama* the following words:

> *Basava*: In my social system there are neither brahmins nor non-brahmins. We are human beings and equal to one another. (Sc. 21, p. 43)

According to Basava there should be no question of difference of gender in every field of life. Commenting on the genderless idea preached by the Socio-Spiritual Academy Basava utters:

> *Basava*: ..Because our principle that a woman should not be afraid of menstruation if she becomes a devotee, the woman in our society has been developing a confidence that she is not 'untouchable'. Her interaction with the Socio Spiritual Academy has been boosting up her confidence further. (Sc. 22, pp. 45-46)

Basaveswara is really against the cruel social practice of *sati* or *masti*. Once commander Marasinga died on the battlefield and consequently his *velevali*, Sankappayya severed his head to attain heroic Heaven like his master. Now his widows were going to die on his pyre. Rejecting such inhuman systems in society and stating the need to abolish them Basava remarks:

> *Basava*: What cruel practice is this?. . . . Who said that the death of velevali and masti are holy practices? These are not values, man. On the contrary, these are exploitations masquerading as values. These are exploitations of common people by royal ones and of women by men. (Sc. 25, p. 53)

Basava in his capacity as a minister of the kingdom declared his order of forbidding the sati and the masti and he also announced that a widow can remarry instead of dying under *sati* or *masti*.

Basava stood deadly against the social evil of untouchability and reservation of cleaning dirty latrines for the untouchable people. So he asks an untouchable boy to stop cleaning latrines:

> *Basava*: Stop going there . . . This is utterly inhuman and barbarous. (Sc. 25, p. 55)

When a *sarana* named Nagimayya requested Basava not to touch him because he was an outcaste while Basava was a great man, Basava, rejecting the caste-division, strongly announces:

> *Basava*: I won't allow it to continue. "The earth is common to the temple of Siva as well as to the love of untouchables. Water is common to ablution as well as to libation. Caste is common to those who knowtheir selves." This is my view. None is low or high by birth. The low is he who created this division (Sc. 26, p. 57)

Basava wanted to emphasize on social welfare than on individual welfare. He said that social welfare should be their target in order to rectify the wrong. His effort had been appreciated by the *saranas*. He also promised to remove the difference between highborn and lowborn. So he accepts the food prepared by the untouchable Nagimayya by saying:

> *Basava*: Sivanagimayya. Where's the difference between the food of your house and that of my house? ... You and I are not different from each other. Both of us are *maheswaras*. The food prepared out of the earnings from hard labour is indeed very great food. (Sc. 26, p. 59)

Because of Basava's new experiment in the use of money from the treasury and the awakening of awareness of *kayaka* and *dasoha* principles in principle there has been decrease in the economic and the class differences. Supporting his idea his wife Gangambika expresses:

> *Gangambika*: Even the gender difference has been decreasing gradually because men and women have been participating freely at homes, in the Socio-Spiritual Academy and the lanes of *saranas.* (Sc. 30, p. 65)

Basava's idea of removing caste discrimination through intercaste marriage is supported by his own wife Gangambika and king Bijjala's sister Nilambika who would like to marry Basava. Gangambika also accepts her as her co-wife. Such an act is also an example of women's emancipation, an aspect of progressive society. Defending her own act of marrying Basava against the censure of her emperor brother Nilambika says that society is a man-made system superimposed upon Nature-made system. Some of the meaningless elements in the society are to be changed. Even wealthy and glorious women are cheated of social justice because of male dominated society. Reiterating her argument for the equality of gender she rightly remarks:

> *Nilambika*: What difference? "If a person has a pair of breasts and long hair on the head, she is called a woman and if he has moustaches

and beard on his face, he is called a man, but the inner soul is neither male nor female". (Sc. 31, p. 67)

In the social revolution of Basava, *saranas* take important role by recognising the human dignity of even the prostitute. When Macideva asks if there is any *sarana* who would marry a prostitute as a mark of recognition her human value and that of her child, a young *sarana* bravely responds:

Young Sarana: I am ready. Whether it is the child of a slave or of a prostitute, they are all *saranas* after theinitiation. I am ready to marry her if she is willing. (Sc. 32, p. 70)

Basava's reformist movement had brought about a free society without gender or *varna* or class-discrimination. In that society brahmin Madhuvayya's daughter was married to untouchable Haralayya's son and this is the mark of an ideal society. Commenting on the significance of this marriage Basava remarks:

Basava: If at all this marriage takes place; it is going to be the first example in the history of the world.

(Sc. 34, p. 74)

Political Revolution

Political revolution forms another important perspective in Kalburgi's *Fall of Kalyana*. In the Kalyana kingdom caste system was prevalent. Lower class people were not honoured and counted. They were not enjoying many of the right enjoyed by the brahmins, i.e., upper class people. They also held lowly professions like the cleaning of latrines, sweeping, etc. They were also manual labourers and workers in the different trades of society. Basaveswara's principle of honouring and recognising the status and professions of the lower class people brought about a great change in the political structure. Raising the status of the workers Basava says:

Basava: I can imagine it, Your Majesty. These are the hard working labourers. Therefore, these are my people. These are the masters not merely of this kingdom, but of the whole world. (Sc. 27, p. 62)

Giving the opportunity of sitting on the *Sunya* chair to Allamaprabhu Basava tried to show the gaining of political right to equality by the lower class people. He claimed that it was a mark of the presence of progressive ideal. When the Pontiff Kriyasakti criticises that act Basava gives a fitting reply in the following words:

> *Basava*: . . . Allama is a great scholar and an able proponent of Sarana philosophy. . . The Sarana philosophy believes in the view that a man, no matter whether he is the son of a maid-servant or of a prostitute, will be the veritable Lord Shiva once he is spiritually initiated. (Sc. 35, p. 77)

Defying the king's authority over the people Basava argues:

> *Basava*: Authority, authority, authority. Whose authority on the kingdom? Authority rests with those who love the kingdom and not with those who love authority (Sc.37, p.85)

One significant example of woman's enjoying freedom and individual right is Nilambika's idea of marrying Basava as his second wife. Without any consent from her brother king Bijjala this girl made her own decision by following Basava's ideal of equality of man and woman and so she bravely expresses:

> *Nilambika*: (Rushing out of the crowd) Though a Ksatriya bride, I am willing to marry Basaveswara. (Sc. 30, p. 66)

Basava's defiance in the political front is also brought into limelight by the talk between king Bijjala and Mancanna:

> *Mancanna*: We defy Basava who has been destroying the
> political system under the guise of political reform.

> *Bijjala*: Of course, I support your defiance. But our problem is how to tackle this. (Sc. 37, p. 83)

Challenging the political authority of the king who is hinted at as a non-believer and an individualist and not a socialist and a humanist, Basava proudly remarks that a believer is greater than a non-believer. The moral victory of Basava over the political authority of the king is very sharply indicated by the fiery speech of king Bijjala:

> *Bijjala*: . . . This is the Emperor's decision: Basava who has violated the royal order and religious order is terminated from his ministership and banished from the capital. (Sc. 37, pp. 86-87)

Economic Revolution

The play *Fall of Kalyana* bears the stamp of economic revolution. Basava, the hero of the play is very much against the squandering of money for useless purposes and for the comfort and luxuries of monastery people. Showing a strong contempt for the habit of monastery people Basava says:

> *Basava*: I have heard about it, sir. It has become a regular habit for the pontiffs to use the money earned from unfair dealings for self-aggrandisement.
>
> (Sc. 16, p. 31)

Basava does not appreciate Pasupati Swami's scheme of enthroning his sister's son, young Sadyojata as his heir in a corrupt manner. Showing a strong dislike of such habit Basava remarks:

> *Basava*: If this habit continues, the monasteries, i.e., the public property which have become the property of one caste will one day be the property of one family. (Sc. 16, p. 32)

Being a wise and resourceful accountant and treasurer Basava wanted to set the royal account right. To bring an economic prosperity he emphasized on honesty and hard work. His idea was planning the work and working the plan. For him what mattered for the honest workers was the work and not the day. That Basava could easily bring a revolution in the economic front is clearly indicated by the speeches of servants:

Servant 1: Yes, six months after his arrival have seen the progress of six years, . . .

Servant 2: Because the policy, "Do the right work at the right time," the speed as well as the efficiency of work has also improved. . . . The treasury has been growing because of the economy and holiness in the matters of spending and stoppage of leakage.

(Sc. 18, p. 36)

Impressed by the efficiency of Basava in his account works which brought about improvement of the treasury office, king Bijjala is very happy and comments:

Bijjala: Yes. Because of your policy, "My honesty is my capital", you have been improving the workings of the Treasury Office.

Satisfied with the improvement brought about by Basava's monetary policy king Bijjala offered the position of Finance Minister to him and says.

Bijjala: Basava, so far, you handle the files of the kingdom. Henceforth you will handle the wealth of the kingdom. You have the maximum power of using it directly. This is a fire-ordeal for you.

(Sc. 19. p. 39)

Basava promises that he will remain clean in the midst of money and which will be a sort of self-examination and spiritual purification. He also says that the caste difference between the privileged and the underprivileged is born out of religion "whereas" the difference between the poor and the rich is born out of "labour". When asked by citizen 1 what the way for overcoming our poverty is, Basava very intensively and instantaneously replies:

Basava: Labour is the only way essential for it.

Basava says that it is the moral responsibility of the kingdom to provide the basic necessities of the life of the primary citizens. So, arrangement is made to supply house, cloth and food to them from the treasury. Citizen 1 asks whether the king will keep quiet if the money from the treasury is used for them. To this Basava replies:

> *Basava*: The royal treasury does not belong to the Emperor, but it belongs to you. You have contributed to it without knowing it. You please come tomorrow and collect your papers for your houses, lands and professional tools. Right now, you may take a little cloth and money for your immediate use. (Sc. 20, p. 41)

According to Basaveswara there is no difference between high and low among the people or even profession. The cobbling work done with devotion is better than even the holy service rendered without devotion. He professes the religion of *kayaka-dasoha*. Such an economic system is highly appreciated by Madhuvayya in the following words:

> *Madhuvayya*: Now we have evolved the concept of surrender of money to *jangamas*. Because of this socio-economic theory, the class-discrimination has been slackening gradually. (Sc. 22, p. 45)

In his new theory of using money from the royal treasury for the betterment of the general public the brahmins are not given additional facilities as was done in the past. When the king asked him whom he consulted for rectification of such things, Basava boldly replies:

> *Basava*: I consulted His highness for a couple of times, but it was of no avail. Because His Highness is influenced by you all. That is the reason why, I consulted my own reason and got the answer that the owner of the treasury is not His Highness but the subject.

Basava also challenged the authority of the king over the treasury. When the king wanted to forcibly take him as the owner of the treasury Basava proudly argues:

> *Basava*: Yes Your Highness. You may be the Emperor, but it is the people who have contributed to the treasury. It belongs to them. (Sc. 27, p. 61)

In scene 36 of the play Basava's economic reforms have come out into the limelight through the dialogue of Lakulisa Pandita and Brahmin Naranabhatta:

> *Lakulisa*: Likewise, king Bijjala and his family are fed up with Basava's economic reforms. It is only the downtrodden who have stayed back in his organisation.
>
> *Naranabhatta*: The merchant class also have stayed back as Basava's supporters.
>
> *Lakulisa*: That is quite natural. On account of Basava's *policy of kayaka,* the productive activities have increased to a great extent. Therefore, the merchants have been earning enormous profit. That is why, these money-minded people have been supporting Basava's movement. (Sc. 36, p. 81)

Basava's new economic policy "Labour for the individual and the fruit of his labour for society" has brought about happiness in the Kuntala country. The *saranas* have recognised and followed this theory while king Bijjala does not recognise the theory and warns Basava to give it up. But Basava fearlessly argues in defense of his theory:

> *Basava*: I am ready to give up even my life, but I cannot leave economic equality, social equality and religious equality and the citizens practising these ideals. (Sc. 37, p. 86)

Cultural Revolution

Fall of Kalyana is a play which can be studied in the perspective of cultural revolution throughout the kingdom of Kalyana. Basava is against the crimes committed in the monastery at Kudala-Sangama. In an exchange of arguments the monastery chairman asks Basava angrily whether he thought that crimes were committed in that holy place. Basava gives a fitting reply:

> *Basava*: Why not sir? You have been dragging the temple and the monastery towards crime. The community- culture is being destroyed in the temple and the monastery. More so in your regime. (Sc. 12, p. 24)

Basava is deadly against the *agrahara*-culrure and also the temple-culture because he knows that both are the places of corrupt practices and exploitations. Showing his rejection of temple-culture to his friend Nandikesa Basava says:

> *Basava*: No, friend. These rich temples and rituals cannot uplift us. The practice of the rich class supporting the rich caste through alms and charity has been going on continuously here. There has arisen a situation wherein the poor people have to borrow money from the rich for offering their devotion to deities. (Sc. 13, p. 25)

Basava is also of the opinion that even the simple temples of the villages cannot uplift people. In such temples, pots and bowls, roadside stones and trees enjoy the status of gods. Barking like dogs after worshipping God, Mailara; walking on cinders, torturing the body, walking about naked after worshipping God Bhairava, sacrificing pregnant women, women in confinement or marriageable girls and such other cruel activities have grown around the village temple. The priests in these temples have brought the evil practices even into the houses in addition to temples. The meaningless rituals of birth, death, initiation and marriage have been dragging people astray. So Basava defies Saiva temples and rituals as he has defied *agraharas*. Giving answer to a question of Isanyaguru regarding his opinion of temple Basava says:

> *Basava*: Yes, reverend sir. We must defy the temples which have become centers of misusing God. Instead our legs should be pillars; our head, the golden crown and our body, the temple. Everyman should be a moving temple. Our personality should be transformed from static to dynamic. (Sc. 13, p. 26)

When Sadyojata blamed Basava for spoiling the holy atmosphere of the temple Basava defends his innocence and argues:

> *Basava*: It is you, not I, who are spoiling the atmosphere. I am staying back from it, that's all. (Sc. 14, p. 28)

Basava was thrashed by the monastery people for not following their traditional systems. His guru Isanyaguru says that the monastery has tortured Basava. That is a sign of cowards. He also asks whether his wounds are cured. Showing contempt of the act Basava remarks:

> *Basava*: It is healing over. But sir, I am fed up of being confined to this spot. (Sc. 15, p. 30)
>
> *(Blankly)* Sir, I am disgusted not only with agraharas, but even with these monasteries and temples. . . Financial business has grown rampant in this monastery. The people who have pledged their land to the monastery have been losing them. As soon as it becomes dark, the monastery becomes a centre of black-marketing. (Sc. 16, p. 31)

Basava is very much against Vedic sacrifice. When a drought hit the land *Vedic* brahmins were going to sacrifice sheep to appease the rain god Varuna along with a lamb. The sheep escaped and rushed into the temple. Basava asks the Vipras if it does not bring rain what will they do. Vipra 1 replies that in that case they can have bellyful food with the meat. Reacting to this Basava asks:

> *Basava*: If you need an animal for your food, why this pretext of a sacrifice? Let it be. Why do you need an animal for your food? (Sc. 10, p. 18)
>
> (Lifting the lamb) Look at this lamb which is bleating yet out of fear. (Sadly) O cruelty! O religion devoid of compassion! (Sc. 10, p. 19)

One clear evidence of cultural revolution brought about by Basava and his followers is seen in Macideva's speech:

> *Macideva*: The temple-culture which encouraged the priestly exploitation was replaced by the monastery-culture which, in turn, encouraged pontifical exploitation. Now the Socio-Spiritual Academy that we have established has replaced those two cultures and been encouraging the collective culture and organisation. (Sc. 22, p. 46)

That Basaveswara strongly condemns and rejects temple-culture and monastery-culture which have been traditionally handed down is very vividly shown by the following dialogue:

Priest: Oh, being born as a brahmin, Basaveswara has started destroying Brahmanism.

(Spits out of contempt)

Guru: Having become a Saiva, Basaveswara has started destroying Saivism also. (Spits out of contempt)

When Basava was blamed for paving the way for the *fall of Kalyana* with his new "pride of Jangama" concept, he aptly defends his new *Jangama* concept by saying:

Basava: If the city of Kalyana is ruined, another ten cities like this could be built. But my concern is with the the welfare of the people. That is why I would like to end the caste-oriented Jangama-tradition and establish knowledge-oriented Jangama-culture.

(Sc. 35, p. 78)

Citing the fine instances of their cultural revolution against traditional temple-culture, monastery culture and palace culture to bring a progressive welfare society two *sarana* followers of Basava conduct a dialogue:

Mallibomma: Jagadeva, we established *dharma* in place of *karma* and formulated the body-temple culture in place of stone-temple culture.

Jagadeva: We established the Spiritual-home culture in place of palace-culture and the Socio-Spiritual Culture in place of monastery- culture. But nobody listened to it. (Sc. 39, p. 88)

Ideological Revolution

The last but not least perspective on the play *Fall of Kalyana* is ideological revolution. Basava's ideology is based on *dharma,* which embraces all mankind without caste discrimination. His theory is that by practicing violence, purity, pollution, chanting of *mantras* and prayers and such like day-to-day *karmas* one has lost one's creativity. His ideology is, "The static perishes, the dynamic perishes not." His ideology is again compassion and humanism. To him compassion is the foundation of religion.

To indicate the need for changing the ideology of wearing the sacred thread into the wearing of *istalinga* after a question of Isanyaguru, Basava differentiates between the two as follows:

> *Basava*: Definitely sir, The principle of *istalinga* is clearly different from that of sacred thread. Whereas the latter gives a man the power to conduct sacrifice, the former paves the way for spiritual purity. The holy service to the *istalinga* is necessary for the transformation of material body into the divine one. (Sc. 11, p. 21)
>
> Yes sir.It means service to self-god. It is a day-to-day self-examination paving the way for manifestation of virtues like truthfulness, peace, kindness, etc., thereby humanising the individual. (Sc. 11, p. 22)

Basava's strong determination and endurance proves the success of his ideological revolution. When Basava gets bruises in the hands of Pasupati his sister nurses him and she expresses her fear of the monastery people. But Basava consoles his sister by bravely saying the following words:

> *Basava*: Why are you scared, sister? These people can kill me, but not my ideas.
>
> . . .
>
> These people seem to think that they can do anything in the name of religion if they happen to have a little money and a few evil followers. But the time is not far when this money, these pontiffs and their followers will prove to be the death of this monastery (Sc. 15, p. 29)

Basava tries tooth and nail to revolutionise *Vedic* philosophy of individual welfare. Endorsing the view of his guru Isanyaguru on the need of social welfare instead of individual welfare Basava gives a justification of this revolution in ideology in the following lines:

> *Basava*: So far I had considered individual purification very important, but now I have realised that the purification of society is equally important. Just as

> society cannot improve unless the individual improves, the individual also cannot improve unless society improves. It is, therefore, not possible for people to be happy until and unless they destroy the old order of society and create the new. (Sc. 16, p. 33)

Basava's opposition against the useless Vedic rituals for inducting in a new ideological system under which people will be treated equally and the society will be a welfare one, is evident from the following dialogue:

> *Cowherd:* The robbers captured and took away your cows which were grazing . . .
>
> *Basava:* Please give them these calves also. The cows should not suffer without their calves.
>
> Poor cows!
>
> *Cowherd:* Master, What's this?
>
> *Basava:* This is the right method. What does it matter whether the milk is enjoyed by us or by them? Both are the same for the Lord of Kudala-Sangama.
>
> *Cowherd:* Master, cows are divine like brahmins. Our religion says that we should bring them back, even if it means fighting.
>
> *Basava:* Religion, religion, religion. Who included them in religion? These are meaningless Vedic rituals. They are not agreeable to me. You take these calves and hand them over to the robbers. (Sc. 21, p. 42)

Basava revolutionised the philosophy of Heaven and Hell. Instead of believing in such false notions he emphasized on the principle: "Good conduct is Heaven and bad conduct, Hell and indulged in *kayaka* which arranged *dasoha* for *jangamas*." Differentiating between *dasoha* and charity to convince a *jangama* he remarks:

> *Basava:* No. You must practice *dasoha*. Charity is quite different from *dasoha*. Charity involves transferring the ownership of an object to others.

> But *dasoha* means ownership by neither one nor others. It presupposes the ownership of an object by God and use of it for another man. There is no chance of hoarding in *dasoha*. By not hoarding material things we can live happily and develop our treasure. (Sc. 21, p. 44)

Basava's ideology embraces mass education by distributing palm leaf manuscripts to other places. The *vacanas* are made to act as the representatives of the principles emerging from the Socio-Spiritual Academy and this will improve the individual as well as the society. He tries to develop the Socio-Spiritual Academy as a Literary Academy.

Basava's defiance of the superiority of Brahmins over other castes is an aspect of his ideology of equality of man with man and caste with caste. Emphasizing the need to remove the superiority complex of the brahmins to bring about a casteless, harmonious and welfare society Basava says to his wife Gangambika as:

> *Basava*: My darling, neither the Brahmins are superior, nor the sudras inferior. These ideas are very artificial. It is only when we destroy these two ideas simultaneously that we can bring in social equality and avoid social exploitation. (Sc. 28, p. 63)

In a dialogue between king Bijjala and his queen Rambha the new revolution of Basava against the age-old ideas of religion is judged to be true by the king. But as traditional society is of Brahmins, priests and pontiffs who are believers in the caste system, so Basava's new ideas are not adopted by them. The king, even though he knows the Basava's path to be right, he objects it in favour of the traditional society. The following dialogue shows how appreciable the reformist ideas of Basava are:

> *Bijjala*: My dear Rambha, the cordial relationship between Basaveswara and myself may not last long. I thought he would build a new religion along the traditional path. But his concept of it seems to be quite different.
>
> *Rambha*: Means what?

Not even politics is different from religion. He is going ahead in the direction of total reformation.

Rambha: Are the people attracted towards his ideas of reformation?

Bijjala: Why not? So far, only the down trodden and the untouchables used to be attracted to him. But these days even courtiers like Soddala Bacarasa have been showing their inclination towards him. Even my sister Nilambika seems to have liked his ideology. The other day, I noticed her reading the *vacanas* of Basaveswara attentively.

Rambha:Let it be. My lord, please tell whether Basaveswara's stand is right or wrong. What does your conscience say?

Bijjala: Dear Rambha, you posed a very important question. truly speaking, his path is the right one, but our society has trodden another path and come a long way in it. We all happen to be part of that society. What to do? Basaveswara is right in his principles, but the harsh reality is altogether different.

Rambha: My lord, I understand your dilemma. But I feel that the right path is to accept Basaveswara's ideology. (Sc. 29, p. 64.)

Basaveswara's ideology is so highly appreciated and liked by many people including the king's sister Nilambika for its dynamic values. Giving the justification for her attraction to Basaveswara and consequent marriage to him Nilambika argues:

Nilambika: It is better to be a slave in the abode of *saranas* than to be a queen in the palace. . . Yes, it is better to be the wife of a poor man with dynamic values than to be the wife of a king with static values . . .

I have married Basava with an intention of becoming his ideological wife.

(Sc. 31, p. 68)

Showing the success and realisation of the ideological principle to Basava's wife Nilambika, Basava boldly remarks:

> *Basava*: Rapid changes have been taking place in Kuntala kingdom. Our dreams have been coming true. The *saranas* who are the embodiments of the principle, "*Kayaka* itself is Heaven", have been converting their lanes also into veritable heavens. . . In *kayaka* there is nothing superior or inferior.
>
> (Sc. 32.pp. 68-69)

Recognising the marriage between Silavati and Silavanta, a marriage between a brahmin and a *sudra* as secular and democratic ideology Basava appreciates Nilavati as:

> *Basava*: You live the ideal taught by Prabhudeva in his *vacana* which says, "If husband and wife align their temperaments like two eyes having a single sight, they will be very dear to Lord Guheswara."
>
> (Sc. 34, pp. 75-76)

Basava's ideology is based on the *sarana* philosophy which believes in the view that a man no matter whether he is the son of a maid-servant or of a prostitute, will be the veritable Lord Siva once he is spiritually initiated. For him *jangama* is an indicator of knowledge and not of caste. Its chief motto is to uphold knowledge and defy caste at all levels—be it social or religious. The main thing in his ideology is the dynamising of the society and not the stagnating of it.

In the ideology of Basava the king is not the authority of the kingdom. In an exchange of arguments between king Bijjala and Basava regarding the ownership of authority in the kingdom, Basava says:

> *Basava*: Authority, authority, authority. Whose authority on the kingdom? Authority rests with those who love the kingdom and not with those who love the authority (Sc. 37, p. 85)

Basava's ideology is permanent and his spirit, indomitable. In the last part of the play, Basava is banished for his reformist activities.

But his ideology has left an indelible imprint on the mind of the people of Kalyana as reflected in Mallibomma's words:

> *Mallibomma*: Jagadeva, Basaveswara must have gone far away from Kalyana, in Bijjala's view. But he will be alive amidst us and in us as long as his principles are prevalent in our lives. He will propel our movement from century to century. (Sc. 39, p. 89)

Indeed, the *saranas* of the Socio-Spiritual Academy have decided to tackle violence with their non-violence only because of their principle that "compassion is the foundation of religion".

To conclude, we see that the play *Fall of Kalyana* ends with the attack of Bijjala's soldiers on the *saranas* of the Socio-Spiritual Academy. This is an act of static force destroying dynamic force, which bears the contemporary relevance of destroying humanity by evil selfishness.

Reference

1. Kalburgi, M.M., *Fall of Kalyana* (Tr. Basavaraj Naikar), Bangalore: Basava Samithi, 2003. All the page references are to this edition.

3

Socio-Ethical Perspectives in Basavaraj Naikar's Fictional World: A Study of *The Rebellious Rani of Belavadi and Other Stories*

— *Bhagabat Nayak*

The last quarter of the twentieth century witnessed a tremendous growth of fiction in the world literatures in general and of diaspora and expatriate elements in Indian English fiction in particular. In recent times Indian English short stories are largely written with diaspora elements by Vikram Seth, Shashi Deshpande, Anurag Mathur and Manjula Padmanabhan. But a few others like Basavaraj Naikar continue to write honestly and diligently on Indian themes in the tradition of the great Indian English short story writers like Mulk Raj Anand, R.K. Narayan, Raja Rao, Khushwant Singh and Manoj Das.

With an extraordinary realisation and fertile imagination Naikar has expressed his primary concern on the existential problems of man and his struggles to achieve finality. Through his restless creative passion and with his zeal of a reformist he presents the characters in the Indian situation and sensibility with their loss of values in life. His characters are typically Indian in their sense of values and concerns, and cannot be separated from the mainstream of Indian life. Thematically his stories are based on the Indian themes, and deal with the social and family matters. Broadly speaking they are pan-Indian in dealing with Indian sensibilities and morals, but they are very much regional in outlook. Unlike his *The Thief of Nagarahalli and Other Stories* (Shortlisted for Commonwealth Fiction Prize for the Best First Book from Eurasia in 2000), the second collection of short stories, *The Rebellious Rani of Belavadi and Other Stories*, deals with the broad spectrum of his thoughts and perceptions ranging from the historical to the contemporary, the religious to the secular, the and the elemental to the academic in a realistic way. The entire oeuvre presents the problems and possibilities of life in perspective of socio-ethical resonance.

Teaching for Naikar is both a vocation and a mission, but he has a creative passion for dealing with the Indian themes and sensibilities in his stories. As a bilingual creative writer and critic he expresses his commitment by projecting his insight into the nature and character of man in the contemporary society. He rejoices at the celebration of Indian sensibility in life but looks at life with a jaundiced eye when its richness is affected by the loss of high moral values. He is aware of the tragedy of human situation and uses smiles and tears together glimpsing through the rainbow magnificence of life. His stories are fact-based rather than the fictions of imagination. The touch of realism is so strong in his stories that they appear to have been based on certain actual events in real life. In some of his stories he projects a part of his personality in order to make them real in a semi-autobiographical way so that they look like disguised autobiographies or camouflaging elements of situations in real life. Diving deep into the human psyche he moulds the social and personal matters into a fictional shape. In the graphical description of the south Indian landscape, like Narayan and Anand, he presents the sickness of modern life and man's suffering in his physical and spiritual worlds. Naikar writes post-colonial and post-modernist blend of fiction that is a fine mixture of autobiography, self-reflexivity and of the revaluation of post-modern tendencies.

Through his thematic apperception it seems that Naikar is both directly and indirectly influenced by the Bloomsbury Group of the Mysore Generation consisting of T.S. Satyan, the photographer; R.K. Narayan, the distinguished Indian English Novelist; R.K. Laxman, one of the greatest cartoonists of the world; C.D. Narasimhaiah, the most celebrated English teacher and critic of his generation; Doreswamy Iyengar, the finest *Veena* player of his generation; B.S. Kesavan, pioneering librarian and historian of publishing; A.K. Ramanujan the great poet, folklorist and translator. He is very sensitive to history and culture and specific in his narrative techniques. With a sound historical sense embedded in historical perspective some of his stories look like historical biographies in his fictive world. Presenting suspicion, rivalry, hatred, jealousy, vindictiveness and murder as the aspects of frenzied life he make his stories micro-tragedies by universalising the human plight in the Indian situation. In asserting Indian sensibility his stories can be read as the understanding and judgement on Indian situations in history and contemporary life. One cannot brand them as the bedtime stories; rather they reflect the niche interest of the mainstream popular fiction.

In an attempt to analyse the Indian sensibility in all the twelve stories the paper aims at examining the Indian society in general: human psyche, historical elements, religious practices, and human vices in particular. The title story "The Rebellious Rani of Belavadi" is a historical biography written in the genre of popular fiction. The diachronic description of Mallamma's life and career from her childhood to becoming the Rani of Belavadi kingdom are marked, like those of many great queens of Indian history and myths. When the Indian kings were lacking worthy male progeny or losing faith in the existing ones, they were choosing their female progeny to be the worthy inheritors of their dynasties. Madhulinga Nayaka, the king and Viramma, the queen of Swadi Kingdom had a son Sadasivanayaka and a daughter, Mallamma, with the blessing of Lord Kartika by conducting *Putrakamesthi yoga*. By imploring yogi Siddhabasava they got necessary spiritual guidance for their lives. In the happiness of having a son and a daughter they granted royal patronage to temples, monasteries and the places of pilgrimage honouring both the Saivaite and Vaishnavaite faiths in their kingdom. This act of noble job made them popular in the Vijayanagara Empire during the reign of Sri Krishnadevaraya. Mallamma, the "jasmine" (3) of their eyes, had classic youth, mythic beauty, exemplary patriotism, "purity of mind and body" (40). The prognostication of yogi Siddhabasava on Mallamma's life with some "trigerish danger" (6) made her parents apprehensive. They thought of arranging an antidote for his predestined ordainment by arranging a *swayamvara* to choose for her a suitable life-partner who would protect her.

In the historicity of the text of the story Naikar has incorporated the military achievements and the geopolitical situations of Swadi and its neighbouring kingdoms, and the arrangement of *swayamvara,* an Indian concept, as the historical givens. In her childhood Mallamma had heard from her father how his kingdom was endangered by the colonial Dutch, Portuguese, and English on the one hand, and the Mughals and Marathas on the other. Thus, in the spirit of a great matriarch she kept "the fire of patriotism ... alive in her right from her childhood" (11), and even after her marriage to prince Isaprabhu of Belavadi kingdom. She felt proud to identify herself with the Rastrakuta dynasty to which her husband belonged. She averted the great tragedy of the tigerish danger and remained busy in religious rituals. She became worried for the peace, prosperity and security of her subjects. She often "dressed herself in the military fashion. She tucked the knot of her sari behind her. She tied her hair into a bun. She hung the sheath and sword by her left side and held a shield in her left hand" (21) and appeared in the battle-field like Goddess Chandi with her hortatory slogans disproving rather the traditional notion that woman is weak and helpless, at the time of external dangers to her kingdom. Her tussle with Chhatrapati Shivaji over the cow issue cost her much dear. She lost her husband and punished Sivaji's mischievous soldiers. In the hour of danger she gave proof of her courage strategically and diplomatically by defeating Shivaji with the help of Sri Siddhavira Yogiraj. Shivaji implored her glory:

> I apologise for my mistake in attacking the king and queen of Belavadi without any discrimination. I feel extremely sorry to know that my soldiers attacked Belavadi when king Isaprabhu was said to be making preparations for my reception and felicitation ... Everything has unfortunately misfired (36).

Naikar has inscribed the best aspects of a woman character in Mallamma as a daughter, wife, mother, well-wisher and protector of her kingdom. Her love for her parents, husband, subjects and kingdom, nostalgia and regalia make her one of the best women-rulers of Indian history. Naikar inscribes all the Indian sensibilities with regional culture and practices in her character. Naikar makes an attempt to portray woman as Shakti, the woman incarnation as the destroyer of evil. His Mallamma appears as Shakti, the destroyer of evil, for her subjects. Apart from loss, shock and suffering in her life Mallamma appears as the fine specimen of Indian womanhood. The story has a colonial setting at the backdrop of history, but in the great historicity of India's past Naikar gives a touch of feminist assertion to his woman characters and influence of saintly persons on the administration of the kingdom.

In "Change of Heart" Naikar's narrativisation of an incident has its holistic approach through magic realism. In this story Naikar conveys the message that forgiveness is one of the greatest virtues that one has to realise and teach. Philosophically it purifies the heart like a solvent and functions like a catalyst for the cause of truth. Through the realistic description of a burglary in the house of Sivalila and Siddhalinga he brings out the essential necessity of truth. Sivalila and Siddhalinga are deeply religious, God-fearing and devotees of Goddess Yallamma and Lord Virabhadra. While Siddhalinga has a passion for reading religious fiction, and poetry, Sivalila has her deep attachment to saris, ornaments, gems and other worldly things. One day they get shocked when three masked burglars enter their house to plunder gold and ornaments at the point of dagger. Sivalila gives them all including her *mangalya sutra* against her husband's desire. She knows that life is more valuable than these terrestrial gold and silver. She advises the tall and hefty man in the group, "see man; don't waste this gold by drinking or playing cards. You start some shop or some other business with that money and settle down to a respectable life instead of leading such an irregular life" (47). Her advice appears obsolete at the instant, but in the long run becomes effective. Siddhalinga becomes self-analytical and assesses his past and present for the misfortune, "I have never cheated or hurt even a fly. ... I really do not understand why such a thing has happened to me" (48). In this *Kaliyuga* he becomes cynical about the police and believes in the unholy alliance between the police and the thief.

Naikar expresses his concern for the deterioration of values in human character and apprehends its cathartic effect on life. The loss of values in life invites danger to life as well as to the nation. When the state framed rules, laws and social institutions fail to safeguard the individual's life and property. Naikar as an optimist and humanist expects that love, forgiveness and sacrifice can help to make life effective. The surprising appearance of three strangers and the tallest one's imploring words to Sivalila, are quite relevant to the point:

> You are not an ordinary lady, but a veritable goddess ... We robbed you of your gold, you advised me ... to make use of that money for some useful investment. I have burgled many houses; but never did I receive such a heartfelt advice ... I have now decided to stop thieving and start leading a respectable life ... please take back this gold and bless me to lead a pious life" (50)

Sivalila's sympathetic words, though had a catalytic effect on the burglars, Naikar presents them through his magic realism. Naikar announces them as a message to the mankind like those of Buddha, Jesus and Gandhi. Naikar is certain that sooner or later human values will earn a lot for life in this *kaliyuga* and goodness in man by making truth stranger than fiction.

"Blood for Blood", a story of different genre, is set in a macabre atmosphere. Here Naikar expresses his concern over negotiation for marriage that often becomes a failure owing to tainted family background. The narrator, who aspires for power and glory, plans to negotiate his second daughter Girija's marriage with the son of Viranagouda, a dynamic leader, social reformer and admirer of Gandhi and Nehru. Before finalising the proposal, the narrator by chance gets hints from his old friend Channappa about Viranagouda's family background, of crime and evil association. He gets disillusioned about the family of Viranagouda. He visualises his daughter's murky future in this prospective proposal. The proposal for marriage settlement gets a shift from the family context to the social context. Very realistically Naikar probes into the psychology of the Indian parents who examine and judge the pros and cons of each other's family antecedents before the finalisation of matrimonial proposals. Family reputation, background and social status become the factors for an engagement. The narrator is surprised to know about Viranagouda's crime record behind the backdrop of his social reputation, concealing reality with the mask of elusive appearance. His illusion for his daughter's alliance with Viranagouda's son is shattered when he hears about

Viranagouda's involvement in Kalappa's murder. Kalappa was accused of Viranagouda's father-in-law, Parvatagouda's murder for which Viranagouda connived with the police subinspector Rangappa who murdered Kalappa on the alibi of forcibly trying to escape from the police custody.

The story has a shift from marriage negotiation to crime investigation. After Kalappa's death his follower Nâgasetty starts taunting and insulting Viranagouda publicly. When Nagasetty gets involved in the rape of a flower vender's daughter, Viranagouda takes the public vengeance against Kalappa, as a pretext and murders him, with the help of his followers. As the public credit goes to Viranagouda for the murder of Kalappa, and Nagasetty, his close follower Allabaksh becomes jealous of his boss and gets flabbergasted in self-glorification before the public, endangering the name and fame of Viranagouda. He thinks of Allabaksh's foolishness that "the brainless ... might go on babbling in public and leak out all the confidential information to the villagers ... he visualised worst possible danger if Allabaksh were, by some chance, to turn against him" (71). By inviting Allabaksh to dinner he gets him choked to death by his men. The disclosure of Channappa of the criminal career and background of Viranagouda forms a story within a story. Girija's marriage proposal with Viranagouda's son is cancelled on the plea that she would pursue her higher education. Naikar transcends the Kannada tradition and culture beyond the boundary of nation and state in the ceremony of bride choosing, an ordeal for Girija which the bridegroom's family prefers with all transparency. The priest

> Panchayya went and sat facing the bride, took her left palm and examined the lines on it meticulously like a scientist examining the bacteria through a microscope. While doing this priestly job he nodded his head by way of approval. Then he asked her to stand up. She lifted up her sari six inches from her feet so that everybody could see the symmetry of her toes and ankles ... Panchayya took out a Siva-string of silk and measured her ten fingers and two palms and compared it with her height, i.e., from feet to the vermilion dot on her forehead ... and asked her for her name" (54).

With the title "Blood for Blood" the story appears to be a revenge story. Naikar conveys the message that no crime solves a problem and each crime prompts another crime of greater intensity and dimension inviting punishment for the receiver as well as the giver. He regrets the people's foolish involvement in such nasty jobs that spoil their lives and careers.

One has to accept life "whether it is natural, or inevitable or necessary"(87) by realising that fate plays a strange role in life. This seems to be Naikar's philosophy in the story "Cross-Road" that deals with the sentimental and melancholic separation of two lovers. The context of the story is Indian while the appeal is melodramatically Tagorean, the approach is Tolstoyeque while the fateful incidents are completely Hardian. Man proposes but God disposes and everything is not right in this world for Sivaraj and Kalpana. Ten years is not a long time to forget one's first love. Ten years ago reasonable Sivaraj and love-sick Kalpana had met each other near Baage Aam Public Garden at Hyderabad and the intensity of intimacy grew more with the former's voluntary help to the latter in searching out her sister Pratibha from the zoo side. From that day Kalpana had become a flower on a creeper for him and he thought himself to have been born as a tree to support it. The affectionate words of Kalpana's mother Saradamma to Sivaraj had made him loyal, faithful and obliged to Kalpana's love for him. Sivaraj became closer with Kalpana and her family when he came to know about the vicissitudes of their life in adversity. His career as a student of Jamia Osmania came to an end and his ambition to build his future home with Kalpana got misfired by the Rajakar Riot. Soon after the riot when Sivaraj returned to Hyderabad he found Kalpana and her family missing from their Gagan Mahal Road Residence. Fate's cruel test in the form of riot separated the two lovesick souls nipping immense possibilities in the bud.

In the Indian context riots cause irreparable loss to life and property impairing the progress of society and the psyche of the individuals. The Rajakar Riot had separated Kalpana and Sivaraj for good. Misfortune softened Kalpana's stand for Sivaraj and she married Mohan, the intermediate friend of Sivaraj just as a compromise for support in life. The story has a well knit plot in its cinematic exposure. Sivaraj's visit to Mohan's garage to rapair his bike is destiny's cruel plan to tantalise him with his past love presently lost in life's labour. Ten years is a long time to forget an incident but how can one forget one's first love for someone? The good old truant memories rushed into his mind. Sivaraj discovered Kalpana in Mohan's house as his wife when the latter invited him to introduce to his wife. In Kalpana's non-existence Sivaraj had existence but now in Kalpana's existence he was non-existent. In Kalpana's enplussing of life he felt his self minused from his body in "a sinking and floating sensation alternately" (87). When Mohan left for a car bargain at Secundarabad in the stormy and rainy night Sivaraj enjoyed his life in the status of a guest with fiery remembrances in an embarrassing situation and with choking sensation. On the one hand he regreted Kalpana's misfortune but on the other hand he is unable to expel from his mind the fond memories of the past. He realised that cruel fate had snatched away Kalpana from him for good. On that rainy and stormy night he saved Kalpana's daughter Sarada (the name in fond memory of her mother) from a snake but he failed to save himself from the inner storm of his heart. The appearance of the snake at the beginning and ending of the story is symbolic as Naikar writes, "The entire day's work will be cancelled if you come across a snake on the road" (76). Thus, suspending the disbelief Sivaraj missed the link of his love life.

The fallacy of the hypothesis that love begets love is brought out in the story "Bloodbath". While narrating the affairs of a royal family Naikar presents the defeat of virtues like moral responsibility, love and values by the vices like jealousy, betrayal, hypocrisy and treachery. The historicity of the fact is fictionalised in the excellent account of King Devaraya II's family of Karnataka Kingdom. King Devaraya II is represented as a man of great learning, idealism and as an upholder of values. His love for his orphan nephew, Jayadeva, after the death of his parents is proverbial, and no less than his love for his own son Sivaraya. It is his moral responsibility to take care of his brother's son though many of his well-wishers think him an impractical fool who accepts love and sympathy as the highest ideology of his life. He does not like to discriminate his nephew for his misery, suffering and misfortune. He compensates Jayadeva's loss with his love and care. But on the contrary Jayadeva develops a secret motive-hunting malignity; "I can be the monarch of this Kingdom" (96). When Sivaraya complains about Jayadeva's ill feeling towards him, King Devaraya evades it with his nobility, "My son, please treat him as your own brother. Never be jealous of him"(91) and "this jealousy and other petty feelings are all passing phases. One should not make much ado about them. You must forget these things ..." (94). King Devaraya deliberately avoids his minister's remark on Jayadeva's deceptive nature. After attaining maturity Jayadeva lives in a separate palace and marries without the knowledge of the king. Prince Sivaraya goes to attend Jayadeva's marriage ceremony on his insistence and just to satisfy his father. The joyous occasion turns into a murky melodrama with the murder of Sivaraya, his minister and captains in a pre-planned conspiracy. King Devaraya is disillusioned when he discovers the dead body of his son in the dining hall now turned into a "funeral hall" (98) but it is too late to mend his mistake. Thus portraying the nobility of Devaraya's character Naikar seems to agree with the dictum that unwarranted love can become disastrous, for human nature is unpredictable. Naikar presents it with Devaraya's shocking realisation, "Had he had some power he would have definitely murdered me long back" (98).

"The Circle of Vengeance" is a story on the contemporary theme of underworld activities. The story raises concern for the failure of societal values that give rise to the unsocial and antisocial activities. It focuses on a criminal's choice of lifestyle that ultimately entangles him in the circle of vengeance. Giving an account of Nagappa's career and lifestyle Naikar presents the long stride Nagappa has taken from a porter to a hardcore criminal in his endeavour to become a man. Nagappa's self-evolution takes place in his ambition and aspiration. He earns money, gets married and settles down for a better prospect in life. But nothing runs smooth and every step he takes leads him to his own destruction. Leaving his porter's profession at the Naragund bus-stop he goes to settle down in Jagapur, the village under the same *taluk* famous for rowdyism, party conflicts and murders. As he has some criminal records in the past he adjusts himself well to the new environment. He finds everything agreeable there and a dozen rowdies support and honour his temperament. He marries a local poor girl and settles down there to a life of prestige and position, enjoying twenty acres of land and its dividends. Though he knows the prevailing tradition of the village that the most powerful of the rowdies would enjoy this privilege until his death or murder by another rowdy he adopts the same. His aspiration and ego go sky high when he is unrivalled and not antagonised by any.

The Day of Judgement comes when Nagappa encroaches on two acres of land of a poor villager, Huchchappa. That sounds his knell and signals his fall. Dharmappa, a lawyer, goes to beg justice from Nagappa for poor Huchchappa. This gets them entangled in the circle of vengeance. Dharmappa, the powerful lawyer, exploits the situation by killing Nagappa's men one after another and easily escaping from the web of law by manipulating and mastering the authorities in the constabulary, judiciary, and by using his shrewd legal knowledge. Studying the goon strategy and psyche Naikar presents cinematic exposure of Nagappa's fall:

> Now that he (Nagappa) had lost his stature as a hero and been reduced to the level of an ordinary man, the members of his gang were losing their attraction for him. Slowly they began to forsake him and join Dharmappa's group one by one. Thus ultimately Nagappa was left with only four to five loyal servants. Dharmappa's party had grown bigger than Nagappa's now (106).

Coming into the circle of vengeance Dharmappa becomes unrivalled in his locality by killing Nagappa and his followers. People began to fear him, revere him and love him for his influence and dynamism. He comes to be endowed with "the title of *The Murderer of the Rowdy Nagappa*" (108). Even Dharmappa is murdered by one Kalinga whose father, the follower of Nagappa, was murdered by Dharmappa. Each one gets poetic justice for the crime and Kalinga, the murderer of Dharmappa, suffers in the prison. Naikar analyses goon psychology and strategy in a realistic manner by presenting the transformation of the protector into the predator, and the destruction of both in the crucible of justice. With a reformative zeal he has done his best to highlight the power of divine justice in this story of crime and punishment. With his firm belief in truth and justice he suggests that the menace of crime cannot make man happy or a society healthy.

"Felicitation" is the story of a new taste. It appears to be based on the writer's study of someone's experience. In the story Naikar has inscribed a creative writer's instinct for writing novels, stories and his desire for availing the opportunity of being felicitated with garlands, shawl, sandal chips, idol of Bidariware, printed scroll of honour and printed certificate. Naikar presents the intoxication of the village rustics with the politics today and their running after the politicians for their promises, neglecting the literary persons and their contributions. The story appeals much for its realistic approach in a comic-serious manner. Though the narrator is "an old-fashioned writer producing ordinary novels and stories" (112) his writings deal with the social evils for which he has been rewarded with the Great Russian Award. His wife Sasikala, like the wives of most creative writers, is very unacademic, repents of marrying such an impecunious writer who only aims at erecting " a building of unsold books" (113). She vehemently opposes her husband's attending functions and sarcastically comments on his love for "the chance of being garlanded" by the ladies.

The narrator feels elated with the invitation of three persons from Channagiri, who invite him to grace a function so as to enable them to felicitate him for his literary contributions. He gloats for being recognised by the larger mass for his writings with an impression that his writings have touched the hearts of the people. He accepts the invitation happily when he comes to know that two important personalities - a poet and a writer-critic on *Dalit* literature are going to be felicitated on the same occasion. Taking it as an opportunity for self-aggrandisement he prepares a synopsis of his speech. He gets clarified about the function and arrangements. He with two other dignitaries moves to the venue on the scheduled date. On the way the three discuss the perspectives of their prepared speeches for the purpose. Funny ideas rush to his mind with his utopian imagination. He thinks of owning a car, which is not materialised in his thirty-five years of writing career. In a flash of recollection he thinks of Sasikala's liking for the shawl, which she would like to give their daughter Daxayini. But the irony is that he discovers everything to his utter desperation to be a fiasco. Nobody is present at the venue to receive them. They are asked to visit the guesthouse as the MLA Saheb is expected to arrive there and everybody is busy there to receive him. They wait at the vacant venue as long as their hope for being felicitated is alive. Being irritated with hunger they decide rightly not to attend such political functions for the sole sake of being felicitated. Utterly humiliated and frustrated, the trio returns with some bitter experience and pay the carfare from their own pockets. In his last bid the narrator fails to convince his wife about his suffering while narrating the plight of a writer in the society of modern days. He thinks of the modern man's hankering after power and pelf at the neglect of art and values in life. In a dystopia he visualises the modern day intellectuals shying away from politics and politicians who try to be popular without ethics.

"Pilgrimage to Kashi" is a story on *moha, maya* and *mukti.* As the former two confine man to the cocoon of a narrow self the latter liberates life through enlightenment to a greater freedom. The irony is that a man who possesses everything laments for having nothing and losing everything. Naikar conveys this message rather philosophically. He narrates the life and experience of Govindacharya, a widower *grahasta* whose expectations are larger than life. He struggles his utmost to get out of the labyrinthine *maya* of his phenomenal existence but fails to achieve his goal owing to his negative thinking. Being extremely traditional and conservative he tends to be patriarchal and thinks that everybody should surrender to him at his desire. He is the type of a man who never finds any positive sign in others. He has three sons, daughters-in-law, grandchildren, affluence and love of others for him but feels lonely owing to his complex psyche that impels him to lose faith in others. He thinks that whatever happens in his family is unbrahmanical and complains that everything has gone topsy-turvy after the death of his wife. His failure to understand his surrounding and fellow beings makes him more miserable and irritable. His desire to preserve the sanctity of his family life is rather prejudiced. He finds pollution in everything and everybody. His daughter-in-law's keeping of eggs in the refrigerator and cooking in the kitchen wearing new clothes during her seven months' pregnancy is believed to be tantamount to pollution. He is torn between paucity of purity and priority for peace in family life. With his conservative, traditional, and patriarchal psyche he does not like to see a wife's influence over her husband. He rather calls this type of woman a "coquettish wife" (121). Even though he does not suffer from any disease he desires to take some injections, visit cinema, theatre and club during his visit to his doctor son Srikanta at Hubli. Now he thinks that sons are loyal to their parents until they are married after which they get swayed and controlled by their wives. During his pilgrimage to Kashi, when his fellow pilgrims talk, celebrate and enjoy the rituals at the holy place he thinks it very mechanical and decides rather to return to his wretched atmosphere of domestic life. He is habituated to think and speak with his own prejudices, and without consideration for others. In his taciturnity he remains cynical, and serious about others. He thinks his fellow pilgrims as frogs in the company of their kith and kin. When he is dragged into conversation by a fellow pilgrim, Nagesharaya, he comes to know about the death of this pilgrim's wife and son long back. To his surprise he finds this man in a happy, joyous and carefree mood. Now Govindacharya's illusion vanishes and he gets enlightened by Nagesharaya's aphoristic explanation:

> We have to generate happiness in ourselves. Happiness lies in being contented with whatever life we have. Happiness and sorrow are two states of our mind. Our happiness lies in what good we do to others ... We can attain peace of mind in feeling contented and satisfied with whatever little is given to us ... in this mortal world ...(13))

In the narrative technique of the story Naikar has made a socio-psychological study of a family-head discovering the complex psychology of obsessed Govindacharya who makes the life of other family members unbearable for his ever insatiable, faultfinding and uncompromising attitude in his traditional patriarchal supremacy.

"The Spider's Web" is a deeply moving story on politics, corruption, and existential suffering of man. The story presents the vicious circle of Indian administration and bureaucracy where many sincere and honest officers are dragged into the muddle to be dishonest, and suffer a lot to satisfy their higher authorities. Naikar delineates the energetic, euphoric and reforming zeal of a newly elected minister who is committed to bring *prerestoika* and *glassnost* in the state administration by abolishing the practice of corruption in the administrative machinery. The irony is that the minister's constructive zeal suffers a set back in his existential dilemma when he fails to protect the innocent and weak from the mighty exploitive high officials. Naikar, like Shaw, Galsworthy and Ibsen, raises his concern for finding a smooth passage for this problem. Narrating an everyday incident in administration he fictionalises Circle Inspector Durgadas's life, suffering and end.

Durgadas is Naikar's representative victim, and an exemplary in the scheme and strategy of state administration. The erosion of ethical values in human character and profession has shocked the writer. With zeal to reform the bureaucracy and check corruption in it the minister visits various offices of his department and tries his utmost to streamline the administration. During his official visit and address in the public meeting at Dharwad he orders the Deputy Commissioner of police to suspend Durgadas on duty there after receiving a complaint against him. This demonstration of action-oriented administration leads to the collapse of Durgadas who finally dies in the hospital.

After his return to the Circuit House the Deputy Commissioner explains to him that Durgadas is innocent and that his involvement in the corruption is a forced one to satisfy his higher officials. Durgadas misuses his power and position to extract money from the illegal hut dwellers near Attikolla to meet the illegal demands of his higher authorities. The minister gets disturbed and gazes at a spider's web. He thinks that Durgadas, an insect, " was ... used to touch the strands of the web and ... the spider waited patiently. The harder it struggled ... the tighter it grew the bond of the web. At last the insect's struggle ceased" (34). The minister tries his best to rationalise the incident and forget his worries but the "hospitality, obligation, festival advance, squandered money ... a family of eight members" (37) intensifies his uneasiness and helplessness. He only sighs with the echo of Deputy Commissioner's words in his mind, "we can see people like Durgadas in every department. But it is unfortunate that there are many leaders who deem it to be a sign of able administration to kill the serpent and feed it to the eagle" (137). Thus evoking a response to the suffering and end of Durgadas the storyteller brings out the effect of corruption to light, to highlight man's failure in the Darwinian struggle for existence.

In the story "Basavanti" Naikar narrates the life and career of a lascivious woman, Basavanti. Her choice of illegal and immoral existence for the sake of pleasure earns suffering and premature death. Basavanti, the wife of Kalmesh, enjoys the euphoria of her married life but snaps it for good with her husband for her paramour Chinnappagouda, the man who has robbed her of her virginity before her marriage. Basavanti's youthful charm on the other hand disturbs the family of

Chinnappagouda. Even though he is married and a father of two children he likes to enjoy the "passionate company" with this pretty belle in a "paradisal pleasure" (140). Basavanti also finds a "new security" with Chinnappagouda and never cares much for the wagging tongues of the villagers. The material and emotional generosity of Chinnappagouda make her rich, happy and arrogant. In their secured privacy both enjoy five years of passionate love. Basavanti's frequent headaches and diminishing eyesight is primarily thought a temporary problem but its gravity is realised when the ENT doctor Somasekhar of Kempegouda Hospital at Bangalore advises her a risky operation for her in the head. Now Basavanti thinks of her fate with cynicism, and spends most of her time with her puritanical widowed mother who reminds her for repentance, "Had you lived with your husband, would he have neglected you like this?" (149-50). Slowly Chinnappagouda narrows down his nocturnal visits and comes occasionally just to hug and console her. In the heyday of her love she had cared for none nor did her close and distant relatives approve of her behaviour. So, nobody comes forward to help her in her misfortune. She suffers starvation, and longs for death as a punishment for her illegal and immoral existence. When the *bhajan* chorus sings about the ephemerality of life Chinnappagouda pays his last homage to her by paying some money for her funeral rites through his servant Siddappa. Women folk of the village start cursing her not superstitiously, but rather on moral grounds that she suffered owing to her letting bathwater across the temple road, abandoning her husband and, worst of all, owing to the curse of Chinnapagouda's wife. The extramarital and promiscuous love affair in any form is immoral in the eyes of law and God, and can become fatal for life. Portraying Basavanti as a victim of poetic justice Naikar leaves a message for the Chinnappagoudas and Basavantis in our contemporary society.

Reading biography beyond personal history is an important feature in Naikar's fictional world. Judging the characters in their respective social milieu and analysing them on an ethical perspective he portrays them as living legends. "The Golden Servant" is an interesting story about a low caste boy Timmappa who with a miraculous spiritual progress becomes a great saint. From history to biography and to legend the shepherd boy undergoes transformation with his indomitable spirit and spiritual endeavour for enlightenment. The social milieu of the Vijayanagara Empire and the personal ethics of the individual characters are narrated in Naikar's story of this shepherd boy.

Timmappa is the victim of rigid caste system but Naikar traces his early education, logical mind, spiritual quest, ethical discrimination and the evolution of his faith in God in realistic detail. After the death of his father this shepherd boy of Bada village in the Haveri district of Karnataka during the days of the Vijayanagara Empire becomes the victim of his father's arch enemy Mallanayaka. He has to leave his village Bada for Kaginele to consolidate his spiritual faith. His *grahastha* life comes to an end with the death of his wife Laxmidevi and son Biranayaka. His essential loneliness, non-possessive nature and holy service in the local temples make him popular as Kanakappa. The Emperor of Vijayanagara appoints him as *Dandanayaka* (the administrator) of Bada and Bankapura villages. He is further designated as Kanaka Nayaka. Being made the servant of Tirumalesa he becomes popular as Kanakadasa. Becoming the golden servant of Lord Adikesava he accepts *sanyasa* for good and leads a spiritual life. Through pain, agony, disappointment and disillusionment he realises the ephemerality and transitoriness of life. His passion for worshipping God, attending festivals and singing holy songs and of divine miracles help him to compose *Haribhakti Sara, Mohana Tarangini,* Vishnu's Ten incarnations, *Bharata Kathamrita* and *Nrisimha Stava.* After becoming the disciple of several gurus like Rangadasa, Tatacarya, Kanakamuni and H.H. Vadiraja he attains enlightenment.

"He had elevated himself from the realisation of *Saguna Brahma* to that of *Nirguna Brahma* and died as "Dasa Supreme" (194) in the year A.D. 1606. In his *advaitic* realisation Naikar is quite sure that "He who chooses the Divine has been chosen by the Divine." He conveys the message that one can achieve purgation and enlightenment through devotion *(bhakti)* and surrender *(prapatti).* He exposes the greater aspects of human life in the character of Timmappa and his spiritual partner Lachumi, the daughter of his father's enemy Mallanayaka who had failed in her ambition to marry him but had succeeded in her mission through her spiritual odyssey.

The story "A Chronic Patient Became a Doctor" looks like the memoir of a scholar, Nandiswar. Exposing the set backs and difficulties in the pursuit of research for the award of Ph.D., Naikar delineates the shocking affairs of *guru-shiya* relationship. Nandiswar, the teacher-scholar, has lost his sanity of mind during his fourteen years of ordeal under a tough and sadist guide for the award of a Ph. D. degree. Being frustrated with his unexpected result at the M.A. level he has made up his mind to excel his friends by doing Ph.D. on a rare topic of international standard. Sympathising with the plight of the scholar at the Post Graduate Centre, Naikar discloses some of the unsolved problems of Nandiswar in the hands of a third-rate, cruel, cunning, non-cooperative, selfish, lazy, egocentric and sadist guide professor Nagaraj. Apart from his quest for knowledge Nandiswar goes for a "holy tirtha" (241) in contemporary pan-Indian *guru-shiya* relationship. He realises the lack of sanctity in higher study and research. He enjoys his suffering in the hands of a moody and incalculable guide, the penal agent of his past *karma*. Apart from pursuing higher study for research he discovers his guide to be a man with a mask who only advises to read more of criticism, philosophy, psychology, indology and research methodology for making a thesis of international standard for such a prestigious degree, without any practical help in the registration, preparation, chapterisation, and in the structure and texture of his thesis. He rather scathingly comments on Nadiswar's writing "as mere trash ... school boyish ... have no judgement and no style" and hurts his sentiments by saying that the "university ruined you all. Besides you ... do not have brains" (211).

The despicable saga of the guides in pan-Indian situation is exposed in the personal suffering of Nandiswar. The scholars often get disillusioned about the nature and behaviour of their guides who at times pretend to be the well-wishers and bemoan like the devils. Even without rendering some practical help they manipulate the system by bargaining their relationship with the experts on the evaluation of the thesis. As the representative Indian guide, Professor Nagaraj harangues at his scholar making an Oxford standard thesis, even though he himself was not educated nor his works evaluated at Oxford. He boasts of his learning and high post not so much for his academic excellences as for his manipulative skill and other affiliations. As Nandiswar says from his experience with Nagaraj, " Even if Aristotle were to come and stand before him, he would insult him by calling him a brainless fellow" (231). Apart from his intellectual shallowness he has also the moral turpitude for hobnobbing with a young lady teacher of the department and asks Nandiswar for celebration with beer, which is quite abominable in Indian academic culture. Narrating the problems of a scholar Naikar impersonalises Nandiswar's personal problems like ingratitude of his brother, financial problems and unhappy married life, all posing obstacles in his pursuit of a Ph.D. degree. Naikar agrees with his authorial creation, Nandiswar, a scholar who in his youth ventures into this project, has to spoil his whole life.

Though Ph. D. is a necessary criterion for promotion it becomes suicidal to waste one's precious youth in such endeavours. At the same time its tricky affairs are inescapable for a genuinely interested bibliomaniac, academically inclined and ambitious scholar like Nandiswar. To get a Ph.D. under such a difficult guide means to enter "the cave, hold dialogues with a tiger and came out safe" (268). The suffering of Nandiswar becomes miserable in the Kafkaesque mystery of the university system and the assessment of the foreign experts with their intellectual honesty. He draws the impression that the British guides are rigid, conservative and uncompromising in their views and academic standard; the Americans are more liberal and humanistic in their approach to the Third World scholars and their. Indian counterparts are superfluous and harassing.

Commenting on guide-scholar relationship Naikar writes, "This is the reason why brilliant Indians want to leave India and settle in foreign countries where they are recognised and respected" (277). He expresses his serious concern over the unprofessional attitude of many Indian professors like Nagaraj, who unnecessarily harass their scholars in the pursuit of their research for Ph.D. Naikar regrets this shocking situation in higher studies and research in India.

With the creative excellence of Naikar's writing all the twelve stories express his concern over the loss of values and morals, the cementing factors and strongholds of human life in a socio-ethical perspective. As a rationalist and humanist he believes in the personal ethics as a potential force that guides and controls the society in the process of evolution. The self has its evolution in the ethics that provides the knowledge of right and wrong, virtue and vice, merit and sin in the theory of *karma*. In the narration of fact and fiction, history and biography he confirms that the violation of moral and spiritual code deviates man from the path of real success. He believes in the rational volitions of man that help him to achieve the freedom of his mind, the *moksha* (liberation). With his authorial privilege Naikar has projected his insight into the human nature giving importance to the basic values of life like love, honesty, nobility and forgiveness. In the narration of commonplace incidents he claims that vices in human character are to be checked as they pose immediate threats to life and society. He deals with the themes of crime and punishment, man-woman relationship, sexual lives, promiscuous love affairs, romance, values, jealousy, betrayal, hypocrisy, treachery, greed, corruption, vicious circle of power and politics, immoral living, spiritual endeavour, idealism and existential suffering of man with the help of historical facts, folkloric elements, semi-autobiographical presentation, humanistic approach and idealism. His characters are chosen from pan-Indian situations and sensibilities. They are presented with a strong touch of realism. He has chosen his characters from different walks of Indian life to fit them within the confines of a multifaceted fictional society created by his imagination.

Works Cited

Naikar, Basavaraj, *The Rebellious Rani of Belavadi and Other Stories*, New Delhi: Atlantic Publishers, 2001.

4

All for Gold and Sex: A Thematic Analysis of Basavaraj Naikar's Short Stories

— *Pashupati Jha* and *T. Ravichandran*

There has been a trend in the Indian English Writing for the last few decades among a few senior academics that after years of slogging through classics in the classroom, they assume a different role by turning themselves into creative writers. Although scholarship and creativity do not always go hand in hand, there are a few successful scholar writers in India. Basavaraj Naikar has made a humble entry to this exclusive club of professor transformed into a creative writer by way of publishing his first collection *The Thief of Nagarahalli and Other Stories.*

That Basavaraj Naikar has chosen to write in largely ignored genre of short stories, while most of his predecessors, be it Srinivasa Iyengar or Shiv K. Kumar, ventured their hands first at poetry, is a laudable one. And that, instead of going for high-brow themes like 'alienation', 'expatriate sensibility', 'exile', 'east-west encounter', 'dislocation of identity', 'search for the authentic voice', etc., the author is unpretentious about the reiteration of simple themes as man's primordial obsession for the possession of opulent wealth and succulent woman, and his subsequent fall from grace, is equally a meritorious one. These are precisely the themes around which our mythical pots were boiling and so many of our master craftsmen were weaving their plots. Naikar's *The*

Thief of Nagarahalli and Other Stories contains ten short stories. Except for two stories, all the remaining ones deal with the ingenuity, manipulation, and coercion that go before the craving for money and sex, and the disappointment, repentance and retribution that follow the accomplishment and satiation.

The hunt for gold happens to be the main occupation, in the title piece, for the central character, Malla, the notorious thief of Nagarahalli. And hoarding the booty happens to be the favourite pastime of his patron and landlord, Marigouda. Malla's artifice has been depicted to such an extent that one is enrapt and gets carried away by his dexterously played games and that one wishes Malla to succeed always in the way one wishes Milton's Satan, evil though he may be, to triumph over the rival angels. Malla, we find like Milton's Satan, has not chosen evil for the sake of evil but he finds the path of good to be less challenging and very uninspiring. Thus in the words of the author:

> He had tried his hand at ploughing, carpentry and masonry and had felt *utterly disappointed*. That was because those jobs did not *thrill* him. Far from thrilling him, they *deadened his sensibility*. Once he even tried to become a Swami at Ranebennur, but found that it did not suit his bent of mind. At last he was tempted to take to thieving and found it after his heart. He practised that art for a couple of years and made a name for himself. He was so clever in his art that no policeman could lay hands on him even once in his entire thieving career... The diverse myths built around him speak of his extreme popularity, indeed his notoriety in all the surrounding villages.[1] (emphases added).

While we find a character like Raju in R. K. Narayan's *The Guide*, on account of his act of forgery and the laboured repentance, moving from the mundane to the sacred, we see Naikar's Malla shirking off from the sacred for the mundane as "Once he even tried to become a Swami at Ranebennur, but found that it did not suit his bent of mind!"

There are two engaging and awe-inspiring episodes of Malla's misdeeds described by the author. In the first one, provoked by his patron, the thief ventures to steal the golden ornaments from a dead lady. The job is terribly challenging since the corpse has been always surrounded by the mourning relatives. Undeterred, Malla deftly makes a hole in the wall just behind the dead body is laid. Malla chooses the right moment to insert his hands inside and he collects the dead hands together and makes them clap. The naïve mind of the villagers which conceives that to be the work of the ghost, and the hue and cry that follows provide ample time for Malla to rob off all the ornaments from the dead body. While we laugh at the villagers' folly along with Malla, we also relish the author's dig at the feeble Indian superstitious mind that finds a devil in every dark tree.

The second exploit is equally macabre; this time he has to steal a copper pitcher full of golden ornaments placed before the family god of Desai of the village Annagiri. Malla manages to hide himself skilfully among the oxen brought into the house and finds an easy entry. Then he paralyses the old lady, who keeps an eye over the gold, with fear by showing her his knife. As usual, Malla executes his operation without any hindrance from the owner. Yet, not just satisfied with his loot, and his self-confidence overflowing, while slipping away from the house with the pitcher, he taunts the house-owner by proclaiming his daring act. He shouts, "Dear Desai, I am Malla of Nagarahalli. I have come to tell you that I am talking your pitcher full of gold. You can take it from me if you have the guts"(20). Malla escapes the big chase that follows and before Desai's men reach Nagarahalli, he is fast asleep in his bed. Thus Malla has transformed the mean act of stealing into something sophisticated and superb, thereby winning the admiration of many:

> He haunted the imagination of the rich Desais, Patils, Deshpandes and Jahagirdars who spent sleepless nights in contemplation on him. He inspired a heroic spirit in the hearts of young men. He kindled amorous sentiments in the minds of young girls. Thus "Success" had become another name for Malla. He had taken an oath that he would stop his thieving profession the day he met with failure in his ventures. (22)

But he meets his nemesis soon when he gets outsmarted by Monappa. When Malla steals the golden bowl from the landlord of Imrapur and hides it in some ditch to save himself from the police, Monappa steals it away from him. Now there is an open challenge between the two—try how much he can, Malla fails to take back that golden bowl from Monappa. Accepting his defeat, one fine day he disappears from Nagarahalli. Thus ends the glorious career of Malla, the legendary thief. In this manner, as Subhash Chandra comments, "There is a folklorish air about the story..."[2]

Most of the other stories in this collection too treat the greed for gold as a recurring motif. The next story is even captioned, "All for Gold". In fact, lust for gold and lust *per se* are blended in equal proportions in this story. Virabhadra is hankering after gold and leaves his young wife, Ganga, behind and goes to Bellary on business where he has to delay his stay for many weeks. In the same village lives Sangappa who has a roving eye for beautiful women. Ganga's 'pretty figure' ensnares and maddens him. He sends his message of love to her through Balappa, who is taken to task by her for this uncalled for errand. Sangappa then bribes an old lady, Paramma, with the 'gift of golden necklace weighing five *tolas*'. Paramma, being an experienced lady in the ways of the world, places the turban of Sangappa in Ganga's house and later manipulates, blackmails and cajoles her into this lustful game. Although Ganga initially thinks, "Sinning once in secrecy would not be a great problem"(46), after yielding to her temptation with the tempter, realises that it could not end as a one-night affair. Naikar here implies that once somebody, even as pure as the mythical Ganga River itself (the choice of the name Ganga is not a mere coincidence) yields to the ways of gold and lust, then there is seldom a comeback. Thus he explains the attitudinal change of Ganga:

> Within a month's time they grew up to be expert paramours enjoying their fill of sex without any inhibition. During daytime Ganga would remember her husband who had gone to Bellary on business and feel uneasy for a moment for betraying him, but would soon manage to forget it by recalling Paramma's secret advice about making the best of the golden opportunities of life. (50)

Needless to say that "the golden opportunities" in practice meant yielding to the prurient urges of her clandestine admirer, Sangappa!

However, in the end, it is again the gold of Virabhadra that ensnares Balappa to betray his loyal friend Sangappa. Balappa lures Sangappa to an isolated place where Virabhadra and his men hack him to death. Gold plays a lot of other roles in the total scheme of Sangappa but finally all his wealth fails to protect him. Though Sangappa commits the deadly sin of coveting his neighbour's wife and deserves to be punished the brutal way in which he gets killed, one cannot but feel some sympathy for him since he has a premonition of his own death and a philosophical outlook towards the ephemeral life. Once in a fair when he happens to see a boy blowing a balloon to its full capacity only to get it burst the next second, he exclaims to his friend Balappa, "See, dear Balya, our life is also like that balloon. We do not know when it bursts."(31)

Rajasekhar, in "Her Husband Went to America", like Sangappa, gives credence to the 'seize the day' motif. In this story, the lust for gold is mixed up with a more dominant passion of achieving a Ph. D. from abroad and thereby enhancing one's worldly prestige and material prospects. Rajasekar's obsession for a Ph. D. from U.S.A., as it would offer him freedom from his drab job of a lecturer in some local college, makes him even abandon his young, innocent wife and old parents. Despite the fact that it is his wife, Girija's strong support, patience, forbearance and prayers that fetch him a foreign fellowship and get him a degree from the Princeton University, Rajasekar gulls 'the semi-educated woman' to sign her own divorce papers. Since he has also married an American woman and has two children by her, without any qualms, he goes to America for good. When Girija's mother suggests her to go for re-marriage, the poor girl refuses to leave her in-laws. Misfortune has taught her courage and contentment. In this way, she represents a typical Indian woman, ready to face her fate with fortitude even if she loses the much- needed support from the spouse. However, her ideal character is rather unusual in this collection which is otherwise full of morally degraded and weak-willed people. But the story, on the whole, is not unusual because most of the Indian young men going abroad remarry there enchanted by the sophisticated white ladies. Circumstances, Naikar seems to reiterate, do not make a man but reveals his true colour!

The moral lapse of degradation is at the lowest ebb in "Mother's Husband" where the author has tried to bring in the Oedipus myth with a strange twist and with little success. Instead of the son killing his father and remarrying his mother, here the mother abandons her husband and has sex with her son. The story begins keeping in mind the mythological tempo. Setavi, a flippant version of the Greek fore-teller Teresias, is 'the celestial scribe' who writes the fate of the mortals to be reborn, literally, on their foreheads. But she is shocked out of her wits to know the future of her yet to be born daughter, Kamalata, "who is going to have sexual intercourse with her own son according to the strange course of her life." (79). As it happens in reality, Kamalata, in a fit of physical passion marries a cobbler and years later, when she knows of his inferior profession, deserts him and their son.

As she is still very engaging, she slides into harlotry and changes her name to Chandrasani. Like mother, the son too is disgusted with the father's profession and becomes a young merchant dealing in precious stones and pearls. Pure chance and sheer coincidence brings the son, Adivesha, to the same town where his mother earns a living and makes him desire her celebrated beauty. As a result of their passionate lovemaking Chandrasani gives birth to a male child. Subsequently, in dream, a woman of her mother's age shows up and admonishes her of this incestuous relationship. Unable to bear the guilt and shame, Chandrasani jumps into a well and commits suicide along with her "son-and-grandson". Deplorably, the story, despite the author's best attempt, lacks in organic growth. There has been very little said why and how Kamalata, who was so devoted to her husband and son, having had her fill of matrimonial pleasure for full five years, could leave them without a backward glance and suddenly become so degraded simply because her husband turned out to be one of the low caste men.

The obsession with wealth recurs again in "The Invisible Face", where Bangarasetty, a renowned merchant of Dharwad turns out to be an accomplice in the crime of printing fake currency notes. Bangarasetty has risked his reputation for the sake of ill-gotten wealth. But there is a double-irony at play; when there is a chance for exposure, all his partners in crime bribe the doctor in the hospital who poisons him to death. Thus, the person who should have saved the life of Bangarasetty is actually responsible for his death. So the greed for gold takes everything away from Bangarasetty. This story is a bitter expose' of the widening gap between the public and the private face, between the man and the mask.

This life of intrigue takes another form in "She Wanted a Child." Here Manjula sacrifices her everything for a child of her own. This type of hankering after child is quite common in Indian society where life is supposed to be worthless without a male progeny. Manjula does not conceive during the first two years of her conjugal life and thus loses her familial and social status in the eyes of her mother-in-law and husband. Her husband, Sankara, even hints at his second marriage, compelling her to mislead him by telling a lie that she has lost her menstrual cycle and hence is expecting a child. A sudden but welcome offer of job in the Dharwad post-office as a clerk saves her from exposure for the time being. She has to leave her family and join the post where Sekhar, her young colleague, is attracted towards her. Manjula's wish for the child is now strangely mixed up with her desire for this smart young man. They secretly meet at different places and make love passionately, yet Manjula fails to conceive. The lady doctor finally tells her that she would need a minor operation. Scared of the operation Manjula prefers an easier way out by stealing a newly born baby from the Civil Hospital. But being a novice, she is caught by the police while she is returning to her husband to impinge on him that the child is their own. The police inspector, moved by her plight and candid confession, recommends for a less severe punishment of three months imprisonment. The one improbable point of the story is the long absence of Manjula's husband who should have, in natural course, visited her very often to know about her well being, more so, when she is expecting a baby.

The sexual depravity, which is the forte of many of the stories described above, surfaces again in "Coffin in the House". It is about the rape and the resultant death of a nubile girl by an elderly man. That hapless girl is Prema and the perverted man is Mr. Patil, otherwise a very respectable man in his society. He has broken his leg and is recuperating in a hospital when his neighbour in the apartment complex finds out some unnatural sound coming out of his room. It finally turns out to be the tinkering of a coffin by a thief. The episode is narrated to Patil in the hospital by Mallikarjuna. But gradually Patil is remorse-stricken by his past guilt and confesses his crime before a stupefied friend that how his carnal desires for that young girl led to that heinous act. It appears that he tempted her by chocolates, gagged her mouth, and raped her so violently that the helpless victim died during the assault. Gradually, the news spreads from one to another and Prema's father exclaims with disgust: "We thought Mr. Patil to be the best friend of our family and could never imagine that he would do such a terrible thing. We simply cannot guess which snake lives in which hole"(159). It should be noted here that the author has used snake symbolism in an appropriate way, for serpent is always associated with sinful lust both in the Eastern and the Western mythology. The police arrests Mr. Patil and he has to face the punishment meted out to him by law that he has to undergo ten years of imprisonment as soon as he is discharged from the hospital. Thus he is punished for his brutal crime but at what cost to that innocent girl and her parents!

Being an academic with decades of teaching, Naikar comes to campus conspiracy in "The Anonymous Letter". The Professor and Chairman of the department of English of a university instigates the students against their own teachers by making them write repugnant letters to them collectively. Without signing any names at the bottom, these students become free in their anonymous garb to hurl abuses at them. For instance, they write:

> Professor Gangadhar dictates notes and does not explain anything. He speaks English like Kannada. We cannot understand Dr. Balachandra's pronunciation. He cracks jokes in the class and kills time. He makes students bring

> cigarettes from the shop. Professor Nagesh is a peculiar man. He never looks at the students but always stares at the ceiling. He does not tell us the meaning of Greek and Latin quotations. Professor Sekhar is a weirdo and helps only the girls by leaking out questions to them. He comments upon his own colleagues and fails the students who are not his *chelas*. (167)

This story is remarkable in this collection for its wide-ranging humour. It is also one of the two stories that is free from lust for gold or woman. Later on, the teachers find out the trick of the Chairman and make him apologise, of course, obliquely.

"When the News Came" is the other story that has a different theme. Here, the reported death of Chennappa, a truck-driver, by the police turns out to be painfully wrong. The one whose death is actually reported is alive and there is yet another by the same name who died accidentally. When the real Chennappa returns safely back to his village, after a week, he is surprised to see the fear on the faces of his people who mistake him to be his ghost. Chennappa also realises the forced widowhood of his wife and her eventual exile on account of his (ghost's) arrival in the village. In the end, the same police who contributed to the chaos make amends by reuniting Chennappa with his family. Naikar takes another opportunity to hint at the superstitious beliefs of the poor people. And the shifting tone of humour and pathos leaves no room for sex or chase for gold.

The last story, "Fulfilment" is a usual stuff of a rich girl falling for a poor boy of low caste and then eloping with him to fulfil her physical and emotional needs. Bharati is overwhelmed by the acting prowess, combined with the physical charm, of Chandrasekhar leading to their secret love affair and subsequent marriage. She is so devoted to her husband that she willingly lives a life of poverty with him in a remote village. They are blessed with a son named Viswanath. But their happiness rankles in the eyes of a few others and Chandrasekhar is implicated in a criminal case. He disguises himself as a beggar and goes to Bombay to escape the dragnet of law. Bharati's father is gradually reconciled to his fate and becomes philosophical. Finally, he donates all his property to a *Matt*. After twelve years, Chandrasekhar returns with beard and moustache. And for a while, even Bharati fails to recognise him. But the recognition dawns on her when she hears his voice and they live happily ever after.

In the "Preface", the author gives his preference for the Indian variety of English. He says: "Like many Commonwealth writers, I believe in the view that we Indians must write in our native brand of English and should not ape the British 'masters'. Our imagery and style should be redolent of our cultural ethos"(5). There are plenty of examples of typical English expression in the collection. For instance, when Malla hears of the countless golden ornaments, his mouth begins "to water at that news"(11). Similarly, when he succeeds in scaring everyone from the dead body of the old woman that would enable him to steal everything, he feels himself in "seventh heaven"(15). And when Balya approaches Ganga to concede Sangappa's secret wishes, she cries out in anger: "I shall have you shoe-beaten..."(39). Again she retorts to Paramma in similar vein, "How can he think of having me as his keep?"(43). When her husband finally finds our her extramarital affair, he shouts at her, "You whore, you have blackened my face permanently and I cannot show my face to the people in the village"(53). Virabhadra, when he gets hold of Sangappa, *boils* with anger (58). When, out of ignorance, Girija signs on the divorce paper, her father-in-law, tells her in anguish,"You have dug your own grave"(76). When Rudravva is wrongly reported by the police of the death of her husband, she suddenly feels, "as if the earth under her feet was sinking" (133). She wails pitifully before her son, "My dear Chandru, your father has left us in midwater" (Ibid.). When Prema's father finds out the misdoing of Mr. Patil, otherwise a highly respected gentleman, he cries out in abhorrence, "We simply cannot guess which snake lives in which hole" (159). These expressions give an earthly touch of reality to these stories. In addition, there are so many references to South Indian customs, rituals, dress codes and food habits, thereby providing an extra edge of naturalness to this collection. Thus we have innumerable references of women adjusting their sarees around their breasts indicating their inherent modesty.

But this naturalness is not maintained in the structure/plot of the stories. There are unnecessary details, self-evident facts and damaging repetitions pointing to the fact that the author needs a lot of practising and polishing of his craft. Every now and then a reader is not supposed to know how *holige* and *bhajis* are prepared, *dosas* and *idlis* are eaten and beetle leaves are chewed or cigarettes are smoked. These excessive details simply distract the mind of the reader from the main theme and often reduce the tempo and smooth flow of the storyline. Moreover, if everything is told by the short story writer to the reader, then what else remains for his 'discovery'?

Printing errors are plentiful and the author should have himself proofread the final draft, particularly when this happens to be his maiden venture. There is then sexual "passion portrayed in its raw intensity."[3] One wonders whether it is this overdose of sex that makes fine female critics like Prema Nandakumar to choose only one story, "The Anonymous Letter", and discuss it at length and shy away from all the remaining stories?[4] None the less, there has been a long and controversial debate in literature as to how much sex should be put into it. D. H. Lawrence has portrayed sexual passion with a particular philosophy of life in his mind. One fails to find any such philosophy in the present collection. Even Arundhati Roy has her own share of sexual interludes in her most famous novel. Yet everything is amalgamated in the fine alchemy of her art; one solely misses this artistry in Naikar. But then, when Henry Miller was accused of putting so much of physical passion in his novels, he simply replied, "Maybe you have to wade through rivers of shit to find a germ of reality."[5] It is equally true for this collection. One fervently hopes that Naikar would hone his craft further in subsequent collections after this apprentice work, which points to his dormant potential that needs further exploration.

References

1. *TheThief of Nagarahalli and Other Stories*. Calcutta: Writers Workshop, 1999, pp.9-10. All the textual quotations are from this edition.
2. "Basavaraj Naikar, *TheThief of Nagarahalli and Other Stories*", review in *The Indian Journal of English Studies*. Vol.37, p.141.
3. Ibid., 142.

4. "*The Thief of Nagarahalli and Other Stories* by Basavaraj Naikar", review in *The Journal of Indian Writing in English*, Vol.28, July 2000, No.2, pp.78-79.
5. *Nexus*. 1960 rpt; Frogmore: Panther Books Ltd, 1974, p.100.

5

A Kaleidoscopic Vision: Short Stories of Basavaraj Naikar

— S. G. Vaidya

Though the most popular genre among the reading as well as writing community of the contemporary times, short story is the most elusive form of literature. It frustrates the attempts of the erudite critics and the persistent practitioners of the form to encapsulate all the features and elements that go in to render a story successful one in a single and neat definition. If one stresses "the economy" of words, other stresses "the impression" and yet another emphasizes "the purpose" or "narrative" and so forth. It is quite incontrovertible that all these are essential factors for a successful short story. Yet for our convenience let us assume that a short story is a monument erected for a moment. It is an attempt to "catch the eternal in the casual, invest a moment with the immensity of time."[1]

Though handled by distinguished practitioners of fiction, though enjoyed by diligent readers, enough critical attention is not paid to the genre. In spite of the widespread immemurable academic journals very few of them publish a paper on this neglected genre. Moreover because of its heftier counterparts like drama, poetry and novel the form however gets elbowed out of the curriculum at higher levels of study.

Due to aforementioned reasons and unquestionable critical ignorance the genre is pushed to the dusty corners of the libraries and many good short story writers remain and rot in darkness of unrecognition. But whatever may be the state of affairs around it the short story has grown in abundance in occidental as well as oriental literature.

Being perhaps the most chameleon form of literature the short story has changed its form, structure; plot design, etc., from nation to nation thereby altering the previous conceptions of its nature. In accordance with the tendencies of readers as well as writers the short story has manifested in the diversified forms, viz., sketch, yarn, marchen, parable, novella, cycles, etc.

Now let us cast a glance at these one by one. Sketch appears to be static in its nature. As Washington Irving wrote, it is "the play of the thought, and sentiments and language: the weaving in of characters, lightly yet expressively delineated; the familiar and faithful exhibition of scenes in common life; and the half concealed vein of humour that is often playing through the whole,"[2] and it also shows some movement towards narrative dimension.

The word 'yarn' seems to be derived from rope making which is much connected with nautical field. Further it seems to have become applied metaphorically for story weaving. It is the most suitable kind of genre for the storyteller who identifies himself more with the oral tradition. It is "an elaborated anecdote or series of anecdotes" presented in colloquial or casual tone. When stretched further it results into a Tall Tale. Its features may be gathered at random as under. (1) It is comic in its tendency. (2) It makes use of vernacular idiom. (3) It attaches importance to external elements, while marginalising the psychological ones.

Marchen is an adopted form of the fairy tale by a modern writer. But in that a Faerie is usually replaced by magic. But the magic it employs is the magic of peculiar mood and power, etc. It also remains close to the outlines of oral narrative. There in marchen we may witness the profuse fusion of supernatural elements. The maximum number of characters does not exceed seven and the number of units of action does not exceed thirty-one.

If a parable is a story, which is didactic in tone and realistic in its approach to life intending to bring home some moral, fable is a story, which again intends to teach some moral. In that it employs animal as characters, which act as though they were human beings. When these two forms refuse to teach some moral deliberately soon they enter into the frontiers of short story proper in the modern sense of the usage.

A novella is another form of literature the aspects of which appear to be different from that of a normal work of fiction on the one hand and short story on the other. There are some writers who opine that on independent status and enough critical attention to this form must be assigned. In other words, a novella is unique form of literature, the features of which cross and go beyond the regulations of the short story proper and also cannot fit properly into the framework of the novel proper. "The narrative task of these forms is quite different,"[3] says Judith Leibowitz. Her view may be summarised as follows.

a) Novel - elaboration

b) Short story - limitation

c) Novella - compression.

One can infuse serious, tragic, comic and satirical elements in it. "The kind of satire which gravitates towards novella is that in which the object of ridicule is a single one rather a compendium of the follies of mankind"[4] (Judith Leibowitz). This does not signify that there is a sort of tacit compromise or agreement or whatsoever between novel and short story.

Man's tendency to have mixed taste seems to be the cause for the entwining and concatenation of one story with the other. And this might have resulted into cycles. But the conspicuous element is that the writer avoids the tight and terse/continuous structure of the novel quite consciously. The best example of the form may be found in Kannada literature, *Vaddaradhane*.

Indian English literature, comparatively a new body of writing, has revealed its all-round growth in almost all forms of literature and has won the acclamation. In the latter half of the previous century short story has grown considerably. Story telling impulse is quite natural to human beings, particularly for Indians because of their being fed upon by grandmother's tales, since their infancy and also because of their hoary, rich and incessant tradition. The seedlings of Indian English short story may be traced in The *Brihatkatha Saritsagara* of Gunadhya and *The Jataka*

Tales of Buddha. Further, with the introduction of Western education and impact of Western writers and their writings, modern Indian writers learnt something new which added up to their knowledge of their own tradition. Begun by S.C. Dutt's *Realities of Indian Life* (1885), the tribe of short story writers has continued to allure the attention of the readers down to present day.

Professor Basavaraj Naikar's second collection of short stories, *The Rebellious Rani of Belavadi and Other Stories*[5] is a welcome addition. A modest attempt is made in this paper to analyse the stories in detail in the light of the theory mentioned above. The book depicts the South Indian life quite vividly. The stories included in the collection present various themes ranging from the "historical to the contemporary, from the religious to the secular and from the elemental to the academic" (Author's preface).

All in all there are twelve stories in the collection, which may be divided into two categories, viz., historical and contemporary.

To condense the historical incidents into a short story great acumen is essential. It requires not only sympathy and understanding of the past generation but also the knowledge of environment and conditions under which people lived and the ideas that dominated their minds and actions. It is not only wrong but also foolish to judge the past life with the contemporary standards of thought and behavioural patterns. Their faith, religion and customs were quite different from ours. Whatever mode of life a particular generation imbibes may have surely had some relevance and meaning to it though they seem strange and different for the other generation. If we look at the past generation with sympathy, understanding coupled with the knowledge of environment, etc., we witness the dead dry bones vivified, teeming with life and buoyancy in their childhood, adolescence and prime in their own suitable clime though very different from ours yet much like us and our own with the same kind of human passions, feelings and failings. It is in this context that we may consider history though not magic but a magic mirror held to the past life.

Of the twelve stories three stories may be listed under the first category, namely, "The Rebellious Rani of Belavadi", "Blood Bath" and "The Golden Servant". Of the three stories the first one deals with the life story of a Warrior Princess Mallamma. Mallamma was a daughter born to Madhulinga Nayaka of Swadi and Rani Viramma with the blessings of Kartikeya Swami. She was born on "ashtami tithi" of Kartika paksha of Sravana month of Salivahana Saka 1580. Mallamma studied under Sankarabhatta. She attained sufficient proficiency in Sanskrit, Kannada, Urdu and Marathi. She could even compose poems in Kannada. After knowing that she had to face a danger of death by a tiger during her sixteenth year, Raja Madhulinga Nayaka arranged a *Swayamvara* to avoid it. Ishaprabhu, Prince of Belavadi married her, as he was a great tiger hunter. This was so done to provide double protection to Mallamma.

After the marriage, Mallamma moved to Belavadi *samsthan* which "extended from Yakkundi to Devarahubballi and Gokak to Halyal"(10). They lived happily for some days. Then they went to Gokarna and came back. On the way they rested on the banks of a lake where she had to encounter the tiger attack. Soon she fought with them lest her husband who was in deep sleep be disturbed. On waking, Ishaprabhu was full of appreciation of the heroism of his wife.

Chhatrapati Shivaji was a strong supporter of the Hindu cause. Hence he waged wars relentlessly. Around A.D. 1676-78 he proceeded towards Thanjavuru and on the way back he attacked the cities of Karnataka also. When he had camped at Yadavada village, Ishaprabhu and his men planned to invite and honour him. But before their plan materialised Shivaji men captured the cows of the *Gollas*. When this was brought to the notice of Ishaprabhu, Rani Mallamma took her army of female warriors and attacked the soldiers of Shivaji when they were sleeping, defeated them and also regained the cows. This defeat was an unswallowable pill for Shivaji. Hence he ordered his commander to attack Belavadi.

Ishaprabhu had sought the help from Gaviappa Nayaka of Huli and Virappagouda of Sigehalli. But before their troops came, Belavadi was attacked. Ishaprabhu died heroically in the protection of kingdom. Hence the responsibility of the kingdom fell on the shoulders of Rani Mallamma. She resumed the battle. She ambushed Shivaji with her women warriors when he was returning from the temple of Jagadamba. Shivaji saw in her his mother Jijabai and also Jagadamba. Hence, he supplicated and surrendered to her. Later peace was made and Shivaji returned to his capital. After he breathed his last his son Sambhaji wished to capture her and keep her as his mistress. But Tarabai, his wife, came forward to protect the chastity of Rani Mallamma and helped her. After the death of Sambhaji she visited his capital. She breathed her last in Belavadi in saka 1639.

The other story, *Bloodbath,* deals with a historical event that took place in one of the dynasties that ruled over the Vijayanagara Empire. Though bred and brought up and provided with all that he needed by his uncle Devaraya, Jayadeva kills his cousin Sivaraya (Devaraya's son) and the latter's father Devaraya II. He conspires against his cousin and uncle with a desire to encroach upon the kingdom. Ultimately everything winds up with his own death.

Another story that deals with historical theme is "The Golden Servant'" which presents the life and achievements of Kanakadasa, a saint-poet of Karnataka. Kanakadasa was not only a saint-poet but also a fighter who fought for the cause of his own people, self-respect and the like. He was a good administrator and above all, a soul that hankered constantly for a healthy society. A woman is not helpless and timorous because she is born as a woman. Woman though tender and tender-hearted by nature at times can surpass any brave man. It is witnessed in many cases of many nations. She can breast-feed the man when she is overwhelmed with motherly affection. When her heart is charged with hatred she can play umpteen numbers of tricks and bring the downfall of man. According to an old saying none equals the mother in protecting and cherishing the man and similarly none can surpass a wife in satiating and subduing the emotions and manliness of man. In both these forms of mother and wife, woman's role in the life of man is of certain altitude.

In the first of the stories under discussion, namely, "The Rebellious Rani of Belavadi", we witness the female heroism of Mallamma displayed lavishly. She fights with the two tigers quite heroically single-handed. Here is Raja Ishaprabhu, her husband, full of applause,"Bravo, my darling Rani, I am really proud of you. You have put the menfolk to shame. You have proved that a woman is never weak or helpless. Our kingdom is really proud of a heroic Rani like you" (14). He is even apologetic for not being able to protect her for which she had married him.

There is no wonder if a woman awakes and arises and answers the challenge of time and tries to protect herself, but if she the people of her own sex and trains them in the art of fighting it becomes worth considering and laudable. Probably Rani Mallamma is a rare person, a first, and a special phenomenon in Indian history to organise the women and train them up in fighting. It is possible only for an Amazonian woman like Rani Mallamma to lead an attack against the Maratha army and put them down. When Rani Mallamma and her female warriors brought back the cows captured by the Maratha soldiers the *Gollas'* happiness knew no bounds. Raja Ishaprabhu once again indulges in her praise, "Bravo... You have disproved the traditional notion that woman is weak and helpless. You have indeed become Goddess Chandi in your military achievements" (22). Even the enemy Shivaji, commended her heroism and displayed his gentle manliness though he expressed his insult and anger later. When the war with Shivaji army was prolonged Raja Ishaprabhu was down-hearted and worried a lot. Again it was Rani Mallamma who ignited the fire of encouragement in him by her fiery words. "... We are the heroes of Kannada Land... we shall achieve either victory in the war or attain heroic death on the battlefield" (25). Though Raja Ishaprabhu died in the war with the Marathas she never lost her heart. On the contrary she steered a plan to ambush Shivaji and teach him a fine lesson. She did it too. He even fell at her feet and said that she was his mother next to Jijabai and she must bless him in his future plans. Thus one witnesses the picturesque description of Rani Mallamma's personality as a good administrator, an able organiser and also as a ferocious fighter.

The other side of the medal of heroism is spiritual heroism. Kanakadasa may be regarded as the pioneer of spiritual heroism among the downtrodden section of the society. To lead a sequestered spiritual life is one thing, which is easy while compared with that of a spiritual life living in the midst of community. The days of Kanakadasa were custom-bound. The caste contrabands were quite impregnable. In such a hostile ambience Kanakadasa's decision to embrace a spiritual life is really laudable one. It requires guts on the part of a man from a downtrodden section of the society. In such a predicament Kanakadasa's growth from political heroism to spiritual heroism becomes not only significant but also recognisable, which demands serious attention. To become a *dasa* is to dedicate and surrender to Lord Sri Hari. Certain qualifications like good health, courage to protest and criticise the follies of people around and inducing correct understanding in society, etc., are required for a man to become a *dasa,* Kanakadasa would have lived a happy life of a ruler as *Mandalika* but he abandoned it along with its glorious aura and embraced the life of spiritualism with its austerities with an intention to bring reformation in society while immortalising himself in the spiritual world. As he was a relentless traveller wherever he went he arranged and addressed the gatherings to improve the people. As a part of his advice to society he has left a body of *Kirtanas* and immaculate poetry, which is in need of critical attention.

Another important element with the dignified dynasties of the past was that of their display of pomp and glory. When Mallamma married Isaprabhu their marriage was performed in a glorious way. Here is the description of their wedding, "The hall was decorated with festoons of various flowers and mango leaves.... She was decked with a variety of flashy golden ornaments studded with rubies, diamonds and jewels and looked like a veritable goddess called Rati... . All the princes offered valuable gifts of golden ornaments and silken garments to the couple. It was followed by a grand feast of a variety of delicious dishes. The marriage ritual continued for *ten days"* [italics mine] (8-9). Their married life was also full of glory.

Though glory adds to the pleasure of an ordinary man in the ordinary sense sometimes it becomes the cause of hatred and tussle. The staunch desire to possess it may also lead one to conspiracy and assassination when one is motivated by morbid desires as we witness in the story "Bloodbath", wherein we see Jayadeva killing his nephew and further planning to kill his own uncle who had bred and brought him up into a full grown man in all respects, to acquire the same glory and the seat of power.

But the case of a pious man is altogether different. Though he enjoys the glorious life and the gifts of glory he indulges in it with a sense of detachment, and very soon gets disillusioned and decides to abandon it. He may even stoop to share that personal glory all around him. Such a noble soul was Kanakadasa. His desire to attain the highest state of bliss goaded him to invest the gold, which he had got for ameliorative purposes. Philosophy in general and Indian attitude in particular holds the view that wealth and glory are *maya*. They are often held to be the hindrances on the path of a spiritual practitioner and his spiritual progress. Hence Kanakadasa's selfless generosity in the story "The Golden Servant". He, like the Buddha, renounced his position as a ruler of a province and the accompanying pomp and glory, and turned into a *dasa* (servant) of God. It holds up a mirror to the life of Kanakadasa. Thus the three stories breathe the ample air of glory of daily life and activities of these glorious characters in their full swing.

Contemporaneity is the most important component of human life. No human being can escape the clutches of contemporary tentacles. And ignorance of contemporary life, especially on the part of a writer, is suicidal. In fact a writer is a child who is vulnerable to contemporary influences. At the same time no writer can ignore the past. This concept of Time has been bothering man since times immemorial. Time is infinite and eternal. Time is, for the convenience again, divided into past, present and future by man himself who lives, thinks and acts in the present. The present is full of pressures, tensions and is concerned more about the instant and the immediate, in other words "here" and "now". Speaking of this phenomenon D. H. Lawrence writes, "Eternity is only an abstraction from the actual present. Infinity is only a great reservoir of recollection or a reservoir of aspiration, man-made. The quivering nimble hour of the present. This is the quick of Time. This is the immanence. The quick of the universe is the pulsating carnal self, mysterious and palpable."[6] Thus to capture and encapsulate the present seems to be the attempt of a writer in general and short story writer in particular, because short story writing is a process of limitation as has already been discussed. Basavaraj Naikar's preoccupation with the present and the contemporaneity in various forms and colours is quite clearly seen in the collection under discussion. Contemporary life is full of complex elements in umpteen numbers. Let us discuss these elements as reflected in the stories in the collection.

"Change is the law of nature" is an oft-quoted statement. Change in itself is neutral. But in accordance with the time, convenience and circumstance man labels the change as 'good' and 'bad'. If the antisocial elements change into pro-social it is good and fortune of the society. Change occurs when one person or a thing comes in to contact with the other. That a good person can transform the heart of a thug or a bad man is shown very effectively in the story "Change of Heart". In the story we see the house of Siddhalinga and Sivalila attacked by the thieves in the midnight of a new Moon Day. When the thieves hold the daggers in their hands and begin to move towards Siddhalinga, Sivalila rushes to the bedroom to bring the keys of almirah. No sooner does she bring the keys than she hand them over to the thieves who ransack their wealth and ornaments. Then they attack the couple again and demand other jewels if they have any. Sivalila muster up her courage and cames before the leader of the thieves and surrender the golden bangles and other ornaments including the sacred *tali* she has on. With tears gathered in her eyes, she says to the thieves who ask for other ornaments, in a piteous voice, that they have given all they have with them even, if they are not satisfied with that they must kill her first and then her husband. Puzzled by Sivalila's words the thieves make towards the door. But soon Sivalila calls them back and advises them in the following words, "See man, please don't waste this gold by drinking or playing cards. You are like *my brothers* (Italic mine). You start a shop or some other business with that money and settle down to a respectable life instead of leading such an irregular life" (47). These words of Sivalila, spoken in the affectionate tone of a sister, affect the leader of the thieves and leave an indelible impression on mind.

Within the period their a fortnight he comes back to the couple and falling at the feet of Sivalila and says that he has decided to stop thieving. These are his words. "Dear madam, you are not an ordinary lady, but a veritable goddess. *You are like my elderly sister* (Italics mine) ... You advised me like a sister to make use of that money for some useful investment ... *Your words have been ringing in my ears, without my knowing. My heart had accepted you as my sister* (Italics mines). I have now decided to stop thieving and start living a respectable life. *My dear sister* (Italics mines), please take back this gold and bless me to lead a pious life" (50). Thus, a humane approach can convert the heart of even a hardhearted thief.

University and college campuses are considered to be pure and untouched by hypocrisy and corruption. Since universities and colleges are the highest seats of learning the human belief in and expectation from them is very high. But the author, it seems, is hurt much by the pollution that has been infested on them. A couple of stories deal with the theme of campus life in the collection under discussion. The long short story that can be classed as a novella is "A Chronic Patient Became a Doctor". The story presents before the reader how Mr. Nandiswar becomes a Doctorate Degree holder. It is a saga of the protagonist. The story is full of satire on the campus life of the Indian educational institutions in general and the university in particular.

The protagonist meets his professor after announcement of the M.A. result. Then he meets Professor Nagaraj who proposes to take him as his research assistant and takes him to the City of Rocks. It is from that day onwards that the protagonist's difficulties commence. He is caught in the triple hot streams of attending the clerical job, teaching the M.A. students and carrying on the research work. In his staunch and unflinching desire to acquire Ph.D. he has to surrender himself to the severe austerities and ordeals. Ultimately his Ph.D Thesis is finished and submitted to the University. Amidst the difficulties Ph.D. is awarded to him after a continuous combat with a cynically tenacious guide. Very soon the advertisement of the university for the post of a Reader is in sight. The protagonist is elated and applies with innumerable expectations. He thinks that he is the only person who deserves the post of a Reader. But much against his expectation and hope he does not get the post of a Reader because one of the candidates is the daughter of a central minister. She has wielded much political pressure and thereby gets appointed. The news is given to the protagonist by a senior member of the department, Professor Sitaram. He discloses the news to the hero of our story.

Here is protagonist Nandiswar speaking about the shallowness of the drama of the appointment: "I was deeply disturbed by the absurd drama called the interview. I experienced and learnt that the idealist U.G.C. Rules were made a farce by the opportunistic practice of the university" (P.276). The mode of appointment followed by the authorities in the contemporary Indian set-up is often commented by the characters in this story. Even the guide of the protagonist, while working on a selection committee of Mangalore University, selects an ordinary woman without a Ph.D., while ignoring the merit of Ramaswamy. Here are the words of the professor defending. "I fought for her vehemently. I pleaded that she should be appointed as Selection Grade Reader because she has a brilliant mind. Besides her father and I were jail mates in 1942. So I had to help his daughter" (237). Today most of the Indian universities, their activities academic as well as bureaucratic administration in every rung, are politicised. Here are the words of the seasoned professor of mathematics,"... But our Universities never follow the UGC norms honestly. They always follow practical and opportunistic methods. You know our Vice-Chancellors happen to be puppets in the hands of politicians. Their sole intention is to please the Ministers, MLAs and MPs and never to maintain academic excellence" (273) which shows the predicament of the rotten academic ambience in contemporary India. Thus the story is full of satire on the hypocrisy and shabbiness of the guides in the P.G. departments and the helplessness of the students who believe them to be their well-wishers and guides, not only in academic life but also in their personal matters, while hinting at the hapless state hurled upon the innocent candidates who anticipate a job and economic security from such institutes.

Though we boast of ourselves as a democratic nation and free people, we are not so in the real sense. We live in a bureaucratic set-up, whether we want it or not. The bureaucrat is a heartless creature. He spreads around him an unpleasant odour of selfishness, ignorance and corruption. When his selfish nature is not satisfied the first weapon he hurls upon the person before him is delay — inordinate delay in attending to the file. In more than one story we come across this evil of delay process in this collection. The bad elements, in whatever walk of life they set in, take their *avatar* first in the elite and educated who are considered to be the cream of the society and then make their movement downwards, spoiling it slowly. Such a kind of degeneration is shown in many of the stories. The delay process reaches its highest point with the guide's unpardonable indifference towards his research student in the story "A Chronic Patient Became A

Doctor" but at the end the guide feels sorry for it. In the same way the Indian examiner of the thesis is equally ignorant and causes inexplicable delay. "Hence, some ten telegrams were sent to the Indian examiner every second day. From the delay in his response I could make that the Indian examiner was a thoroughly callous and indifferent person. In my imagination I visualised him an elder brother of my own supremely indifferent guide"(257). The carelessness of the clerk of the department of English of Bombay university is equally noteworthy in this regard.

Another evil that accompanies delay process in a bureaucratic set-up is corruption. Corruption lurks even in the immaculate personalities of university academicians in the modern days. A research guide expecting his student to provide for his drinks, etc. is nothing but degeneration of values. There are ample examples of corruption prevalent in the society. Naikar spares no opportunity in holding up a mirror to reflect the interior of such corrupt characters. Especially when it comes to the Department of Police who are supposed to be the guardians of law and order in the society. When the theft takes place in the house of Siddhalinga the neighbours call on him to console; one of neighbours suggests lodging a police complaint. Here is Siddhalinga's reaction to it, "Perhaps you do not know these fellows. They not only do hunt for the thieves, but also on the contrary, extract money from us. I am not the sort of person who would visit the police station. As far as possible I would like to be away from the police fellows, lawyers and even doctors" (48).

In the story "Blood for Blood", Viranagouda arranges the murder of Kalappa through the police people themselves under their own custody. The Inspector agrees to undertake the risk for the handsome amount of money he is getting. Here are the words of Viranagouda as spoken by him to the Police Inspector, " I need your co-operation for this task. Please don't think that I am asking for any favour gratis. I shall give you Rs. 2,000/- if you oblige me" (61). Herein we witness the callousness of the police firing at a snoring man, which they do much against their own conscience. Though the call of conscience warns them they repress such calls considering the economic gains.

Many times the society, the environment and the political as well as bureaucratic set-up itself propel the corruption motif among the officials. This can be vividly seen in the story, "Spiders Web". In the story we come across a character called Durgadas working as Circle Inspector. The Deputy Commissioner under whom he works has made him arrange grand parties whenever any V.I.P. visits the district headquarter. The parties would be grand and vegetarian as well as non-vegetarian. Everybody who attends them, including the D.C., dines and drinks sumptuously and never bother about the bills. How can a low salaried person like Durgadas meet the expenditure of such expensive parties? Hence he finds his own way of raising money from the dwellers of slum threatening to demolish their shacks. This money would be sufficient for Durgadas to arrange a couple of parties. Though the complaints are lodged to the Government, they are referred to the District Commissioner who is again involved in it. Thus the desire of the District Commissioner to devour the dignified dinner leads to the dire circumstances in the story. Gluttony is a sin. It leads to corruption. Sin leads to sin. There is only an entry into the world of sin but no exit. This harsh truth is seen in the story.

Politics is a part of public life. He who responds to the contemporaneity around him must take into consideration the activities that take place in public. If for political people politics is a game where from they derive diversion and benefit, for an innocent and also a subordinate it is a vortex, which ultimately suffocates and kills. People in politics can entice as well as enforce control on the people from a layman to the learned professor and poet. There are a couple of stories in the collection that deal with the theme of politics. The story "Felicitation" shows how even the learned professors and popular poets become a prey to the brainless politicians and their petty politics. Since politics is a process of dehumanisation, the politician shows no real concern for any one. In the story a poet, a critic and also the protagonist are invited by a group of petty politicians to be felicitated. The trio travels by a car to the village and is puzzled to see the people showing much indifference and engrossed in a mood to give importance to a political personality rather than to these writers. They are totally ignored and kept in abeyance. Finally the person who has gone to invite these people sents a message that he is very busy with the M.L.A. who is to address the public at the Guest House and that the trio, must go there to be felicitated. The trio since they are illustrious, take it as a sort of mortification and decide to go back to their place unfelicitated. Thus, the story holds up the mirror to the state of things in the academic world. The desire of writers and critics, to be recognised and honoured, thus becomes the cause of their insult. The desire of such persons (men of letters) to be felicitated ultimately lands them into difficulties, because it is the brainless politician who enjoys the highest respect by the public.

Another story that deals with the theme of politics is "The Spiders' Web", wherein we see the narrator becoming the cabinet level minister by virtue of his caste. Caste/religion plays a vital role in politics at least in the matters like issue of tickets by the parties to contest in the appointment and then adjusting the portfolios. The narrator in the story says that he is an idealist by nature and hence desires strongly to improve his department. He undertakes a visit to many of the offices of his district. Then he eats the sumptuous meal of fried fish. The dinner is grand. But he never bothers to pay. When addressing a public gathering as a response to the complaint of the people against a local Circle Inspector he orders for the suspension of the said officer. As soon as he announces it this man collapses near the dais and is carried out for medical aid. Later on, the protagonist learns from the District Commissioner that the man who collapsed was none but the man (Mr. Durgadas) who had arranged the grand dinner of fried fish. The District Commissioner also narrates the story of how Durgadas had arranged for the money to meet out the expenditure of such expensive parties. The protagonist feels inexplicably sorry for the predicament in which he was thrust by his own desire. How politics and politicians together play with the lives of laymen is shown in the story heart-rendingly.

The desire to grow and prosper is quite natural to human beings. If an individual grows personally by dint of hard work and diligence it is good for a nation in general and the individual in particular. When such a growth is motivated by the malevolent selfishness and is intended to suppress the growth of other individuals it leads to tussle and rivalry. In a rural atmosphere so many times such rivalry leads to factionalism. There are stories in the collection that deal with the theme of rural rivalry. The story "Blood for Blood" begins with the marriage proposal and bride examination by Viranagouda and family. Viranagouda is a political leader. Afterwards the narrator goes to Naragund and meets an old friend named Channappa who is working in the revenue department. There the narrator asks about the background of the family of Viranagouda. Then Channappa narrates the story of Viranagouda's life.

Viranagouda has developed enmity with Kalappa, a rural rowdy. After Kalapa's marriage with Parvatagouda's daughter, Parvatagouda is murdered by Kalappa and his men. When he is travelling in a bus, Kalappa and his men preclude the bus by piling some logs and boulders across the road. When the bus stop they get into the bus and attack Parvatagouda, who soon jumped out of the bus and begins to rush across the fields. "He thus ran continuously for nearly half a mile" (59). But Kalappa and his men chase him like mad dogs. In spite of his beseeching to leave him, Kalappa "hacked Parvatagouda with his big and sharp axe. His followers also hacked the enemy indiscriminately. Blood sprouted out of the inert body of Parvatagouda. They had mangled his body as if it was a vegetable" (59). Therefore to revenge his father-in-law's death, Viranagouda gets Kalappa arrested and by bribing the Sub-Inspector of Police sees that he is shot dead in the jail. Further the police people spread the news that the culprit tried to escape from the jail and hence he was shot dead by the constable on duty.

But there is a staunch disciple of Kalappa called Nagasetty. He is a cold-blooded murderer and a savage sadist. Hence his name is closely associated with dark deeds in the area. Nagasetty decides to revenge the murder of his master. Hence he challenges and taunts the followers of Viranagouda.

In the meanwhile Viranagouda receives a complaint against Nagasetty by the *hugar* (flower vending) community that Nagasetty has raped a girl of their community near the village tank and therefore he must be punished. Viranagouda takes it as an opportunity to finish Nagasetty under the pretext. Hence he plans his murder. Though later he changes his mind on the spot seeing the enemy in a pitiable condition, his follower Allabaksh kills Setty. But when the people take it to be an adventure by Viranagouda, Allabaksh, being envious of Viranagouda's popularity, begins to spread the news of self- glorification.

Viranagouda therefore decides to kill him. This time he planns to play a different trick. Instead of attacking the enemy on the face itself he asks his wife to invite Allabaksh for dinner with affection. Then he sets the murderers on him who kill him instantly. Then his dead body is taken and thrown into the brook called Bennihalla. All this is done by Viranagouda with a fear that his position may be disturbed on the one hand and on the other his son might be attacked in future. Thus the harsh truth that the desire to assert the self and self alone many times leads to the downfall and disintegration of personality is shown very effectively in the story.

Another story, "The Circle of Vengeance", wherein we see Nagappa who work's as a coolie on Naragund bus-stand, seeks shelter in Jagapur. He chooses Jagapur village only because there is a patch of land of about twenty acres unaccounted for in the rural documents. Moreover according to the conventions in the village the greatest rowdy can become the owner of the land and enjoy the status or benefits whatsoever. Hence Nagappa, a born rowdy, decides to go there, exhibit his heroism, capture the land and begin to live. Adjacent to that land-patch is another patch of two acres owned by Huchchappa. By his high handedness Nagappa merges that land also into his twenty acres land and begins to cultivate it. Soon he becomes wealthy and open three canteens and own a herd of sheep. Hence Huchchappa met a lawyer called Dharmappa who was also a native of Jagapur but settled in Dharwar practising law. When Huchchapa approaches the lawyer he gaves him *abhaya* and then goes to Jagapur and ask Nagappa to give back the possession of that land to Huchchappa. But Nagappa who is an incorrigible fellow by nature was angry with the lawyer as well as Huchchappa. Then a quarrel ensues. There is factionalism in the village. Dharmappa brings a revolver by way of precaution. There murders occur. Dharmappa shoots a man of Nagappa's party at Navalagund. Though a case is registered against him, Dharmappa bribes the judges and lawyers who investigate the case and escapes the punishment. Meanwhile the entire wealth of Nagappa melts in spending for the court, the lawyer and the police station and also in maintaining the hefty group. He is forced to close down the canteens and sell his herd of sheep. Therefore his followers leave him and join the group of

Dharmappa. In the meantime some men of Dharmappa's party pretend hatred towards him and join Nagappa's group. They begin to show extraordinary fidelity to him. Now Nagappa becomes confident.

One day he is attacked by Dharmappa and his men. He becomes furious and begins to shoot. As there are only three cartridges in the revolver, they are lost soon in the encounter. Now Nagappa comes to know that his hours are numbered. Hence he throws away the revolver and begins to run. He takes a taxi and gets into it. No sooner does he get into it than the men of Dharmappa catches him and pulls him out. "Nagappa fell on his back on the earth and before he could get up, some one in the group dealt a heavy blow with a big axe. The axe fell on Nagappa's forehead and the bleeding skin turned down and fell on his eyes and blinded him. Nagappa's body sagged to the earth" (107). After the death of Nagappa, Dharmappa, the lawyer, becomes the uncrowned monarch of Jagapur. But Kalinga, the son of the villager who is shot by Dharmappa at Navalagund, has grown into a strong and angry young man. He is sharpening his axe against Dharmappa.

Once there is a fair of the temple of Kalmeswara. That night Dharmappa sleeps outside the house due to stuffy weather. Kalinga waits for the opportunity and hack Dharmappa who is in deep sleep. The circle of vengeance is thus completed. In this way the stories discussed above show the writer's power of depiction of the rural life and rivalry in all its elemental reality.

Human relations form one of the major themes taken up by the writer. Human beings, as they live amidst the people, will inevitably come in contact with other human beings. That the relationships are the results of necessity is a known fact. Of the human relations man-woman relation is conspicuously delineated in the stories "Cross-Roads" and "Basavanti". In the first story the protagonist is estranged from his beloved Kalpana due to Razakar Movement whom he meets accidentally while he drops in at a garage to get his motorcycle repaired. Then he learns that his friend and classmate has married her. As the friend has some urgent work at Hyderabad he leaves Sivaraj at his home and goes away. It is then that the protagonist's past beloved engages him in a conversation and says that she has accepted life as it, made her to act. She says, "We come across so many things, whether it is natural or inevitable or necessary; we come across so many kinds of persons. We compromise with them in one-way or the other. If we fail to do so, we see our life slides away from us. That is why I accepted life. And that itself is life" (87).

In another story we see the protagonist Basavanti, a young girl of fancies confronted with a predicament. Though she is wedded to Kalmesh her connubial life with him is not a happy one. For her husband ill-treats her, and moreover she longs for the company and caress of her former lover. As per the latter's secret advice she even severe her relationship with her husband and goes back to her village Nagarahalli without telling him. Chinnappagouda, her former lover, feels ecstatic about her return and renew his visits to her house. He continues his diurnal as well as nocturnal visits to Basavanti's house. He gives her golden bangles, necklace, earrings and other ornaments. He gives her economic support. Their illicit affair becomes the talk of the village. Both Chinnappa and Basavanti grow unmindful of the talk and comments of the villagers.

Nearly half a dozen years go by like this in amorous enjoyment. But one day Basavanti's eyes suddenly grow dim. She can see nothing around her. When Chinnappagouda comes to know about this in the night he is shocked and gives her some money asking her to consult some doctor immediately at Hubli. But the gravity of the situation demands that she must go to Bangalore. When the news is made known to Chinnappagouda he is terrified by the gravity of the situation. He then assures her that he will supply her enough money that would suffice for the journey as well as the doctor's fees at Bangalore. But on Basavanti's asking him to accompany her to Bangalore his reply to her in apologetic tone is, "Dear, please try to know my difficulty also. I cannot stir out of the village because I have to attend to the farms. This is the sowing season. I must see that all the farms are sown in right time" (145). Instead, he deputes his faithful servant Siddappa to escort her and her mother to Bangalore. But on their consulting the doctor it becomes clear to them that there is less chance of success of operation even if carried out quite dexterously. Hence they come back to their village helplessly.

When Chinnappagouda comes to know about this he grows restless and lessen his visits to Basavanti's residence. Basavanti grows restless and feels insecure. As Chinnappagouda's visits become rare she is short of money. Therefore she is forced to sell the ornaments one by one. "Basavanti decided to live on only one meal per day as a punishment for her illegal existence with her lover" (150). Finally she abandons that single meal also. As a result her health deteriorates completely and she dies. When Chinnappagouda hears that his ex-beloved is no more, he rushes immediately to her house and offers his "last homage" to her. Then he pays enough money to Siddappa and ask him to arrange Basavanti's funeral rites properly. Thus the story of Basavanti's love and life came to an end. What becomes noteworthy in the story is Chinnappagouda's lust towards Basavanti. It is he who motivates her to separate from her husband permanently so that he can remain her permanent paramour. It is his selfish desire that sucks away from Basavanti, her youthfulness, her beauty, the social status as a respectable woman in the society and ultimately her life itself. This is so, because of Chinnappagouda's possessive nature. Thus the male possessiveness and female gullibility become important elements in spoiling the human relations. This is seen in a majority of the stories in the collection.

If a novelist has a vision of life a short story writer has reflective moments. Contemplation leads forward the thought towards reflection at the first stage and when reflection receives reaffirmation from the conscience and gets firmly established in the mind it becomes a vision. Since the canvass of a novelist is vast he proceeds to envision whereas a short story writer has a limited space and time he rests at the stage of reflection and stares at life with an analytical look. There are a couple of stories, which show the writer's mettle in writing the reflective stories.

The story "Pilgrimage to Kashi" happens to be reflective. In the story we come across a character of Govindacharya who is irreformably orthodox, who goes to Kashi but never feels free from the tangles of mundane life. A person like Govindacharya, living in the evening of life, can enjoy a pilgrimage. By his adamantine nature he has forced his sons to send him to Kashi, for they fear that he might not adjust with the co-pilgrims. But ultimately they yield and wave him off at the railway platform.

"He had a purseful of money and a strong desire to eat, nearly a month had elapsed after he had left his place, but he had never befriended any co-pilgrim in the compartment. He never participated in their chatting and laughing. He used to remain ever serious thereby showing off his riches" (127). He remain so with his contorted and morose face in spite of repeated attempts of Nagesharaya, another pilgrim to Kashi. He says, "see Acharya, you have not laughed even once during these days and never relaxed your contorted face ... shall I show it to you by holding a mirror?" (129). All along the journey Govindacharya remains introverted. The party reaches Kashi, bathed in the holy waters of Ganga and has the *darsan* of Lord Vishwanatha. Acharya participates in these pilgrimage formalities mechanically. Later during the conversation with Nagesharaya, Acharya says that they have all finished their pilgrimage happily and will go back to their homes to stay happily but his lot is quite different and he is compelled to go back to that hell house of his sons. At these words of Acharya, Nagesharaya says, "Who doesn't want happiness? But can one get happiness if one goes in search of it? We have to generate happiness in ourselves. Happiness lies in being contented with whatever little we have. Happiness and sorrow are two states of our mind ... But people remember how we live our life.... our happiness lies in what good we do to others...." (130). These words cause the dawn of awareness in Acharya. Thus the story is full of reflective dialogues.

Likewise the story "Cross-Roads" is also full of reflections. The protagonist Sivaraj reflects again and again on time. "Time is a strange thing indeed. Time, they say, has stood still. It moves neither backward nor forward. It has no limits to this side or that. Is it then infinite? ... Time is travelling eternally ... We breathe but an infinitesimal moment of this eternity and thread our sensations and disappear into oblivion"(77). In the same way the other story, "The Golden Servant" being a life story of the great saint, poet, philosopher of Karnataka, Kanakadasa, is full of reflective passages.

Technique heightens the effect of the story. While helping the narrator, as an effective tool in building up a proper rapport with the reader and in making an impact on him through indelible impressions of men and their manners, it alone cannot suffice in making a story a memorable and successful one. Basavaraj Naikar emerges as a successful reconteur by making use of diverse devices to suit his purpose.

It seems most of his stories are plot oriented. Plot may be taken to be schematisation of events in a linear form. It shows, in other words, a proper beginning, muffled middle and an exact ending. Most of the stories in the collection under discussion fall in line with the above observation. But setting predominates over plot and character as in "Cross-Roads" very rarely. As far as the effective use of setting is concerned the story is comparable with that of Chinua Achebe's "Marriage is a Private Affair".

As for narrative mechanism he makes use of various narrative manners, such as flashback technique, stream of consciousness technique, point of view technique and also first person narration. He handles these narrative techniques quite dexterously. The flashback method is very effectively used in "Cross-Roads" again.

Very often the characters created by the writer seems to be types, a common feature of Indian English short fiction writers. One wishes the kind of multiplicity in the types of characters as the author does with his manner. What becomes quite noteworthy is his power and inventiveness he reveals in creating the typically South Indian ethos. To show his attempt to convey the typically South Indian atmosphere the following lines may be quoted.

> (1) My sons offered water to the guests in small tumblers. Each one of them sprinkled water on their feet, washed their faces and rubbed them clean with towels offered to them (53).

Here is the picturesque depiction of bride examination prevalent in the Lingayat community of northern Karnataka. "The Priest Panchayya asked her to be seated on the wooden seat with her face to the east. She touched the floor with her palms and symbolically saluted all those seated there and sat on the wooden seat in a lotus posture. Then Panchayya ... took her left palm and examined the lines on it meticulously like a scientist examining the bacteria through a microscope ... he nodded his head by way of approval. Then he asked her to stand up. She lifted up her sari six inches from her feet so that every body could see the symmetry of her toes and ankles... Panchayya took out a *Shiva* string of silk and measured her ten fingers and two palms and compared it with her height i.e., from feet to the vermilion dot on her forehead" (54). Likewise he makes references to South Indian dishes and food items and food habits to make the atmosphere living and real. Here is the list of food items, which we come across almost invariably in every story in the collection. *Uppittu,* sweet balls, mirchis, fried-parched rice, puffed rice, *kadabu, holige, shyavige, sandige, rottis,* brinjal curry and curds—a fine and typically North Karnataka staple food item.

He even makes reference to many rural games like *Tiger-House, Chakka,* etc., which one can come across if one undertakes a tour across Karnataka and especially North Karnataka, the locale of which forms the prominent picturing in his works. The rural games and the participants in such games he alludes to, often in his stories, are held in the afternoon siesta or lounging in the temples or in the *chavani* (veranda) of *Gourimani* (a place where village rustics spend their leisure hours and indulge in the rehearsals of village drama and *Yakshagana* and *Doddata*) during hot summer afternoons.

The author's desire to create the atmosphere has so many times motivated him to coin the archaic Kannada words in italicised forms. Here are some words, which he uses, in his historical stories to create the administrative atmosphere of antiquity: *Paragana, Dhandanayaka, Palegar, Darbar, Karbhari, Subedar, Sarot* (a horse drown cart), *Pathashala, Swayamvara, niskha* etc.

As though he is not satisfied with the mere use of words many times Naikar employs the similes and metaphors which are peculiar to Indian life that go a long way to create Indian sense and sensibility in general and that of Karnataka in particular. Examples culled at random can suffice to show this, "bird of his breath had flown away" (29), "bewitching figure of Goddess Rati and handsome like the mythical Lord Kama" (11) and "Mallamma fought with the enemies like the terrific Goddess Chandi" (27) and also his description of the furrowed land in one of the stories as "The ridges of mud in the field looked like the folds of a black Ilkal Sari" (67).

One more striking feature of Naikar's prose style, like Raja Rao's, is the translation and even sometimes transliteration of Kannada idioms. Here are some Kannada idioms translated/ transliterated, "We must speak ten lies to arrange an alliance"(57); "The villagers had not kindled their ovens for three complete days" (58); "even a single hair of yours not hurt" (67); "the sun rose to an elbow's length from the horizon" (68); "Viranagouda had warmed the palms of the police authorities" (70). Such and many other elements in the matter of style as well as theme make the reader reminiscent of the stories of Bhabani Bhattacharya and Raja Rao. It would be interesting to study how an author makes use of his mother tongue and incorporates it in his English thereby making it typically Indian English.

The above-listed achievements of Naikar as a short story writer show him as a renowned raconteur. It wouldn't be tantamount to sacrilege either to consider or point out that there could be some areas of darkness in 'the resplendent corpus' of the short stories by him. It is a reiterated fact that brevity is the soul of short story and it depends for its success on suggestion rather than exposition or explication. If there is one enemy of whom a short story writer must be wary and always try to subdue, it is superfluity. There are a couple of stories, which seem to suffer from superfluity. My reference in this regard is to two stories selected at random. The story "Blood for Blood" which has already been discussed in detail has for its subject the bride examination. The narrator, who after the bride examination goes to Naragund, meets his friend Channappa, collects the information about the background of Viranagouda's family. He decides personally not to marry off his daughter into that family. After coming back home he consults his family, specially the bride, who dissents and his wife is also angry and refuses the alliance flatly. Actually the story ends here but the author has elongated the story with addition of one more paragraph, "A weeks later Viranagouda's messenger came to our house ... a great burden had been lifted off our chest" (74), which does not contribute any thing to the effect of the story. In the same way in the story "Basavanti", the eponymous protagonist forsakes her husband and comes back to Nagarahalli on the secret advice of her former lover Chinnappagouda. After her arrival he visits her continuously and renews his former love to her. During his visits he engages her in long conversations: "She would tell him all the stories and hearsay that she had heard or could remember and make him laugh, similarly he would narrate to her all the adventures of his younger days and keep her in good humour" (141). Here the author could have stopped the description and gone ahead to the next point. But instead he proceeds to make Chinnapagouda indulge in circumlocution: "When I was a young boy of about sixteen," he said to her one day, "I had observed the purity ... until he had his fulfillment for the day" (141-2). So also another paragraph, "Basavanti never attended ... in the enjoyment of their glorious love affair" (143). And also the last paragraph in the same story, "After three days when the sepulchral gravity had thinned ... said Lingavva" (151). The excision of the above-quoted paragraphs would certainly not hinder the pleasure of the reader but on the contrary would enhance it. In other words, their excision does not cause any harm to the total effect of the story. This is only to show that the sparsely scattered dross enhances our reverence for the veritable gold mine that the collection really is.

Thus the range and variety in theme and technique and the kaleidoscopic view that Naikar uses in his short stories shall surely secure him a firm position of honour and recognition in the realm of Indian English short fiction.

References

1. M.K. Naik, *A History of Indian English Literature,* New Delhi: Sahitya Academy, p.179.
2. Quoted by Ian Reid in *The Short Story: The Critical Idiom,* London: Methuen & Co. 1977, p.31.
3. Quoted by Ian Reid, op.cit. p.44.
4. *Ibid.* p. 45.
5. Basavaraj Naikar, The *Rebellious Rani of Belavadi and Other Stories,* New Delhi: Atlantic Publishers, 2001. All subsequent references to the stories are to this edition and have been absorbed in the text by giving page references in parentheses.
6. K. R. Hayagrivachar, *Selected Essays From D. H. Lawrence,* Chennai: Macmillan India Ltd. 1986, p.43.

7. C.V. Venugopal, *The Indian Short Story in English: A Survey*, Bareilly: Prakash Book Depot.

8. T. R. Sharma, (Ed.), *Perspectives on Rabindranath Tagore*, (Ghaziabad : Vimal Prakashan, 1986).

6

Basavaraj Naikar's *The Sun Behind The Cloud:* A Typical Indian Historical Novel

— Jibesh Bhattacharya

In India there has been a distinguished past tradition of historical novels. Most historical novels of the past were written against the background of the reign of rulers of some particular lands. The writers collect some facts of history and use them for their imaginative reconstruction. While writing a fiction, a good historical novelist researches the chosen period thoroughly and strives for verisimilitude. The main aim of a historical novelist is to present human characters showing the life and manners of a bygone age. Such a novel may be truer than history because it recreates the spirit of the time, not objectively, but subjectively. It is not concerned with mere facts or chronology, not mere spectacle or pageant, not merely the humour of the ancients but with the changing physical, intellectual and spiritual environment and the spirit of the ancient people.

English has become, in the present time, a common language of expression to the writers of various nations of the world. Because of the British Empire that extended its fold over almost the entire world, the English language, the language of the British, was understood by most nations of the world. In India, too, writers are using today this medium of expression to reach a wider audience and a larger number of readers. Among the Indian writers of the present day, who use English as their medium of expression, the name of Basavaraj Naikar may be mentioned.

Naikar, however, has not trodden the conventional path of restricting his vision merely to the exploits of a particular king, rather he looked back nostalgically to the past and tried to present before his readers a picture of the first ever battle of independence by the Indians against the British, while at the same time unfolding the glorious past of a place named Naragund. The author has a sentimental association with the period he is writing about, as he himself has stated in his preface that his great-grandfather Virabhadranayaka was one of the army officers and also a confidant of Bhaskararao Bhave, king of Naragund, whose rise and fall he narrates in his novel. This is his first attempt at writing a historical novel in English, although he has to his credit a number of critical works and translations in his own native tongue, Kannada, as well as in English.

The Sun Behind The Cloud (2001) presents a native king's revolt against the powerful British rulers, and may be treated as an account of the first battle for freedom by the Indians during the first half of the nineteenth century. The novel is a wonderful recreation of the age and the locale where the incidents took place. A historical novel gives an artist's view of a thing and not a photograph. It is an imaginative recreation of events or characters giving out the secret aroma of the past. As W.H. Hudson writes: "The historical novelist is evidently compelled to rely upon indirect information for the specific characteristics of any period he undertakes to describe and it is the sheer power of realistic imagination which will often enable a writer to see more clearly and depict more convincingly a scene he has only heard or read of than could an ordinary person who had himself witnessed such a scene or even taken part in it."[1] The historical novelist provides us with the human side of great events. And in this respect, Naikar is quite successful. He describes common incidents of daily life in so much detail that the readers are able to visualise the period in which they took place. Naikar uses his creative imagination to present his own vision of the world he portrays. Walter Alien observes: "Every novelist, then, gives us in his novels his own personal idiosyncratic vision of the world."[2] A wide knowledge of history and a romantic interest in the past are very essential for a historical novelist. Mr. Naikar has certainly gathered the relevant historical facts from different sources about the important events of Bhaskararao's time. This is evidenced by the various dates of occurrences he has mentioned in different parts of the novel. This adds to verisimilitude.

Naikar has not divided his novel into various sections or chapters, giving subtitles, as generally the novelists do. Instead, he seems to have created breathing spaces in the continuous narrative by putting five star marks in between the narration, at sixty-nine places. I call them breathing spaces as the breaks in many places appear to be rather arbitrary. It would have been better if the entire narration were divided into several sections with such subtitles as: (i) The birth and early youth of Bhaskararao, (ii) Bhaskararao's confrontation with the British on the question of adoption, (iii) Krishnaji Pant and Bania Bapu-chief conspirators against Bhaskararao, (iv) Manson and his men killed by surprise attack of Bhaskararao' s army, (v) Malcolm's attack of Naragund and Bhaskararao's defeat, (vi) Escape of Bhaskararao and his family from Naragund, (vii) Death of Yamunabai and Savitri, (viii) British atrocities after the capture of Naragund, (ix) Raghopant's capture by the British and his death, (x) Bhaskararao's arrest and death sentence by the British, (xi) The end of the traitors Krishnaji Pant and Bania Bapu, (xii) Bhaskararao's providential escape and his last life.

The entire novel, however, has its own organic unity. It tells the story of an illustrious son of Naragund from his birth till death. The various ups and downs in his career have been meticulously dealt with. Naikar mostly used the common method of narration, which is the epic method in which the author distances himself from the main story and narrates it as an omniscient narrator. R.J. Rees has described this method in his own inimitable manner: "Plain narrative is, of course, the technique most commonly employed by the novelist. He takes the position of an 'omniscient observer," and describes not only the events of his story, but the thoughts and feelings of his characters, taking a sort of 'God's-eye view' of them.[3]

Naikar has used dialogues in many places. He has made the narration lively, no doubt, but had there been appropriate variations in the dialogue according to the nature and status of the speakers, it would have been more realistic.

A historical novel may necessarily have a large number of characters. *The Sun Behind The Cloud* is no exception. But Naikar has introduced only those characters that are relevant to the main action of the novel and are somehow related to the main character, Bhaskararao Bhave. The golden rule for the historical novelist is to give a subordinate position to real historical persons and incidents and to allot a prominent place to imaginary characters and invented situations. For the danger of introducing important historical personages lies in the fact that existing records or traditional conceptions would hamper the creation of a truly living or a transcendentally imagined character. That is why historical characters are assigned a minor part or a subordinate position in historical novels. But Naikar's novel is somewhat different from the conventional historical novels. Here he has attempted to portray the life history of a glorious freedom fighter. Hence all his attention is focussed on the protagonist, Bhaskararao Bhave. And for this he has painstakingly gathered detailed necessary information available in print. As he himself writes in his *Preface*: "I made a systematic study of the topic by reading the major recorded material in print and tried to reconstruct the history of the colonial encounter in a realistic manner without resorting to sentimentalism or glorification."[4] In fact, there been scope for glorification of the principal character as the author himself has an emotional connection with him. For, his "great-grandfather Virabhadranayaka happened to be one of the army officers of Naragund and a confidant of Babasaheb" (viii).

Yet the novel does not exactly read like hero-worship. With his historical imagination, Naikar has presented before us a complete man in flesh and blood. By referring to minor and insignificant incidents he has been able to point out the various facets of the character of Bhaskararao. Thus we can have an idea of courage and boldness when on a day of 'Holi', a Hindu religious festival, he jumped, riding his horse, over the burning effigy of 'Lord Kama', that blocked his way, and also when he defied the orders of the British Deputy Commissioner of Dharwad to surrender to the British Government all the arms he and his men possessed. His heroic demeanour is further illustrated by his attempt to capture Manson and compel him to sign the order of adoption.

That Naikar has not attempted hero-worship in his novel is amply illustrated by the fact that he is not blind to the human weaknesses of his protagonist. Bhaskararao is heroic, brave, courageous, patriotic, and yet a bit sensuous too. Naikar has, at least, given two instances of his hero's weakness for feminine charm when he mentions Bhaskararao's affair with a danseuse named Bhimasani and later, Bhaskararao's lust for Annapurna, daughter-in-law of Gangadhar, a merchant and friend of Bhaskararao. This may remind one how Marlowe humanised his king Edward II, the eponymous hero of his tragedy, although a comparison of the two works is not exactly tenable.

Besides presenting the graphic figure of the protagonist, Naikar has taken much pain to portray the loyalists and the conspirators. Bhimaraya, Vishnu Kulkarni, Virabhadra Nayaka, Raghunatharaya and others are bright examples of loyalty, obedience and heroism and they never deserted their king in times of need. But, Krishnaji Pant, Bania Bapu, Chandralal Deshpande and others, who secretly joined hands with the British and brought about the ruin of Bhaskararao, have been portrayed in the darkest colours. Their cupidity, selfishness and meanness have been brought out by their behaviour and activities. Naikar has shown his imaginative perception of such characters.

Naikar has also portrayed the British officers like Manson, Thomson, Malcolm, Oglivey, not with any patriotic rage, but with the calm and dispassionate outlook of a psychologist. The British officers were in an alien land. Besides they were duty bound to serve their superior authorities. Hence, although sometimes they were sympathetic to the natives who had been arrested for some alleged crimes of sedition, they could not but give those natives the severest of punishments, including capital punishments to satisfy the whims of their superior masters. The presentation of this human side of some of the British officers makes them realistic and convincing.

There are only a few female characters in the novel. But less attention has been paid to the development of those characters. Yamunabai and Savitri are pathetic figures. When left to their fate, as Bhaskararao escaped from the palace to save himself, two women became panicky and to save their honour they committed suicide by drowning in the river Malaprabha. Towards the end of the novel, we meet one Kashibai whose only role seems to be giving her niece, a young girl, in marriage to Bhaskararao an old man of sixty-two. The other female characters are just passing figures.

The title of the novel, *The Sun Behind The Cloud,* is symbolic. 'The sun' as a symbol is applied to both Bhaskararao and the East India Company. This is said by the author himself in the *Preface*: "Bhaskararao means 'the sun' who, shines brightly and then is hidden behind the clouds as it were. Similarly the East India Company or the British Government, which believed that the sun never sets on the British Empire was behind a cloud as it were until it annexed the kingdom of Naragund and began to shine brightly" (viii). Considering the spirit of the novel, the second interpretation of comparing the British Government to the sun seems to be rather inappropriate. For, certainly the writer's purpose is not to glorify the British Government. He has made an effort to show how an Indian king bravely stood against the mighty British for gaining freedom of his own people. The word 'Bhaskar' means 'the sun', and this sun of Naragund went under the cloud of ignominy of defeat and lost all his brightness of kingly splendour and power and ended his life incognito, unwept and unsung, just as the sun covered by a dark cloud may pass unnoticed by people, to the western horizon and set. In this respect the title may have got some significance.

The use of many native words in the novel makes smooth reading and comprehension of the text by a foreigner rather difficult. The glossary of eighty-six native words appended at the end of the novel does not give the English equivalent of many more native words used in the novel. Instead of this glossary it would have been more convenient for a reader if the English equivalent of the native words used in a page are given at the end of that page, with their indication numbers. Another small addition to this book would have made it more helpful to a reader. This is a list of characters introduced into the novel with their mutual relationships. It might have been placed after the *Preface.* Again, the novel would have been livelier if some sketch of some significant incidents and characters were depicted at the relevant places in the novel. Last but not least, the medium of expression used for the narration of such a glorious tale needs careful attention, power and smoothness.

But despite all this, the novel as a whole is engrossing in its narration. The writer's patriotic zeal, ancestral pride, romantic imagination and attention to trivial details make the novel interesting reading. E.M. Forster says that the final test of a novel will be our affection for it, as it is the best of our friends, and of anything else, which we cannot define. And we feel affection for Naikar's novel for the qualities already mentioned. The patriotic Bhaskararao's betrayal by some timid, selfish and unscrupulous hypocrites has been dealt with, with extraordinary skill. The past glory of an almost unrecognised place and its brave patriotic king has been effectively presented by Naikar before a large number of readers eager to know about this almost unknown chapter of India's freedom struggle.

REFERENCES

1. William Henry Hudson, *An Introduction to the Study of Literature*, 1913; London: George G. Harrap, 1961, p. 136.
2. Walter Alien, *The English Novel: A Short Critical History*, 1954; Middlesex, England: Penguin, 1962, p. 17.
3. R. J. Rees, *An Introduction to English Literature*, London: Macmillan, 1968, p. 131.
4. Basavaraj Naikar, *The Sun Behind The Cloud*, New Delhi: Atlantic, 2001. p. viii.
5. E. M. Forster, *Aspects of the Novel*, 1927; Middlesex, England: Penguin, 1968, p. 30.

7

Turning Historical Material into Art: A Study of *The Devil's Wind* and *The Sun Behind the Cloud*

— S.B. Singh

In the vocabulary of Romantics 'history' becomes 'story' and stories of history prepares the ground, for the novelists to pick up and re-create out that story, a history which might appear to many, fictional Utopias (which is the beginning and end of fiction itself if it is good fiction) about what happens and where a past reality has happened. We accept the same as history, but the how and why of the historical moment viewed and or interpreted by the novelist is the fiction created by the creative writer re-creating the past. The sum total of story of the war, the peer, the general, the statesman, the soldiers, the spy, etc., in the historical relics or remains of the past is accepted as historical fiction. But this act of re-creating the past that is dead, the creative writer, has to live and breathe the ruins, imagine himself and others, as part and parcel of that point of time in order to extract the truth that existed, and sharpen and shape his sensibility and imagination.

The observations of Lukacs on the historical novel, even on a novel dealing with remote Biblical history such as Thomas Mann's *Joseph and His Brothers*, concentrate in a typically modern manner on the business of the novelist to recreate the past and make it contemporary. One might think of such an attitude as a revolution in the concept of the historical novel. It involves the paradox of turning the fluid nature of fiction into clear outlines of history. Written history has a pattern of certainty, whereas the pressure of innumerable details which has yielded such a pattern in course of time is the ground of all fiction. Fiction as history is a concept of the historical novel which designates the actual process of taking on the full challenge of events, and turning them into the kind of significance that history has instead of dismissing them as peripheral and dealing with the essential drift underneath. This latter process might easily lead to subjective or philosophical distortion of history. As Collingwood observes about the writing of history :

> This conception of 'turning into' the conception of becoming is ... the fundamental idea of all history.[1]

Fiction as history at its best is turning events into history just as it is turning the historical material into art. What G.M. Trevelyan defines as the requisites of a historian are equally applicable to the novelist treating fiction as history :

> He will give the best interpretation, who, having discovered and weighed all the important evidence available has the largest grasp of intellect, the warmest human sympathy, the highest imaginative powers.[2]

The paradox of freedom of fiction and the form of history yields an insight into the nature of events and what they mean in relation to history. Writing fiction as history involves an effort which is similar to Collingwood's reflections on the nature of event and history:

> For history, the object to be discovered is not the mere event, but the thought expressed in it. To discover that thought is already to understand it.[3]

Reading history is more or less like reading a story. Living and writing history is like finding a plot or a pattern of significance. Fiction as history, therefore, is extra-ordinarily rich in potentials both fictional and historical. It is the ultimate truth, realism and awareness of a particular time of which the novel is capable. One would as such agree with Georg Lukacs:

> The great realism depicts man and society as complete entities, instead of showing merely one or the other of their aspects.[4]

At the same time it is the deepest and broadest foundation that history can acquire in the unresolved variety of facts and events at anytime.

History and fiction do not blend easily. It is an act of great genius implying great liberties particularly in matters of imaginatively interpreting history in order to suit the purpose of the creative writer. Both these forms are dominant forms capable of overshadowing each other without letting either know that they are being overshadowed. However, there have been great masters of this form who have taken great liberties with history and have successfully managed to maintain a perfect balance to contribute in their own ways towards the development and enrichment of this literary form. They have known their histories intimately and moved among scenes of past as if natural and have reconstructed the atmosphere, the habits, the prevailing psychology of a generation or a race, etc. The versions of history proliferate endlessly; every version being a provisional reconstruction, that it is never possible to know all the facts about anything even the smallest act. "The things done vanish with their doing".[5]

Both these stories of Malgonkar and Naikar are stories of national histories aiming to give a comprehensive and comprehensible form to documentary history. Both supplement to the incompleteness of official histories. Both these authors use historical events and documentary evidence for their framework, operating on margins of preferentiality introducing other stories— concocted, fantastic, even private stories—which put the official historical records in question. However, they do not deny the official historical records, but by offering "so many different stories" they refuse any claim to absolute truth in the official versions. Both these novelists have stated in more or less the same way their concern with history and probably very much in agreement with Ruby Wiebe and hence adopting more or less the same method.

> When you start looking at the actual stuff from history from a slightly different angle you start seeing so many different stories there than the standard ones we have been given.[6]

However, it is beyond doubt a compulsion to ones who wrote about history when one is distanced by time, place or some other factors.

The period 1857-1858 has offered to writers like Malgonkar and Naikar a wide ranging portrait of a nation moving through a time of crisis of hope, misery, terror, slaughter, riots, loot, arson, rape of women and history. Nana, the protagonist of *The Devil's Wind* sums up in a very apt manner.

How often during the months that followed, did we sense the nearness of victory? And yet the pattern remained unbroken. At the last moment something would happen and victory would slip out of our grasp. Slowly I began to think to myself that we were not just fated to win, that it was in pursuance of some divine purpose unfathomable to us that Mother India would go on being prostituted by an alien breed; that her sons and daughters for some unforeseen sins would go on remaining slaves.[7]

Naikar's description of British soldiers under the direction of Sri Malcolm taking possession of Bhaskararao's palace and indulging in the pleasure of looting the houses of the natives not locked or properly closed, entering puja rooms with their boots on, drinking milk and curd in the deserted kitchen, getting silk clothes, silver and gold. They were simply thrilled by the huge quantity of wealth, in the cupboards and left behind boxes. Naikar remarks:

> ... the enormous wealth of Naragund was looted within a couple of days. But the only piece of luck for Naragund was that there was no slaughter of native inhabitants or molesting or raping of women. (But they) rushed into the famous library called Saraswati Bhandar (Treasure of knowledge) and burnt all the valuable Sanksrit books and manuscripts. Some of them took sadistic pleasure in butchering the cows on the sacred yard of the temple.[8]

There is evident in these novels a unique kind of imagination, a historical imagination. Both these materials show man in time and place, show him as both maker and product of history, show him in full and complex historical context and above all depicts them as a part of social turmoil. Apart from the protagonists other characters, may be imaginary ones who pass over into history as they are usually embodiments of forces or trends in Indian history. General Wheeler and Nana, Mason, Lt. Thomson, Sir Malcolm and Bhaskarrao Bhave to a great extent dramatise the tensions and conflicts of the time.

Both these novelists with their scholarly interest in history are pre-eminently equipped to handle the historical themes they have chosen. *The Devil's Wind* and *The Sun Behind the Cloud* are concise historical sketches of the Revolt cf 1857 without departing from the factuality of history. Both these novelists are fascinated by the fate of their protagonists Nana Saheb of Bithor and Babasaheb of Naragund. Both of them have sincerely felt that the stories of their protagonists have never been told from the Indian point of view. For this Malgonkar states to have spent two years on research, read over 150 books by Britishers and Indian on the Revolt of 1857. But he lets nothing of his research overburden his fiction. Naikar on the other hand is inspired by his parent's narration of the heroic feats of Babasaheb and his great grandfather, Virabhadranayaka. The process of selecting and reconstructing the theme of the novel continued for more than thirty years, and for the same he indulged in reading major recorded material in print and went collecting stories retold by many of his relatives friends and scholars in versions. But in narrating the story of Babasaheb he claims that he does not resort to sentimentalism or glorification. As such, both these books bear witness to the range and depth of the novelists' historical reading, in depicting the colonial conflict between Indians and the British.

At a time when a separate nation was slowly emerging, quite a number of native suns were rising to dwarf or negate the alien sun rising on the Indian horizon, the British East India Company. The negative and anti-Indian policies of the East Indian Company and Lord Dalhousie's exercise to implement the provisions of the Disarmament Bill and the Doctrine of Lapse with a view to plant firmly British imperialism in India made many kings including Nana Saheb of Bithoor and Babasaheb of Nargund revolt against the British. Dalhousie's policies aimed at annexing the native states by hook or by crook, by application of divide and rule, by suppression and oppression and so on. All these created an atmosphere of revolt which finally broke on Sunday, May 10, 1857 when Indian soldiers called 'Sepoys', stationed at Meerut, killed their British Officers, their women and children, marched to New Delhi, fifty miles away and captured the city without much difficulty and proclaimed the Mugal Emperor, a helpless, bent man of eighty-two, as their leader. The East India Company and the British were fleeing to the fields and jungles as fugitives, or as described by Paul Scott in *'The Raj' Quartet,* were reduced to lead an existence like a scorpion within a ring of fire. The Rebellion swept across India from May 1857 to July 1858—a period in which terrible atrocities were committed by both sides: men, women and children both British and Indian were massacred. About half a million people died, about 3,000 Britishers and the rest Indian. By the end of the year the Company's authority was restored, but the relations between the British and the Indians were never the same. Initially the mutineers received popular support in areas of Uttar Pradesh and Bihar. Fortunately for the British, the mutiny spread slowly. At this point of time most parts of southern India remained unaffected, but the news of the mutiny and the messages of the leaders of the Revolt like Nana Saheb, a victim of the British who had refused to recognise him as the Maharaja and denied him of his family pension as per agreement with Baji Rao II brought into action. Persons like Baba Saheb, of the Peshwa dynasty, a victim of the British policy due to heirlessness rebelled against the British and finally declared war.

British historians have portrayed these Maratha kings as monsters of evil, which recent historians like R.C. Majumdar and S.N. Sen have rejected. But, both these novelists have filled the blanks which the historians were incapable of filling through their narrative. Narrative in itself is the life-blood of history. The important thing is the story, and the wonder of how, what, when and who. The 'why' they both assume would come out in the telling of the story, by way of placing lumps of analysis in the story to help the reader understand 'why', and in both these narratives, *The Devil's Wind* and *The Sun Behind the Cloud,* these analytical digressions do not obstruct the flow of the narrative. In explaining 'how' both these novelists communicate what the past felt like, what it looked like and what emotions drove people to decisions and actions. Here is history as 'heritage' hallowed with nostalgia, and sustaining the intimate psychology of their characters, the Indian rebels and their British masters. They are both scrupulously true, to the period and the nature of human beings.

They remain faithful to the feel of what had happened, the inner dynamic, the core truth while maintaining fidelity to known facts of history.

Both these novelists have picked up historical personalities who enacted their roles in the hour of crisis and then disappeared from the scenario, leaving behind scholars and historians ponder and account little about them in the prescribed limits of history and historicity. So paucity of historical materials in respect of their protagonists became an advantage to them. The feelings, thoughts and experiences of Nana and Babasaheb before and after the actual historical occurrence, after a historical distance of about one hundred and sixty/seventy years provides a resulting ability to the whole event clear and whole. Both these protagonists come richly alive, marvelously 'felt' and 'observed', created from a sense of withinness from an 'inner' vantage point. Yet, none of those novels read like stories of hero worship. With their historical imagination in full display, both these protagonists are presented as men in flesh and blood, suffering from human weaknesses very much like common human beings. None resort to glorification. Bhaskararo is heroic, brave, courageous, patriotic but is also sensuous. Nana lacks according to Malgonkar the heroic virtues or qualities but he has been made a hero by circumstances prevailing. He has been declared the hero for giving effect to Satichaura and Bibighar incidents. However the fact is that he is always away from carnage. He is also a very sensuous person. This exercise adopted by the novelists to humanise these protagonists attracts comparison with Shakespeera's practice in King Edward II. Both these novelists have paid almost no attention towards the development of female characters. They are depicted as nothing but pathetic figures.

One of the remarkable things about both these novels is the accurate and convincing portrayal of mid-nineteenth century British India. Malgonkar has a historian's eye for facts, so does Naikar. They make dead bones of the period live by making them move. Every effort has been made by them to reconstruct the feeling, the emotional and moral atmosphere of an earlier period with deliberate patience and care of a humanist. They also don't turn the history of Mutiny inside out, but they work with their imaginative insight into the established historical material for the clarification of their protagonists' motive and point of views. They have broadened our understanding of the Sepoy Mutiny and the contribution of the British in creating such a situation by adopting unnatural policies from a novelist's perspective, probing the protagonist's psyche which of course lies beyond the historian's domain. The novels are 'meditations on history' and succeed as historical novels by being a stimulus to the imaginative and critical faculties and an education in human sympathies. Both these novels, apart from being a historical rendering of facts, acquire great significance as the psychological story of individual's intense quest for fulfilment which is sought in the values of friendship, patriotism and love. Both these protagonists have been trapped in identical situations and compelled to be wanderers. Both make a voyage to Nepal, meet each other, admire each other, discuss the causes and consequences of the mutiny and the opportunistic behaviour of the British in India. In exile Nana gets the company of Eliza and Babasaheb of Kashibayi's niece. Babasaheb gets married and becomes a father in his post-sixties. Both return from Nepal to their motherland Kanpur and Nargund only for a very short time, only to lament for what has been lost. These are where both the novelists give full objective description plus subjective or emotional life of the main characters in relation to the events of history.

Malgonkar and Naikar as historians are not distanced with the histories they have fictionalised or presented through their fictions, very much like Ruby Wiebe, Paul Scott or Salman Rushdie who are distanced, although they are also narrating stories of national histories. Both Malgonkar and Naikar are novelists very much 'in' the history racially, Naikar coming more closer by tracing his family link, Vidarbhadranayaka being his great grand-father. As such, they are more successful in presenting a comprehensive and comprehensible form to documentary history, supplementing the incompleteness of official histories. Historical events and documentary evidences are used within the framework of the story, and interpenetrated in it are other stories—concocted fantastic even private stories—which put the official records in question. However, they do not deny the official historical records, but by offering 'so many different stories' they refuse any claim to absolute truth in the official versions. Such practice is not at all new which can be seen only in these novelists. All novelists concerned with history, fictionalising history or writing historical fictions have accepted this as compulsion. In these books both Naikar and Malgonkar fall in line of novelists like Ruby Wiebe, Paul Scott, Salman Rushdie, Taslima Nasreen and others in showing their concern with history. The following novelists have stated:

> Wiebe When you start looking at the actual stuff of history from a slightly different angle you start seeing so many different stories there, than the standard ones we have been given.[9]

> Scott... the best is only history and between our history and our lives there is this vast dark plain where the rapt and patient shepherds drive invisible flocks in expectation of God's forgiveness.[10]

> Rushdie... there are so many different stories to tell, too many, such an excess of interwined lives, events, miracles, places, rumours, so dense a commingling of the improbable and the mundane.[11]

However, as readers and interpreters of history these writers although having much in common also differ among themselves.

So far as Naikar and Malgonkar are concerned they have interesting similarities as historical novelists apart from selecting a common point of historical time 1857, protagonists of the common racial stock — the Maratha clan, protagonists having more or less the same fate—striking and then disappearing into oblivion, never to rise or stage a comeback. Some other striking similarities may be accounted as follows:

1. Both share epic aspirations, though expressed in different images.
2. Both are novels of multiplicity and duplicity of history which contains events capable of making many histories and many silences—capable of giving birth to many fictions.
3. Both seek to make visible/audible what has been pushed to the margins and forcibly silenced.

4. Both seek to deconstruct the opposition between fiction and history, to make available what has been suppressed and by doing so reveal the official interests at stake in this suppression.
5. Both are revisionist history which subvert the official view and offer a critique of authority.
6. Both are constructive/deconstructive and creative reworking of history which supplement historical facts in order to give a more comprehensive account of historical processes and of the continuum between lived experience and recorded history.

On the whole, without being partisan, it can be held that both Naikar and Malgonkar have opened the gates for others to march in the grey area by taking up and fictionalising history for clarifying and presenting their own points of view, because what they have presented is not complete. There are still many tales to be told and many histories to be created and highlighted, precisely because *The Devil's Wind* is more history than novel or story, whereas *The Sun Behind the Cloud* within its symbolic manifestation is more story or novel than history. Whatever is left out or is incomplete has to be filled up by the coming generation of novelists and historians, without charging these novelists of having presented something historically inaccurate or writing a fiction round of facts—Malgonkar writing in the form of fictive autobiography and Naikar in the form of biography.

References

1. R.G. Collingwood, *Essays in the Philosophy of History,* p. 74.
2. Quoted, Richard Langhorne, "Historiography," *The Twentieth Century Mind,* Vol. I, p. 107.
3. R.G. Collingwood, op.cit., p. 214.
4. Georg Lukacs, *Studies in European Realism,* p. 6.
5. Rubey Wiebe, "A Novelist's Personal Notes on Frederick Philip Grove", *A Voice in the Land,* p. 219.
6. Shirley Numan, "Unearthing Language : An Interview with Ruby Wiebe and Robert Kroetsch," *A Voice in the Land,* p. 230.
7. Malgonkar, Manohar, *The Devil's Wind,* p. 220.

8. Naikar, B.S., *The Sun Behind the Cloud*, pp. 134-35.
9. Shirley Numan, op.cit., p. 230.
10. Scott, Paul, *The Raj Quartet, The Day of the Scorpion*, p. 318.
11. Rushdie, Salman, *Midnight's Children*, p. 9.

8

Fiction and Faction in Naikar's *The Sun Behind the Cloud*

— *Aroonima Sinha*

The Sun Behind the Cloud is a historical political novel that deals with the conflict between Bhaskararao Bhave, the King of Naragund, belonging to the Peshwa Dynasty, and the authorities of East India Company. This is a first novel by Basavaraj Naikar of Karnatak University, Dharwar, who has written besides others, two short story collections one of which *The Thief of Nagarahalli and Other Stories* was nominated for the Commonwealth Fiction Prize from Eurasia in 2002.

As Basavaraj Naikar himself says, "writing a historical novel is not so easy as that of a contemporary novel. The novelist has to do a lot of research and locate a logical thread in the mutually contradictory pieces of information thereby reconstructing history in a convincing if pleasing manner" (Preface, pp. viii–ix).

Indeed, the writer of a historical novel treads on a narrow path where he cannot let his creativity over rule historical facts. All he can really do is to give us a glimpse into the inner workings of the protagonist's mind and dwell on the circumstances that led to the making of that particular fragment of history.

This paper attempts to examine the tensile connection between fiction and faction that the novelist has woven into his novel, with his vast panorama of characters and the turbulent historical events of the period.

The times when the central character, Bhaskararao, ruled, i.e., the middle of the nineteenth century is best described from the point of view of the East Indian Company as an era of Acquisition. It was a period of the trampling of the 'native' spirit and oppression of the masses. It was a time when the avarice of the East India Company knew no bounds, and various cruel Acts like the Disarmament Bill and The Doctrine of Lapse were introduced much to the chagrin of the people. The culminating point was the Sepoy Mutiny in 1857, about which Naikar has given a very flimsy picture concentrating more on the locale of Naragund and its unfortunate king.

Why Basavaraj Naikar has chosen a well-known legend of Bhashkararao amongst the vast panorama of Deccan Kings is made clear by the author himself. It is because Virabhadranayaka, one of the author's ancestors, was in the army of Bhaskararao and a close confidante of the latter. Along with the main character, there are a number of well-known historical figures that make a fleeting but lasting appearance in the novel. The lesser-known characters especially the women characters make a deep impression.

The whole novel can be divided into two parts. The first part deals with the birth, the opulent adolescence and the accession of Bhaskararao, whereas the second part deals with the conflict of the king with the authorities of the East India Company and consequently his downfall, his flight and his arrest, his escaping the death rope by a quirk of fate, and his life as an ascetic in Varanasi. Bhaskararao marries again at the age of sixty and his craving for a son and heir is at last fulfilled. But the irony of the whole situation is that now Bhaskararao is no longer a king and has no kingdom to bestow upon his son. When he needed an heir he was at the zenith of his glory and a son born to him would have changed the history of Naragund because the Doctrine of Lapse would not be applicable in the case. The story compels us to think about the strange ways of providence and creates an aura of pathos around Bhaskararao.

Bhaskararao is certainly not a marked character but he does have a 'fatal flaw', which happens to be self-respect. The much-awaited son of the Naragund royal family, he is considered a blessing of Lord Venkateshwara, a splendid temple of whom has been built by Bhaskararao's ancestors. It overlooks the capital of Naragund, which lies on a leonine hill having the "grand look of a sleeping lion" (p. 1). The festival of car pulling, i.e., the *Rathyatra* during the *Navaratri* festival, is a major event of the kingdom. The building of the temple itself has a hair-raising story behind it, which was handed down to Bhaskararao at quite an early age.

When Bhaskararao becomes king, after the demise of his father he has no choice but to follow in the glorious footsteps of his ancestors. The last round of advice to Bhaskararao by his father is, "Don't be afraid of anybody or anything in life. Never be a slave to anyone. Nothing is greater than self-respect" (p. 17).

The last words of Apparao is like the general advice of a father to his son but it becomes the 'mantra' of Bhaskararao's life, and leads to an era of conflict.

After the initial reluctance, Bhaskararao proves to be an able administrator. He soon gets the feel of absolute power and gives in to the cravings of lust.

Bhaskararao's consort, Savitri, "a beautiful girl of good family," has been selected by Appa Saheb Sarkar himself. She belongs to the well-known Manjrekar family of Ajara of the Western Ghats. Married early, Bhaskararao is not dissatisfied with his pretty wife and spends five years without worry or anxiety. "He used to spend half of his time in military exercises and the other half in the arms of his pretty wife" (p. 5).

No other women enter his life until he ascends the throne. His roving eye, however, falls upon a temple dancer during the holy service at the temple, and he happens to observe "the details of her beauty as he had never done before. Her hair had been secured on top of her head, the mischievous light in her eyes, her drooping shoulders, her shapely breasts and her protuberant posterior charming in themselves assured an additional beauty when twisted into different postures and gestures..." (p. 21).

The burning desire for the danseuse use leaves Bhaskararao in agony, and he soon sends for her. Bhimsani, as her name is, is overwhelmed by her "unexpected turn of luck" (p. 23) and tries to make most of the situation by securing a position for her guru, Keshar Prasad, and herself. A palace for her and her guru is built which is only a quarter of a furlong from the king's palace. An underground tûnnel, connecting Bhimsani's palace to the king's, is built at great cost. This is to facilitate the king's nocturnal visits to his beloved without facing the scrutiny of the palace guards and without hurting the sensibility of the neighbours of Bhimsani.

The other woman who is mentioned by the author also appears during the time when Bhaskararao is at the peak of his reign. She is Annapurna who is the young daughter-in-law of Gangadhar, a close friend and confidante of Bhaskarao. He espies her when she is fetching water from the well, and without knowing anything about her identity, he is besotted by her. He discloses this to Gangadhar who is shocked beyond measure when he realises that it is his daughter-in-law who has caught the king's fancy. A loyal subject, he however cannot stoop this low to please his king. He thinks, "Can he allow her to be an adulteress? Can he give her upto the king ..? What would be the consequences is they refused to surrender his daughter-in-law to the king ?...(p. 47)

Gangadhar takes advantage of the king's ignorance about the whereabouts of the woman and decides to dispose of his daughter-in-law. First of all he sends his son away on some errand and then digs a huge pit in his backyard on the pretext of performing a special *puja* to appease Goddess Laxmi. A huge cauldron is placed in the pit with all the paraphernalia of worship and Annapurna is asked to climb down into it and squat in the cauldron along with an idol of Lakshmi. As soon as she begins the *puja* with her head bent down, a copper lid is placed on the cauldron, with a big stone on top. The pit is then filled with mud, ignoring the muffled cries for help by Annapurna. This tragic incident involving the deliberate murder of a innocent women only proves that women were mere pawns in the political game, and there were no qualms in doing away with them on the altar of self-respect but mostly, self-gain. Savitri and Yamunabai (Bhaskararao's step mother) also end their lives by drowning themselves in the river when Bhaskararao flees his land and Naragund is captured by the British. These episodes involving the women are perhaps deliberately inserted by the author to give a humanitarian angle to the political drama depicted in the book.

Bhaskararao rules peacefully for fifteen years, which go by in "royal luxury and merriment" (p. 25). But he cannot rest in peace because of his heirless state. In spite of many astrological consultations and *yagnas* he fails to become a father. He decides to adopt a son from amongst his relatives in Pune but the Doctrine of Lapse has already been promulgated, according to which Bhaskararao's kingdom will be confiscated by the East India Company in the absence of an heir. The Disarmament Bill is also not far behind, and its outrageousness leaves every self-respecting individual seething in anger. All kingdoms, according to the Bill, have to surrender their areas to the British. But Bhaskararao's approach to it is more pragmatic than to the Doctrine of Lapse. He bids his people to hide their weapons and welcome the rude British soldiers with cool drinks and sumptuous food. This makes a great difference in their behavior towards the common people as they refrain from being their usual discourteous selves.

Bhaskararao's meeting with Mason, the East India Company Deputy in charge of the Deccan states, is disastrous. Mason cannot give him any assurance to calm the agitated king of Naragund on the Doctrine of Lapse. The latter, therefore, connives with other Deccan ruling chiefs, especially those who like him do not have an heir, and plan to revolt against the Company.

Therefore, Bhaskararao's association with Nana Saheb and his sympathy for the proposal of "coming together to fight for the cause of saving their country and honour from the British people" (p. 54) seems justified. A little before the Sepoy Mutiny of 1857 a new consciousness among ruling chiefs of belonging to a common fraternity was taking birth. A feeling of nationalism was being born and the majority believed the Britishers to be 'kafirs' and oppressors. Now the ruling chiefs were looking beyond their own kingdoms and broadening their mental horizons.

Another incident of Mason's meeting with the sixty-three Deccan rulings chiefs is an interesting one, and it only proves how well the British understood the 'native' pre-occupation with notions of valour and prestige, and had found ways to strike at its very roots. Mason orders sixteen gates to be erected, each smaller than the other, so that the kings, as they enter the smaller gates, would have to get down from their horses and bow their heads. Sarnayaka, the aide of Bhaskarao, with his sword demolishes the gates in order to facilitate his king's grand entry. This gives rise to admiration among other royal guests and angers Mason who however is placated by the forthright answer of Bhaskararao.

Mason is ultimately killed by the soldiers of Bhaskararao in a hot-blooded impulsive act. The murder sounds the death knell for the king of Naragund. "He knew inwardly that this event was the beginning of disaster, although he could not visualise all the details. He thought that the snake of British power, which he had wounded now, would bite him to death any time in future" (p. 108).

The Britishers continue keep a close watch on Bhaskararao with the help of the Naragund clerks, Bania Babu and Krishnaji Pant, who, for the lure of gold, supply the company with all the information. A war with the British is now imminent, and meticulous preparations are made by Bhaskararao.

The characters of Bania Bapu and Krishnaji Pant in the novel are found galore on the pages of history. Their services are enlisted by the British to send important information on the affairs of Naragund. They are also responsible for the defeat of Naragund at the hands of the British because they mix ragi and oil into the gunpowder kept in the armoury. History, it is said, would have had a different face had it not been for the avarice of some employees. It is imprisonment, not gold, which is given to these two traitors clerks in the end, and this is the usual treatment meted out by the British to all traitors in their colonial rule.

If there are traitors and rebels in Bhaskararao's kingdom, there are people like Vishnu Kulkarni and Virabhadranayaka besides others, who do not desert their king and fight to their utmost ability. When Bhaskararao has to flee, having lost the battle, he is accompanied by a handful of trusted followers who never betray him. But the spy system of the British is so efficient that Bhaskararao is captured and sentenced to be hanged to death. He escapes death by a quirk of fate when a loyal subject Sankara, who used to take lunch and dinner for Bhaskararao in jail, points out about the uncanny resemblance between himself and the captive king. He also coaxes the king to escape, wearing his clothes and, agrees to die instead of the king.

Bhaskararao escapes to Nepal and then lives the life of an unknown ascetic in Varanasi. He is unable to regain his kingdom because all his men have been put to death by the British. His remarriage to Kashibai's niece, his becoming father after the age of sixty and his unsung death in Vasai, near Mumbai, makes us wonder at the dexterity with which Bhaskararao is tossed about on the two extremes of recognition and anonymity, of fame and ignominy. He accepts his fate and seems to have found a certain measure of peace and contentment towards the end of his life.

Naikar has merged both fiction and faction to tell an interesting story. He leaves the reader in suspense about the identity of the hermit who stays in the 'ashram' and dies an anonymous death in the last chapter of the novel. He could have been a close relative of Bhaskararao. The ploy, however, fails to create the required effect, as the reader already knows it is not Bhaskararao. Perhaps the novelist has tried to show through this how people close to Bhaskararao faced the consequences after the insurgence. Being a historical novel, dates and facts dominate the whole book, sometimes wearing thin the tensile connection between fiction and faction. The solar image, as embodied in the title, does suggest the contrast between light and darkness in the life of its protagonist and the fortunes of the East India Company. But unfortunately for Bhaskararao the sun never shines again, and his dream of regaining his kingdom is never realised. The novel can be termed a period–piece because of the detailed attention to the rituals and customs of the times and the coverage of the manipulations of the East India Company which was successful in subjugating the princely states of a land of multi-varied cultures.

Reference

Basavaraj Naikar, *The Sun Behind the Cloud,* New Delhi: Atlantic Publishers and Distributers, 2001. (Futher references to this edition are parenthesized within the text of the paper).

9

From Static to Dynamic: A Critical Study of M.M. Kalburgi's *Fall of Kalyana*

— S. John Peter Joseph

> A true play is three-dimensional; it is literature that walks and talks before our eyes. It is not intended that the eye shall perceive marks on paper and the imagination turn them into sights, sounds and actions; the text of the play is meant to be translated into sights, sounds and actions which occur literally and physically on a stage. Though in fact plays are often read in silence, if we are to study drama at all intelligently we must always keep this in mind.
>
> (Marjorie Boulton, 3)

Of all the genres of literature, Drama happens to be the most powerful and effective medium in world literature. As an impressive audiovisual means of expression, it represents joys and sorrows, hopes and despairs, successes and failures and in total the entire human affairs on the stage. Being an integral part of culture, drama highlights customs, moral edifications, philosophical reflections, religious beliefs and social and political vicissitudes of a country. Apart from depicting general human experience on the stage, a drama seldom fails to provide instruction, entertainment and enlightenment to people. As a well- established genre, it has a close link with other fine arts such as music, dance, painting, sculpture and architecture. Describing the unique nature of drama, Girish Kaṛnad observes: "There is no maxim, no learning, no art or craft that is not found in drama. For it is the joys and sorrows of human nature expressed through gestures and other techniques" (71).

India, known for its long cherished art, culture, varied customs, languages and literatures, has a glorious dramatic tradition of her own. With its splendid and illustrious history of dramatic literature and elevated stage performances India has undeniably made remarkable contributions to the world's dramatic literature. The exceptional dramatic creations of genuine and gifted playwrights of ancient India like Kalidasa, Bhasa, Visakhadatta, Bhavabhuti and Harsha marked the real flourishing of classical Sanskrit drama which can be compared only with the much acclaimed dramas of ancient Greece and Rome. In spite of having such a glorious tradition of dramatic literature and performances Indian Drama in English has not prospered as much as it should have done. Regarding the slow growth of Indian Drama in English, K.R. Srinivasa Iyengar rightly observes:

> Modern Indian dramatic writing in English is neither rich in quantity nor, on the whole, of high quality. Enterprising Indians have for nearly a century occasionally attempted drama in English— but seldom for actual stage production (226).

Though Indian Drama in English has not fared well, the rich and varied Indian dramatic tradition has been kept alive by such renowned playwrights as Rabindranath Tagore, Sri Aurobindo, T.P. Kailasam, H.N. Chattopadhyaya and Bharati Sarabhai. These playwrights who wrote noteworthy dramas in English during the pre-Independence era liberally borrowed themes and characters from Indian mythology and ancient Indian literature. Moreover, the *Ramayana*, the *Mahabharata*, the *Puranas* and The *Bhagavad Gita* are permanent sources of themes for the playwrights. The *Upanishads* have also a great source of inspiration for a number of playwrights. Deeply rooted in Indian culture and Hindu religious thought and mythology, some of the playwrights depict the themes of philosophical, religious, social and political problems in their plays. But the growth and development of Indian Drama in English is certainly far greater in the post-Independence period. Playwrights like Asif Currimbhoy,

Gurucharan Das, Girish Karnad, Pratap Sarma, Shiv K. Kumar, Mahesh Dattani have, of course, enriched Indian Drama in English. Their plays deal with the themes of contemporary social, political and economic problems, corruption practised in the name of religion, evils of the caste-system, widow - remarriage, psychological conflicts, the East-West encounter and religious problems. Though they have used new methods and innovative techniques some of their dramas lack stageability.

It is quite unfortunate that Indian Drama in English has not achieved the status that Indian Fiction or Poetry in English enjoys in the realm of Commonwealth Literature. Compared to other genres, the general output of Drama in Indian English is quite scanty and inadequate. Several reasons can be cited for the paucity of drama in Indian Writing in English. Firstly, English does not happen to be the mother tongue of Indians. Though English is now accepted as the second language in schools and colleges in many parts of India, English is still treated as an alien language. Natural and spontaneous conversation is an indispensable aspect of a drama. But in Indian Drama in English the vigour and vitality of a spoken language is miserably lacking when two or more characters are speaking in English on the stage. As a result the conversation often becomes highly artificial. Secondly, it is not as easy to write dramas in English as in one's mother tongue. That is the reason why many talented and commendable dramatists first write dramas in regional languages and then translate them into English. Thirdly, the role of the audience is an important factor for a drama. Unless the audience is English-knowing and matured, a drama in English seldom succeeds in eliciting the proper response from it. Fourthly, since a drama is a performing art involving techniques of stagecraft it is basically meant to be staged. The real success of a play can be judged only on the stage since "a drama is a composite art in which the written word of the playwright attains complete artistic realisation only when it becomes the spoken word of the actor on the stage and through that medium reacts on the mind of the audience" (M.K. Naik, 225). It is quite appropriate to quote in this context the words of R.K. Dhawan:

> It is a well - known fact that the real success of a play can be tested on stage. A playwright needs a living theatre to put

> his work on acid test, evaluate its total effect on the audience and thereby get a chance to improve upon his performance. This handicap has not allowed him to pursue playwriting in a systematic and comprehensive way (19).

It is an acknowledged fact that many plays written in English do not get staged. In this connection what Rama Sarma has observed in the preface to his *Collected Plays* holds good: "Any play written in India in English has an inherent disadvantage in the sense that it is not very often staged. Stage-worthiness being a basic test for a play, most of the plays written in English do not fulfil this requirement" (IV).

Indian Drama in English undoubtedly relies considerably on the translation of regional plays into English. Compared to the translation of novels written in regional languages into English, the translation of Indian Drama in English is quite limited in number. The dramatists who have translated their plays from their regional languages into English are Rabindranath Tagore, Badal Sircar, Mohan Rakesh, Girish Karnad, R.S. Badal, C.C. Mehta, Mahasweta Devi and Gurujada Apparao. Several plays written in Bengali, Kannada, Hindi and Marathi have been translated into English. These transaltions have unquestionably enriched the oeuvre of Indian Drama in English. Quite incredibly the fame and reputation of Indian Drama in English is characteristically based on translations than on original plays written in English. Basavaraj Naikar's *Fall of Kalyana,* an English translation of M.M. Kalburgi's original play in Kannada entitled *Kettitu Kalyana* is undoubtedly and exceptional addition to the realm of Indian Drama in English Translation. The play is an outcome of Kalburgi's research findings on the noble life and the determined pursuit of Basaveswara.

The dynamic and charismatic personality of Basaveswara is so admirable and magnificent that it has inspired many writers from the twelfth century down to the twenty-first century. Several poets like Harihara, Bhima Kavi and others have endeavoured to depict the character of Basava in their own style. Moreover, some of the playwrights of Karnataka have also tried to portray the versatile personality of Basava in their dramas. But unfortunately their treatment of the grand personality of Basava happens to be only partial and incomplete. For instance, in *Sankaranti* P. Lankesh mainly focuses his attention on the issue of inter-caste marriage raised by Basava. H.S. Shivaprakash's play gives a picture of the kind of recognition and treatment given to Basava by his fellow *saranas*. Girish Karnad's play, *Tale Danda*, highlights only Basava's fight against the evils of the caste system prevalent in the twelfth century Karnataka while ignoring other important aspects of his work. It is quite obvious that "all these three playwrights have failed to portray a satisfactory picture of Basava's social, economic and mystic philosophy and progressive thinking as it emerges from his own vacanas . . . ." (R.M. Girji, 125). But the play by Kalburgi quite successfully depicts the wholesome and multifaceted personality of Basava. In the words of Basavaraj Naikar:

> He (M.M.Kalburgi) has tried to distil the quintessence of Basava's philosophy — including a rejection of Vedic brahminism, the concepts of kayaka, dasoha, istalinga, jangama, social equality, gender equality, etc and present it through the dramatic form. He has placed Basava in the right perspective which acts as a corrective to the partial picture of Basava presented by other clever dramatists (IV).

Fall of Kalyana dramatises the magnificent life of Basaveswara, a great and renowned social reformer and mystic of the twelfth century Karnataka. It deals with the theme of the conflict between Basava's progressive and dynamic ideology and the static principles of orthodox brahmins, Skivites and King bijjala of the Kuntala kingdom. It vividly portrays the emergence of the dynamic environment from the static environment and finally the decline of the dynamic environment due to the inevitable forces of the static environment. It graphically depicts the memorable life of Basava in three significant phases: the first, the caste-oriented agrahara-culture of Bagewadi, the second, the dogma-oriented exploitative and corrupt monastery-culture of Kudala-Sangama, and the third, the power-conscious and money-oriented palace-culture of Kalyana. The play begins with Basveswara, a fifteen-year-old brahmin boy, son of Madarasa, the Mayor of Bagewadi in Karnataka, snapping up the sacred thread, a symbol of the brahmin caste. He does not want to wear the sacred thread because it "makes him a brahmin instead of a human being (*Fall of Kalyana* 1). He wants to defy the agrahara culture and the age-old brahminical tradition because the caste system creates divisions among people and, moreover, the concepts of *karma* and rebirth strengthen the division. He protests against the brahminical authority and tradition because "the loss of creativity and dead mechanicality start from the day one puts on the sacred thread" (2). He feels that wearing the sacred thread has stifled his vision, growth and inner potentialities. He reasons that following the path of *dharma* and Truth is greater than adhering to the ethical codes of Vedic brahminism. Though his parents and relatives urge him to retain the sacred thread and to follow the *agrahara* culture Basava does not heed their advice and reiterates his stand that he is fully determined to reject both the brahmin society and the *agrahara* culture. Consequently the entire family of Basava is excommunicated from the brahmin society because Basava is found guilty of insulting the *Manusmruti* by tearing off the sacred thread. Defying the authority of the Brahmin Council and the *Manusmurti* Basava leaves for Kudala-Sangama in his quest for Truth.

In the monastery at Kudala-Sangama also Basava is not happy for he finds that the dull and mechanical reading of the *rudra*, the habitual recital of *mantras*, the routine offering of a thousand leaves of bel and other similar rituals, have failed to awaken intelligence in him. He feels that the monastery, apart from being dominated by the selfsame priestly culture as in the agrahara, remains a static force. He understands that just as the stagnant water is impure the static mind also is impure. If the impure water should become pure it should flow. Likewise, if the impure mind should become pure it should become dynamic. Hence "the static perishes, the dynamic perishes not" (13) becomes the *leitmotif* of the play.

Basava is a lover of peace and embodiment of compassion. In the monastery he vehemently protests against animal sacrifice. He does not accept the view of the temple authorities that animal sacrifice is quite necessary to appease Gods in order to get rains. By preventing the evil practice of animal sacrifice Basava earns the wrath and the displeasure of the Shaivite priests in the monastery. He also advocates the worship of *istalinga*. According to him "one should consider one's soul as God and worship its symbol, i.e., the *istalinga*" (20). He says that though both the sacred thread and the *istalinga* are worn around the neck by the orthodox they are different from each other. While the sacred thread classifies society into brahmin, kshatriya, vaishya and sudra, the *istalinga* removes this social division established by Vedic concepts. Moreover, the sacred thread empowers a man to conduct sacrifice but the *istalinga* enables a man to attain spiritual purity.

Basava does not like rituals which are meaningless and are conducted in the name of religion. He understands that the rituals of the *agrahara* have entered the temple and the monastery also. He does not like "the dance service of the Devadasi system, the practice of libation, the cross-palanquin procession, the purchase of puja items and other such activities" (25) which have been attached to the temple. He firmly believes that the rich temples and the senseless and illogical rituals cannot certainly uplift the common man. He feels that in village temples even "pots and bowls, roadside stones and trees enjoy the status of gods" (25). He has a contemptuous attitude towards rituals such as barking like dogs after worshipping God Mailara, walking about naked after worshipping God Bhairava, walking on cinders, torturing the body, sacrificing pregnant women, women in confinement or marriageable girls and such other cruel activities (26) which flourished in the village temples. Moreover, the meaningless rituals to be observed at birth, death, initiation and marriage have made people static. Basava believes that the problems of people would be considerably reduced once the rituals at the temples and the households are discontinued.

Basava who has defied the brahminical agraharas and revolted against the caste-conscious brahmins is now determined to defy the Shaiva temple culture and its rituals also. He makes it clear that the temples which have become centres for misusing the name of God must be rejected. He is disgusted to see that financial business has grown unbridled and rampant in monasteries. They have, of course, become centres of black marketing and money-lending business. He also finds that monasteries have lost their secularism, and the public money of the monastery has been used by the pontiff for self-aggradisement. Basava observes: "If this habit continues, the monasteries, i.e., the public property which have become the property of one caste, will one day be the property of one family" (32).

In the second phase of his life Basava has grown more spiritual and society-conscious. He pleads that wisdom and discretion should be used for the betterment not only of an individual but of the entire society (33). He further illustrates :

> Universal experience is nothing but socialisation of spiritual experience. Every individual should partake of the universal experience. So far I had considered individual purification very important but now I have realised that the purification of society is equally important. Thus as society cannot improve unless the individual improves, the individual also cannot improve unless society improves. It is, therefore, not possible for people to be happy until and unless they destroy the old order of society and create the new (33).

Basava sees that corruption and exploitation have grown rampant in society. The corrupt kings have been exploiting the people, the fraudulent priests have been exploiting the gullible devotees, and the arrogant men have been exploiting the innocent women. According to Basava the entire society has been obviously divided into two categories: the exploiters and the exploited. Keeping this in mind he decides to work for the unity of the divided society and establish a corruptionless and exploitation-free society.

As in the agrahara of Bagewadi Basava undergoes both physical and mental torture in the hands of the authorities of the monastery at Kudala-Sangama. He is subjected to severe torture by Pasupati, the pontiff of the monastery. When Nagalambika, the sister of Basava, says that "this society is not allowing you, the flowing water to go ahead," Basava replies that "these people can kill me, but not my ideas" (29). Basava's unflinching and unswerving determination reminds one of Santiago in *The Old Man and the Sea*. Realising the hidden potentialities in the character of Basava, Isanyaguru, a priest in the monastery, tells him: "Basava, like others you were born as the child of the age, but you have been growing as the father of the age. If your thoughts are translated into action, this age would definitely turn from static to dynamic" (26). Basava moves to the city of Kalyana to continue his mission of working for the welfare of humanity which would certainly be an advancement of individual welfare started by him in the monastery at Kudala-Sangama.

In the third phase of his life Basava strives to bring about economic equality, social equality and religious equality in society. Appointed the Finance Minister of the kingdom, Basava advocates collective work and collective feeding. He also introduces the concept of *kayaka* which means "not only physical labour but mental labour as well. It means one has to work not only for oneself but also for the society" (43-44). He, moreover, advocates the practice of *dasoha* which means "ownership by neither one nor others" (44). He is of the opinion that *dasoha* "presupposes the ownership of an object of God and use of it for another man. There is no chance of hoarding in *dasoha*. By not hoarding material things we can live happily and develop our treasure" (44).

In the city of Kalyana Basava establishes the Socio-Spiritual Academy. The members of this Academy are called *saranas*. The work-culture that emerged from the Academy started taking roots in the entire kingdom. The principle of *kayaka* emerging from the enjoyment and glorification of labour combined with that of *dasoha* brings cheer and hope to people. According to Basava's new economic policy money happens to be "one of the causes for the division of society into high and low" (48). He, therefore, believes that "bringing equality in matters of money automatically paves the way for social equality" (48). In his social system all human beings are equal to one another. Moreover, the Socio-Spiritual Academy now replaces the temple culture and the monastery culture, and encourages the community culture and organisation. Since the priests of temples and the pontiffs of monasteries are reactionary forces and both have created caste discrimination and underprivileged class in the name of religion, Basava, through the Academy, introduces a new concept of religious worship. According to him, "One's home is monastery. One's body is the temple and one's soul is the deity of the body temple . . . . *Istalinga* is the symbol of the deity. Daily service to this symbol will help people to attain spiritual elevation" (40). *Istalinga* also emerges as a symbol of social equality since it is worn by people irrespective of the castes they belong to. The social and the spiritual discussions of the Academy through serious utterances are brought out in the form of *vacanas.*

Basava fights against caste discrimination vehemently. To him the existence of the caste-system is one of the social evils which would always end in exploitation and social injustice. He is of the view that untouchables have been exploited by the high caste people for ages. He calls the practices of tying the thickets of thorns to the backs of untouchables and the hanging of skeletons beside the wells of untouchables as cruel and inhuman. According to him untouchability is a serious social crime. On entering the lane of the untouchables he even touches the feet of an untouchable as a mark of respect. While addressing an untouchable he says:

> The earth is common to the temple of Siva as well as to the lane of untouchables. Water is common to ablution as well as to libation. Caste is common to those who know their selves. This is my view. None is low or high by birth. The low is he who created this division (57).

He affirms that he is ready to sacrifice anything for the abolition of caste discrimination in society. To remove this evil system is his mission in life. To bring about social equality he even eats food in the house of an untouchable. He says: "I have to sanctify myself by feeding on your food" (58). He further says, "You and I are not different from each other. Both of us are maheswaras. The food prepared out of the earnings from hard labour is indeed very great food" (59).

Basava suggests that to remove *varna* discrimination inter-caste marriages should be encouraged. He even invites young Saranas to come forward to marry daughters of slaves and prostitutes. The Socio-Spiritual Academy is not a centre for a mere discussion on the eradication of caste discrimination, *varna* discrimination and gender discrimination but a holy place for the practice of these ideals. Following the philosophy of the Sarana Movement a young Sarana willingly marries a forshaken prostitute in the presence of Basava and others in the Academy. The prostitute tells Basava: "You who wrought the miracle of converting the impecunious fellows into rich people, have worked the miracle of converting me, a prostitute, into a respectable wife.

You are the veritable lord supreme for me" (70). The Academy feels that since society is responsible for forcing women into prostitution it should rectify that wrong and enable prostitutes to lead a respectable life. When Basava happens to see the widows of a Velevali going to die on the funeral pyre of their dead husband he prevents them from performing this cruel practice. When the officer in charge of this ritual tells Basava that the practices of Velevali severing his own head with a sword after the death of his master in the battlefield and his widows dying on his funeral pyre have been handed down from ancient times. Basava tells him that these are not social values but are mere exploitations of common people by royal ones and of women by men. To remove this heartless and inhuman practice Basava introduces very boldly the idea of widow remarriage. He suggests that like widowers, widows also can remarry.

The *sarana* culture has been introducing social changes with regard to gender discrimination. A woman may have wealth and glory yet she has been deprived of social justice in the male dominated society. The Society of Saranas feels that though there is a biological difference between man and woman the inner soul is neither male nor female. Owing to the emergence of the Sarana Movement woman now enjoys self-respect. She who suffered a lot due to orthodox views and conventions established by male dominated society once has been able to lead a dynamic life now. Because of the Sarana Movement women begin to cherish not only social values in their domestic life but they also enjoy freedom in their spiritual life. Owing to the reformist movement and ideas propagated by the *saranas* the Kuntala kingdom grows into an ideal one. Social inequality and economic inequality are considerably reduced. Gender discrimination and class discrimination start disappearing. Society has been undoubtedly progressing from diversity to unity. To remove *varna* system a brahmin gives his daughter in marriage to the son of a sudra. This marriage between a man of low-caste and a woman of high-caste proves to be the culmination of the reformist spirit of the Sarana culture.

By way of introducing another progressive social and religious reform Basava enthroned Allamaprabhu, a shudra, on the Sunya Chair—a religious institute. Allamaprabhu is a great scholar and an able proponent of *sarana* philosophy. The pontiffs and the jangamas express their protest against Basava and his action. Basava makes it clear that the institute the *saranas* have established is not of caste but of knowledge. Since the *sarana* Movement has brought about a comprehensive global view regarding several important issues concerning society they need an institute to pass on such ideas from generation to generation. Moreover, this institute represents a pro-civilian philosophy. He further justifies his stand that he would promote the Sarana culture to uphold knowledge and to challenge the caste system at all levels whether it is social or religious. Raising a strong protest against Basava's bold and courageous initiative the Shaiva pontiffs express their view that the policy of Basava may lead to the fall of Kalyana. Brushing aside the threat of the pontiffs Basava observes: "If the city of Kalyana is ruined, another ten cities like this could be built. But my concern is with the welfare of the people. That is why I would like to end the caste-oriented jangama tradition and establish knowledge-oriented jangama culture" (78). The pontiffs also express the view that in course of time the institute established by Basava too may become stagnant. Basava replies:

> It is the nature of water to freeze in winter and flow on in summer. Likewise, it is the nature of society to stagnate on account of *Karma* and grow dynamic on account of *dharma.* We cannot prevent society from being dynamic now with the fear that it may stagnate in future. Our experiments in dynamising must continue. We have developed our philosophy in such a way that it does not allow for stagnation of the individual or society" (78).

In the trial conducted in the court of King Bijjala the brahmins accuse Basava of destroying the *varna* system under the guise of social reform. The Shaiva Pontiff and the Shaivite priests strongly defy Basava who, according to them, has been destroying the religious system in the name of religious reform. The royal dignitaries oppose Basava as he is, according to them, destroying the political system in the name of political reform. The king finally charges Basava that he has been destroying both the social ethic and the royal ethic without a qualm. But Basava reaffirms that he would continue his mission of establishing economic equality, social equality and religious equality. The king finally gives his verdict that Basava who has violated the royal order and religious order is dismissed from his ministerial post and banished from the city of Kalyana. The king also orders that the brahmin and the dudra who conducted marriage between their daugther and son should be punished by being dragged to death by an elephant on account of their violation of the *varna* system. The king also bans the *vacana* literature which questions the imperial authority and the *varna* system.

Though the *saranas* are basically peace-loving and non-violent some of them get enraged with the king's verdict. They know that they have established "*dharma* in the place of *karma* and formulated the body-temple culture in the place of stone-temple culture and the spiritual-home culture in the place of palace-culture and the socio-spiritual culture in the place of monastery-culture" (88). Despite their peace-loving nature some of the Saranas feel that they must encounter a sword with a sword since the city of Kalyana grew bloody with the blood of *saranas*. Finally they assassinate the king in a cruel manner. The play ends with the king's soldiers going to the Socio-Spiritual Academy and attacking the *saranas*. Many *saranas* are slaughtered and some of the *vacana* literature is consigned to fire.

Thus the play, *Fall of Kalyana*, remarkably dramatises the eventful life of Basaveswara. The play is undeniably a visual representation of the integrated and comprehensive personality of Basava. It memorably illustrates the message and the humanitarian values preached and practised by Basava. It exemplifies very effectively the total revolution which Basava intended in social and religious spheres. With a combination of true scholarship and creative imagination the playwright successfully brings out Basava's social as well as spiritual philosophy. He also depicts in a compelling manner the way Basava attains wholesome maturity by way of making tremendous progress in the first phase from *karma* to *dharma* and in the second phase from physical to spiritual and in the third phase from spiritual to social *(Fall of Kalyana, 1)*. In all the three phases of his life Basava struggles strenuously and resolutely to change people and their environment. Hence the playwright uses the *leitmotif*, "The static perishes, the dynamic perishes not", in several places in the play in order to reflect the energetic and creative personality of Basava. While commenting on the achievement of the play R.M. Girji observes:

> The picture of Basava that emerges from the present play is very comprehensive as it gives due importance to all the major aspects of Basava's liberal and humanist philosophy . . . . It is a realistic presentation of Basava's life of struggle and ethical nobility against the backdrop of religious dogmatism, political authoritarianism, communal segregation, gender discrimination of the twelfth century Karnataka (126).

The play, *Fall of Kalyana,* can be compared to T.S. Eliot's *Murder in the Cathedral* in some respects. Both the plays depict the eventful life of two remarkable and significant historical characters namely Basaveswara and Thomas Becket. Both belong to the twelfth century. Though the central theme of the play, *Murder in the Cathedral,* is the significance of martyrdom one cannot deny that the recurring theme of the play is the conflict between the Church and the State. In other words, the conflict is between Thomas Becket, the Archbishop of Canterbury and King Henry II. Similarly, the major theme of *Fall of Kalyana* is the conflict between Basava, a great social reformer and mystic, and King Bijjala of the Kuntala kingdom. Though *Murder in the Cathedral* is basically concerned with the assassination of Thomas Becket at the instigation of king Henry II, *Fall of Kalyana* portrays vividly the events which lead to the banishment of Basava and finally to the fall of the city of Kalyana. King Henry II appointed Thomas Becket the Archbishop of Canterbury because the latter would be less authoritative, less independent, less arrogant, a useful adviser and, moreover, a fine and welcome ornament of the court. But after assuming power Thomas started realising his real spiritual responsibility and inevitable loyalty to the Pope in Rome. As a result, a wide breach between the king and the Archbishop developed. The enmity between the king and the Archbishop ended only in the cruel and inhuman murder of the Archbishop right in the cathedral. Similarly, King Bijjala too appointed Basava the Finance Minister of the Kuntala kingdom thinking that he could use Basava's influence and exceptional intelligence for his selfish ends and for protecting his sovereignty. But unfortunately a tug-of-war between the King and Basava develops when the latter tries to establish economic equality, social equality and spiritual freedom in the kingdom. When Basava becomes very popular among people due to his reformistic zeal and spirit the king begins to be apprehensive of his own future. Unable to accept the social and spiritual reformation brought about by Basava, King Bijjala banishes him from Kalyana and destroys the Socio-Spiritual Academy. Both *Fall of Kalyana* and *Murder in the Cathedral* depict the contemporary social, political and spiritual problems faced by people. While Thomas Becket fights against the temporal authorities in England, Basava fights against the conservative religious leaders and the power-hungry king. There is undoubtedly an evolution in both the characters. While in *Murder in the Cathedral* the tempters, especially the first three, try their best to prevent Thomas from achieving martyrdom, in *Fall of Kalyana* the orthodox priests and the royal dignitaries deliberately obstruct Basava from fighting against social and spiritual inequality. It is needless to say that both the protagonists certainly move from static to dynamic in order to achieve something extraordinary in life.

Drama may be defined as a comprehensible and meaningful story in action. The story should be unquestionably intelligible and well-spoken but it must also be in action. For an effective drama, conflict of some kind is quite indispensable. There should be some conflict or clash between the protagonist and his surroundings. *Fall of Kalyana* is unmistakably an effective drama which dramatises the conflict between Basava and the Vedic brahmins when the former snaps up the sacred thread. This conflict sets in motion a series of conflicts which follow one another in a logical sequence. The resolution of the conflicts is the banishment of Basava, the cruel assassination of King Bijjala and the eventual fall of Kalyana. Since "a play is an integral part of a performing art and not literature" (Vijay Tendulkar, xxiv) it should give due importance to structure, dialogue, characterisation and other theatrical techniques. In the words of Vijay Tendulkar: "A playwright must possess two skills. One: the skill of characterisation. The other one: the sense of structure" (xxvii). Unlike a conventional drama *Fall of Kalyana* has forty scenes some of which are short which naturally enhance the stage-effect. With his theatrical craftsmanship the playwright presents the situations and the episodes which are impressively dramatised. Though the entire play is divided into scenes, all of them are interlinked with one another keeping the sense of structure as well as the unity of action in tact in the play. With a keen sense of theatrical aspects the playwright maintains a striking balance between dialogue and action in order to keep the tempo of the play and make it stageworthy. Moreover, the framework of the play is not static; its flow is unimpeded.

In order to communicate his ideas effectively to the audience the playwright takes utmost care in the depiction of theme, dialogue and the language well suited to the purpose. The careful selection of the plot and the theme clearly demonstrate the commitment of the writer. He has taken great pains to give adequate stage directions. Moreover, a careful blending of vision and stagecraft makes the play more natural and logical. In order to make the play effective he uses symbols and images. Water is used as a constant symbol in the play. While the flowing water symbolises the pure and the dynamic state of mind the stagnant water symbolises the impure and the static condition of mind. Any great drama requires genuine and like-life characters who perform their actions on the stage in front of the audience. With his power of observation and his deep sense of understanding human nature the playwright is able to create true-to-life and authentic characters in the play. Almost all of them are quite lucid and unambiguous. He gives them life and authenticity. His insight into human nature lies in creating an immortal character like Basaveswara. The playwright successfully breathes life into this timeless and imperishable character and brings him to the twenty-first century with flesh and blood on the stage. With a great historical sense and imagination the playwright succeeds in revitalising the past. He effectively carries the past to the present and by commendably connecting the past and the present, he admirably projects the present into the past and quite successfully humanises the characters who lived nearly eight hundred years back. With a creative mind he is able to reconstruct a convincing picture of the twelfth century.

Basavaraj Naikar's translation of M.M. Kalburgi's *Fall of Kalyana* originally written in Kannada is indeed a landmark in the realm of Indian Drama in English Translation. Himself a novelist, short-story writer and critic, Naikar introduces the play to the English-speaking audience. As a writer with a true sense of craftsmanship he shows his great ability by composing a crisp and thought-provoking dialogue in English. He does not introduce lengthy speeches and bombastic rhetoric. He employs effective spoken-language which reveals his capability to dramatise a situation appropriately. A quick and cursory survey of Indian Drama in English reveals that language happens to be a great hinderance to some of the playwrights. For instance, the plays of Sri Aurobindo have lengthy speeches in verse which ultimately impede the central action in them. Similarly playwrights like T.P. Kailasam, H.N. Chattopadhyaya, A.S.P. Ayyar and some others with their ostentatious rhetoric, obsolete and quaint diction and high-flown words mar the reality of the language in their plays. Hence some of their plays lack stage-sense and are primarily meant to be read.

In *Fall of Kalyana* the language used by Naikar is quite natural. Moreover, there is no artificiality in the spoken-language. The dialogue, of course, has the force and the vitality which mark the real dramatic quality and the theatrical craftsmanship of the translator. As a writer with a genuine feeling for drama and theatrical values Naikar creates convincing dramatic dialogue in English. In fact, the dialogues throb with passion and intensity in several places in the play. As a writer who knows the basic principles and the nuances of translation Naikar has spared no pains in giving elaborate end notes to illustrate the technical terms typical of the Sarana culture. They certainly help the non-Kannada readers who need clarification for several references in the play. His true insight into language subtleties and flair for expression and vocabulary undeniably make the play a real *tour-de-force.*

With his effective and admirable translation Naikar is able to bring about the image of the illustrious and outstanding personality of Basaveswara who can be compared with "Buddha, Jesus Christ, Karl Marx, Mahatma Gandhi, Ambedkar, St. Augustine and Nelson Mandela in different aspects" (*Fall of Kalyana,* v). Unlike the 'closet' dramas of Rabindranath Tagore, Sri

Aurobindo, T.P. Kailasam and H.N. Chattopadhyaya *Fall of Kalyana* in English translation with its action-oriented scenes and persuasive and convincing dialogues can be effectively staged. On the whole, Basavaraj Naikar's translation is certainly a welcome addition to the corpus of Indian Drama in English Translation.

10

Dynamics of Spirituality in Kalburgi's *Fall of Kalyana*

— P.Obula Reddy

Indian Drama in English Translation is, unfortunately, very limited in quantity as compared to fiction. It is indeed regrettable that the rich regional literature of multilingual and multicultural India is not made available in English translation in large quantity even after the lapse of sixty years after independence. One of the ways of resisting the colonial hegemony and Eurocentric thought, is the discovery of abundant regional literature through translation, especially English translation. The Indian dramatists who are available in English translation are so limited in number as to be counted on one's fingers: Tagore, Badal Sircar, Mohan Rakesh, Girish Karnad, Mahasweta Devi and Gurajada Apparao. Basavaraj Naikar's *Fall of Kalyana*, an English translation of M.M. Kalburgi's original play in Kannada entitled *Kettittu Kalyana is* a welcome addition to the realm of Indian Drama in English Translation. Kalburgi, former Vice-Chancellor of Kannada University at Hampi, Karnataka State, has compressed his research findings on the life and mission of Basaveswara in this play. Basaveswara happens to be one of the greatest free thinkers and mystics of the world.

The personality of Basava is so grand, noble and multifaceted that it has tantalised many a writer from twelfth century down to the present one. Recently a few fashionable playwrights of Karnataka have attempted to portray the picture of Basava in their plays, but alas! They have turned out to be miserable failures on account of the superficiality of their modernist vision. For example, P.Lankesh's play, *Sankranti* cleverly concentrates on the intercaste marriage inspired by Basava's vision of a casteless society, but ignores the other aspects of Basava's elevated personality and mission. H.S. Shivaprakash's *Maha Chaitra* highlights the reception of Basava by his contemporary *saranas*. Basava, therefore, recedes into background. The point of view adopted by the ordinary characters is rather irreverent, vulgar and irritating. Girish Karnad's *Tale Danda* tries to reduce Basava to less than his grand and magnificent stature thereby making him a small and helpless man with a confused mind. Thus all these three plays have failed to portray a satisfactory picture of Basava's social, economic and mystic philosophy and progressive thinking as it emerges from his own *vacanas* as well as the poetry written by others on him. Kalburgi's play is far better than these plays because it foregrounds Basava and his encounter with orthodox brahmanism and King Bijjala and highlights Basava's protestant ideas which are discussed below.

Enlightened few always returned to *karma* and selfless service after spiritual epiphany. The whole exercise of life is fulfilled only when the life is lived with all its variety with a sense of detachment and selflessness. To achieve this poise of mind one must pass through the necessary steps of renunciation. It is only when one dies to the past and prejudiced present that the real life begins. Dr. Kalburgi's *Fall of_Kalyana* is a play about the life of Basava. He is a twelfth century mystic who started interrogating himself and his life quite early in his childhood. He breaks the thread that binds him to the community of brahmins in Bagewadi *agrahara*. He dislikes the thread that makes him a brahmin and prevents him from being a normal human being. He comes to this conclusion after examining his life for six years as a brahmin. The thread ensures a sure bondage to *agrahara*.

Basava says the thread arrests his growth. He feels his creativity is lost. No doubt it got him the prestige of being a God on earth. He is not for any honour disproportionate to one's own work. It detaches him from the community of human beings. The thread ceremony begins the deadening process. Life becomes a series of mechanical rituals. He cannot accept it as a bettering device.

Basava could not endure when the brahmins say that the working people, the shudras are unholy. How can men become holy and women unholy? The sacred thread becomes a symbol of contempt. Basava convinces his father that the rituals are not progressive. He is in search of *satya* (truth), which is the greatest. His mother's expostulations for conformity are of no avail. He decides to defy the *agrahara* culture. When the priest threatens him with excommunication he says that he is rejecting the community itself. But the priests resolve to excommunicate Basava's family as a whole as compliance to *Manusmriti*.

Basava decides to leave for the monastery of Kudala-Sangama. He surprises the mentor Isanyaguru thereby his assertion that God does not inhabit the vicious and the evil. Basava is soon disappointed by the monastery, which practises the same rituals like that of *agrahara*. He avers that the monasteries too need purification. He cannot sleep in the monastery.

Basava is attracted by the democratic principles of the temple culture. But he cannot tolerate the priestly culture. The mechanical readings of *rudra*, the recital of *mantras*, the offerings of thousands of bel leaves do not help the awakening of one's intelligence. The Shaiva *karmakanda* is like that of brahminical *karmakanda* of the *agrahara*. He could not read even the Shaiva literature as it is for the priests and pedants.

Basava undergoes an epiphany in this crisis. Suddenly it occurs to him that the water becomes dirty when it stagnates. It becomes pure and remains pure as long as it flows. This resolves into his life long refrain, "The stagnant is impure and the flow is pure. The static perishes, the dynamic perishes not." He calls this awakening his mentor and it drives him and decides his future life.

Back at Bagewadi Basava's father Madarasa is about to die. He recalls the death in life they had all these days. Basava's mother left for her brother's place and breathed her last there and received a bramhinical funeral. Madarasa hopes for a relaxation of the excommunication at least after his death. The priests relax but Basava does not allow them to touch his father's body. He carries it himself and cremates. When he leaves the *agrahara* Basava leaves behind all the property to the servants. His comment on his property is worth all attention. He tells the servants:

> This property has grown on account of your sweat. I am giving it back to you. You release me from the debt I owe you. Later you distribute the land, the house, the open site and the cattle among yourselves. Now, come on, you take this money. You take this gold and silver; you the sweeper, take these ornaments: you take these utensils (p.17).

Basava and his sister Nagalambika move out of Bagewadi with a bundle of their clothes as the servants shed tears. Basava's refrain "The static perishes, the dynamic perishes not" is heard repeatedly.

Basava does not believe in animal sacrifice. He protects the sheep that the High Priest has ordered to be sacrificed risking his own life. Basava's worship is peculiar. Basava's teacher Isanyaguru is surprised to find him with his back to the idol. His aim is to purify himself inwardly. He agrees with Basava that exterior worship is a waste if there is no inner purification. Basava says that the idol worship has separated spiritual meditation. In order to prevent this rift one should consider one's soul itself as God and worship it as *istalinga*. His *istalinga* is different from the Shaiva practice though both are called *istalingas*. *Istalinga* acts like a symbol of the invisible soul. It is not like the sacred thread that he broke as a child. A brahmin after wearing this classifies society as brahmin, kshatriya, vaishya and shudra. *Istalinga* removes this social division. Basava observes:

> The sacred thread classifies people on the basis of their birth, the *istalinga* does on the basis of merit... According to Vaidicism not only a sudra or vysya even a kshatriya cannot become a bramhin...But Lingayatism is quite opposed to that. According to it, a man who is considered as a non believer on account of his bad conduct can become a believer in this life itself by virtue of his good conduct (P.21).

The worship of *istalinga* transforms the material body into a divine body. The human soul is covered by the moss. It can be purified only by meditation. Regular meditation humanises the individual and takes him nearer to God who in fact is with in his own soul.

The chairman of Kudala-Sangama does not like the independence taken by Basava. He demands conformity to the established procedure. The monastery becomes cruel to Basava. But Basava knows well that the rich and ritualistic temples cannot uplift the people. Worship makes the poor poorer as there is material investment in temple worship. Basava decides to reject the temple in order to ward off the financial deterioration built into the system. Even the simple temples of the village practised their own vices and sacrifices. Temples are the seats of negative activities in the name of rituals. Basava says:

> We must defy the temples, which have become centres of misusing God. Instead our legs should be pillars; our head the golden crown and our body the temple. Every man should be a moving temple. Our personality should be transformed from static to dynamic (p. 26).

Basava does not care for the hostility of the temple authorities. He is not scared. At the most they can kill him but not his ideas. He is quite convinced of his method. He aims at universal betterment by the socialisation of spiritual experience. Purification of the individual should lead to the purification of the society. They cannot be separate. Basava's teacher advises him to shift to Kalyana. The lamp of Kudala-Sangama has to become the leading star of the whole society.

Basava enters Kalyana at a time when King Bijjala is worried about the treasury accounts. Basava convinces the emperor that he could set right the accounts with his honesty and hard work. Basava's work style transforms Bijjala's court. His office as an accountant realises his motto, "Work is Heaven". His work precipitates into memorable axioms like — "Do the right work at the right moment," "Earn the money profusely like water and spend it economically like *tirtha.*" These precepts are simple and practical. They do not break one's head for meaning. Basava himself works hard and receives a low salary and thus sets an example. King Bijjala says:

> He is a divine person. He is an embodiment of trustworthiness and honesty. The circle of his charisma has been widening day by day. His arrival is like a ray to the capital city of Kalyana and light to the Kingdom of Kuntala (p. 38).

Basava realises that the caste and poverty are the two factors, which set the peace of the society at bay. Social welfare can be ensured only when the society is released from these twin sorrows. He diagnoses that this can be best done by labour. He opines that the monasteries and temples created an underprivileged caste. He advises the people to reject the monasteries and convert their own homes into monasteries and temples and make their soul the reigning deity. People can attain spiritual elevation by meditation on *istalinga* symbolising one's own soul. *Istalinga* becomes a symbol of social equality. This is a sure way to attain equality.

Poverty is another hurdle. People can overcome it. Basava's solution for this is labour. He makes the necessary tools available for people from the royal treasury. He also arranges for their collective work and collective feeding. He feels, it is the moral responsibility of the kingdom to provide the basic necessities for the citizens. He takes liberty to provide houses, clothes and other essentials from the treasury. He feels that the royal treasury belongs to the people and not to the emperor.

Basava's ideas on justice sound peculiar when the cowherds complain that the robbers have taken away their cows. He asks them to send even the calves to the robbers. He does not hold that loss of cows is an affront to the sentiments of religion. He says:

> Religion, religion, religion, who included them in the religion? These are meaningless Vedic rituals. They are not agreeable to me. You take these calves and hand them over to the robbers (p. 42).

Basava washes the feet of jangamas when they come for work and salutes them. They shy away from him. They are surprised that a brahmin by birth and a minister can ever touch their feet. Basava says:

> The Lord of Kudala – Sangama would simply laugh at me if I say that I am a Brahmin. Neither am I a brahmin nor are you nonbrahmins. This feet worship is meant to remove inequality. This is the way for the soul to respect another soul. In my social system there are neither brahmins nor nonbrahmins. We are human beings and equal to one another. (p. 43)

Basava does not believe in discriminating people as masters and servants. Workers are the gods. He feels their visits make his home sacred. He considers them holy. He says that ministers are servants and the emperor should know that he is the greatest servant. *Kayaka* is not only physical labour. It leads to mental purity. There is no difference between the kinds of work. A cobbler who does his work with devotion is superior to even the brahmim who does the holy service with out devotion. *Kayaka* is the most sacred of religions. Workers are the real gods who produce food and comforts for the people.

Kalyana becomes the abode of work culture. People are elated by their work and purity of mind. A new religion of *Kayaka-dasoha* springs out of divinisation of labour. *Istalinga* has bulldozed all caste discriminations. Basava is quite aware of the consequences. This may lead to another religion. Machideva expresses his happiness:

> The temple culture, which encouraged the priestly exploitation, was replaced by the monastery culture, which in turn encouraged pontifical exploitation. Now the Socio-Spiritual Academy that we have established has replaced these two cultures and been encouraging the collective culture and organisation (p. 46).

The spirit of the Academy is propagated through *vacanas*. *Vacanas* serve the people with good precepts. The force, purity and simplicity of *vacanas* is amazing.

Basava imposes tax on *agraharas* and cuts the grants for the temples. As people are turning to *istalinga* worship devotees became less in temples. Brahmins instigate King Bijjala against this. Brahmins try to enter the abode of Basava as jangamas. But Ghattivalayya objects and says they are not pure. When they contest he explains:

> Blame not the earthen pot, if it is broken.
> The milk in it is sweet and the ghee fragrant
> And are holy food for the Linga Supreme.
> The *Saranas* of Lord Kudala-Sangama
> Cannot be called handicapped ones
> Lest it should lead us to Hell.

This is the supreme ethics of Basava. The body of *saranas* is not a measure. Their feelings are sublime. Gattivalayya establishes their superiority as they do not eat without working like brahmins.

Basava dismisses *velevali,* the practice of the servant cutting his head with a scissor to follow his master in death and *masti,* the practice of a devout wife dying on the funeral pyre of her husband. Basava explains that these are exploitations masquerading as values. Basava advises the women:

> Matrons "you cannot spoil your holy body consecrated for Lord Kudala Sanga". Your husband's severing his head for exhibiting his loyalty to his master is inhuman practice, indeed. Similarly your dying on the funeral pyre is another inhuman practice. The concepts of Heaven and entry into Heaven are all false notions and illusions. You have to live on." (p. 54).

Basava feels that the citizen is the basic unit of the kingdom. *Samboli* is another inhuman practice that Basava could not like. Why should the untouchable warn others of his arrival and wear a thicket of thorns? Basava removes the skeleton hung beside the well meant for untouchables. As he removes the skeleton he listens to the *vacana* of Jedara Dasimayya, the super *sarana*:

> People see a skeleton
> By the side of a well
> And call it the well of untouchables.
> If they talk sinfully
> With their mouths made of many a bone,
> Their mouths are worse than
> The well of untouchables
> O Ramanatha (p. 56).

Basava regrets the treatment meted out to the untouchables. None is low. Caste is decided by one's work. No work is superior or inferior. He takes oath to remove untouchability from the confines of Kuntala kingdom. He eats food from Nagimayya's house. He says that food becomes sacred when it is received with a sense of Shiva-consciousness. The food got from the hard earnings of the labour is always great.

Princess Nilambika, King Bijjala's sister is thrilled by Basava's exemplary nature and attitude towards women. She marries him as his second wife. Basava releases a prostitute from the tormentation and makes her marry a young *sarana* opening a new life for her. The Socio-Spiritual Academy established by Basava brings a sea change in the attitude of people. *Saranas* come forward to marry across the castes. This enrages the priesthood. They approach King Bijjala to curb intercaste marriages. They are further enraged when Allamprabhu occupies the *Sunya* chair. Basava sees nothing odd about these things. He says in a dynamic society changes are inevitable.

In a debate with the King Bijjala Basava makes it clear that he does not believe in any authority of anybody. Authority always rests with those who love the kingdom and not with people who love authority. *Saranas* say that Kuntala kingdom flourished because of Basava's lesson: "Labour for the individual and the fruits of labour for the society." King Bijjala cannot adjust to the reality. He terminates Basava from his ministership and banishes him from the capital, Kalyana. He also orders Haralayya and Madhuvayya to be dragged to death. The *vachana* literature of Basava is also banned.

Once Basava leaves Kalyana. All the ideals of Basava's philosophy recede. The Socio-Spiritual Academy becomes weak with the withdrawal of brahmins and Saivajangamas. Basava leaves but he is always present in spirit among the hearts of *saranas*. His concept of body temple is superior to stone-temple culture.

Fall of Kalyana is a dramatisation of Basava's life, which brought sweeping changes in the society. Basava's life and ideals gain everlasting presence in the hands of a resourceful dramatist, Dr. M.M. Kalburgi. Professor Naikar's English translation opens a significant chapter for the world community in assisting the cause of world literature. Significant ideas of human life should not stagnate in local languages. Dr. Naikar's translation successfully brings the nuances and niceties of the play from Kannada to English. World literature is richer by the combined effort of both Dr. Kalburgi and Dr. Naikar. Naikar's translation of the play is admirable on account of its readability and crisp dialogues which appeal to the target-language reader. The play may easily be prescribed for study at postgraduate level of the Indian universities. It easily offers a challenge to the director, who can present it on the national or international stage or even on the silver screen. The detailed notes offered at the end of the play help the non-Kannada reader to understand the technical terms, which are specific to the *sarana* culture. The play offers ample material to religious philosophers, comparative critics and translation-theorists to codify their knowledge and sharpen their perceptions.

Cited Work

M.M. Kalburgi, *Fall of Kalyana*, tr. Basavaraj Naikar, Bangalore: Basava Samithi, 2003. All the page references are to this edition.

11

Basavaraj Naikar's Kannada Translations: An Overview

— Mallikarjun Patil

Dr Basavaraj Naikar is a well-known translator in South India today. Since he is a bilingual scholar he can translate English works into Kannada and Kannada works into English. He knows that translation is a difficult business and that it is an art, a science, a craft and a creation. It is a linguistic and cultural activity. It is interlingual. Translation is concerned with the business of meaning. It is an understanding process. It is reporting, sometimes, an explanation and an analysis. Translation is a means for acquiring knowledge.

Dr. Naikar has translated J. M. Synge's four plays—*The Playboy of the Western World, Riders to the Sea, The Shadow of the Glen* and *The Well of the People.* Unfortunately he has left out Synge's last two plays *The Tinker's Wedding* and *Deirdre of the Sorrows.* Anyway what strikes us is Naikar's translation. Naikar's translation is more a cultural adaptation than mere translation. Those who have read Dryden's adaptation of Shakespeare's play *Antony and Cleopatra,* as *All for Love* will imagine about Naikar's adaptation of Synge's plays. But the point is that Naikar has adapted them in Kannada. Had he done it in English, his works would attract the readers of the English-speaking world. No wonder Shankar Mokashi- Punekar, a great scholar of English language and literature, expresses the view that Naikar has done a commendable work in doing so. Though Professor Punekar did not like Naikar's transcreation in *Paduvana Nadina Premavira* because of the difficulties of cultural transplantation, he likes the very adventure undertaken at the young age of twenty-six. Another English Professor, Chandrashekhar Patil, has a similar appreciation for Naikar's adaptation. Dr. Basavaraj Naikar has not only done Synge's work into Kannada but he has adapted it to Kannada taste and culture. He has changed the names of the characters and locales to suit the taste of Kannada audience and invested them with the aura of North-Karnataka culture, especially the Lingayat culture of which he has an insider's knowledge.

Edmund John Millington Synge (pronounced as Sing) was born in 1871, in Dublin of Anglo-Irish Protestant landowning family. His father was a Barrister-at-Law and his mother was a rector's daughter. He spent his childhood days in the hills and mountains of south Dublin. He had a Wordsworthian taste for the countryside. The same is shown in the imagery and description of his plays. He studied at Trinity College and he had an interest in music. In fact, he became a sort of wandering singer among the peasants of Aran and Kerry Islands. Soon he left music and left for Paris where he read widely in European literature. He studied great writers and literature. Once when he met Yeats the latter advised him: "Give up Paris: you will never create anything by reading Racine, and Arthur Symons will always be a between critic of French literature. Go to the Aran Islands, live there as if you were one of the people themselves, express a life that has never found expression."[1] Synge, therefore, went to the island in the days of Irish revival headed by Yeats and Lady Gregory and collected folk tales and songs from the islands.

Soon the Irish National Theatre was established in 1902 helping the young dramatic talents. People like Gregory, Yeats, Mrs. Horniman, Edward Martyn and George Moore helped the Irish renaissance. This theatre was against Ibsenite theatre. Yeats and Synge wrote: "We must make a theatre for ourselves and our friends, and for a few simple people who understand from sheer simplicity what we understand from scholarship and thought."[2] Synge, in the preface to his play *The Playboy* said, "Ibsen and Zola used 'joyless and pallid words.'" H. H. Anniah Gowda says, "Synge endeavored to give humanity in his plays, he differed from the existing 'upholstered drawing room-like shapelessness of an English theatre.'" The first such play was Yeat's *Countless Cathleen* with William Frank Fay and Florence Fair as star attractions. This was followed by Synge's plays, *Shadow of the Glen* (1903) and *Riders to the Sea* in 1904. Then came *The Well of the Saints* (1905) and *Deidre* (with Yeats's preface) in 1910. *The Tinker's Wedding* was not staged. Synge could not live for long. His poetry is about the people of the Aran Island. Unfortunately Synge died young at the age of thirty-seven.

Dr Naikar's translation of Synge's first and best play *The Playboy of the Western World* is as follows. He has changed all the names of characters and locale in accordance with the North Karnataka culture. The Kannada names of Synge's characters are given in parenthesis here: Pegeen (Girija), Shawb Keogh (Chandru), Michael (Shambhulinga), Jimmy (Shivananda), Philly (Prabhu), Christy (Sidda), Widow Quin (Nilamma), Susan (Mahadevi), Honour (Asha) and Nelly (Jayashri). Of course, he has changed the names of locales. He locales are his childhood places like Naragund.

The Playboy takes place in three acts. The scene is that of a wild coast of Mayo. The second and third acts take place on the following day. The characters are few and far between. The beginning serves to show the scene of the play as well as its language:

> Country public house or shebeen, very rough and untidy. There is a sort of counter on the right with shelves, holding many bottles and jugs, just seen above it. Empty barrels stand near the counter. At back, a little to left of counter, there is a door into the open air, then, more to the left, there is a settle with shelves above it, with more jugs, and a table beneath a window. At the left there is a large open fireplace, with turf fire, and a small door into inner room. PEGEEN, a wild-looking but fine girl, of about twenty, is writing at table. She is dressed in the usual peasant dress.[3]

The story of the play is as follows:

> One evening a young man arrives at a small inn on the wild Mayo coast of Ireland and announces that he has run away from home. He says his name as Christopher Mahon and

> that he is running away because he has killed his father during a fight. The farmers who are passing the time in the inn are very much pleased by his exhibition of courage. Christopher is especially admired by Pegeen Mike, the pretty young daughter of Michael James Flaherty, the innkeeper. She, along with the others, presses the young man to tell his story over and over again.

At home Christopher has been a meek and obedient son, domineered by his father. He accepts the insults of his parent until the latter tries to force him into marrying a rich old woman. At last, in desperation, he hits his father over the head with a log. Seeing the old man fall, Christopher presumes that he is dead.

The experience at the inn is something new for Christopher, who for the first time in his life is looked upon as a hero. When the news of his story spreads among the villagers, they flock to look at this paragon of bravery. The young women are particularly interested in him. Dame Quinn, middle aged widow, is much taken with the young hero.

But Christopher is attracted to pretty Pegeen. He is flattered by her admiration and attempts to live up to her attitude of bravado. Before long he himself believes that he has done a courageous deed.

Each year the village holds a festival in which the men compete with each other in various sports. Christopher is naturally expected to take part in it. His early timidity having long since disappeared, he makes every effort to appear a hero in the eyes of Pegeen, to whom he is now openly betrothed. She has broken her engagement with a young farmer, Shawn Keogh, soon after Christopher arrives on the scene.

While her playboy, as Pegeen calls him, is taking part in the sports an old man comes to the inn. He is looking for a young man whose description fits Christopher's look. Dame Quin, who still has designs on the boy, deliberately misdirects the stranger. But the man recognises his son shortly when the latter wins a mule race. Old Mahon, not dead from his son's blow, flies into a rage. He insults his son and he asks him to go home with him.

But the young man Christopher strikes at his father again and the latter falls unconscious. This however does not make the young playboy a hero now. All the people consider his act as stupid and wrong. Even Pegeen, his beloved, does so. His father gets up good and well and when the people want to punish the boy, he likes to run away. At this time the heroine screams tragically: "Quit my sight. (*Putting her shawl over her head and breaking out into wild lamentations*). Oh, my grief, I've lost him surely. I've lost the only Playboy of the Western World." (p. 96). Dr. Naikar has tried his best to bring out the theme of parricide and the artificial heroism of the protagonist and his final exposure in terms of Kannada culture. Christy Mahon, who is a Christ-figure in the original Irish play, has been intelligently converted into Sidda, a short form of Siddharama, a man of miraculous powers in Kannada literature. He has successfully achieved linguistic equivalence between the Irish dialect and the North-Karnataka colloquial dialect, which contributes to the playability and theatrical effect. But the cultural transplantation of Irish theme into the Kannada context does not seem to be very convincing simply because such a theme of parricide and false heroism does not agree with Kannada culture.

Naikar's second play is Synge's *Riders to the Sea*. Synge wrote the play *Riders to the Sea* in 1904 and it was staged at the Abbe Theatre in the same year. He published it in 1905. The play is about his experience in Aran Island in the West of Ireland. It is about a woman called Maurya who loses several of her sons, one after another, to the sea. The characters include Maurya, her son Bartley, her two daughters Cathleen and Nora and men and women. Here too Naikar adopts the play to the Kannada culture. He uses Kannada names for the Irish. Maurya is Parvatamma, Bartley is Virabhadra, Cathleen is Manjula, Nora is Vimala, and the like. The Aran Island is changed to Javur, a village in Naragund *taluq* of Dharwad district. The sea is changed to a village tank. Of course, everything goes smooth and fine.

As in Synge's play when the play opens Nora asks her sister Cathleen as to where her mother Maurya is. They talk of Michael's disappearance in the sea. Some speak to them that Michael is lost in the Irish Sea. But nobody knows exactly where he is lost. Still, efforts are made about it. The young ladies have got his probable clothes and think that somebody must have performed the last rites for him. Then Maurya comes from the inner room. Shortly

Bartley meets her and tells her that he should go for selling his horse in a fair of Connemara. The mother insists upon him not to go. Her misapprehension is that she has already lost five of her sons to the sea and the only surviving son Bartley should not go and get lost. This is the genuine mother's concern and it is right so. But the boy says he must go. Of course, he assures her his safe return. He tells,

> "*Bartley* : (*Beginning to work with the rope*). I've no halter the way I can ride down on the mare, and I must go now quickly. This is the one boat going for two weeks or beyond it, and the fair will be a good fair for horses, I heard them saying below."
>
> ...
>
> *Bartley*: (*getting his purse and tobacco)*. I'll have half an hour to go down, and you'll see me coming again in two days, or in three days, or maybe in four days if the wind is bad.
>
> *Maurya*: (*turning round to the fire, and putting her shawl over her head*). Isn't it a hard and cruel man won't hear a word from an old woman, and she holding him from the sea?
>
> *Catheleen*: It's the life of a young man to be going on the sea, and who would listen to an old woman with one thing and she saying it over?
>
> *Bartley*: (*taking the halter*). I must go now quickly. I'll ride down on the red mare, and the grey pony will run behind me..The blessing of God on you.
>
> *Maurya*: (*crying out as he is in the door*). He's gone now, God spare us and we'll not see him again. He's gone now, and when the black night is falling, I'll have no son left me in the world. (pp. 10-11)

The old woman Maurya is sure of what she says. She tells,

> There was Sheamus and his father, and his own father again, were lost in a dark night, and not a stick or sign was seen of them when the sun went up. There was Patch after was drowned out of a curagh that turned over. I was sitting here with Bartley and he a baby lying on my two knees, and I see two women, and three women, and four women coming in, and they crossing themselves and not saying a word. I looked out then, and there were men coming after them, and they holding a thing in the half of a red sail, and water

> dripping out of it- it was a dry day, Nora—and leaving a track to the door.

Shortly after Maurya expresses her agony over the loss of her sons to the sea, some women arrive there with Bartley's dead body. One of them says, "God rest his soul."

Maurya's grief is unbounded now. She bursts with sorrow. She says, "They're all gone now, and there isn't anything more the sea can do to me... I'll have no call now to be up crying and praying when the wind breaks from the south, and you can hear the surf is in the east, and the surf is in the west, making a great stir with the two noises, and they hitting one the other". (p. 17). She says, "May the Almighty God have mercy on Barley's soul, and on Michael's soul, and on the souls of Sheamus and Patch and Stephen and Shawn; and may He have mercy on my soul, Nora, and on the soul of every one living in the world." Maurya's final words are words of stoic resignation that "Bartley will have a fine coffin out of the white boards, and a deep grave surely. What more can we want than that? No man at all can be living for ever, and we must be satisfied." The Kannada equivalent given to the Irish setting and theme and language is very convincing because the tragic theme is quite plausible in the Kannada context also. Nothing looks artificial in this cultural adaptation.

Likewise, Naikar's adaptation of Synge's third play *The shadow of the Glen* has come up finely. Here too he has transplanted the names as follows: Nora Burke as Shantavva, Dan Burke as Mallappa and Michael Dara as Somashekhar, and Tramp as Hanumantappa. The locale is a glen in County Wicklow. Naikar's locale is Attikolla, a place in the town of Dharwad. The cultural transplantation is very successful in this attempt.

The theme of the play is the business of life and its monotony. The theme of female loneliness and dependence on men and of male indifference to the sufferings of the female are dramatised here. The play is a comedy. The gist of the play is that Nora and Dan are a herding couple living in a lonely place. They look after cattle and sheep. Yet they are not happy. One of the reasons for this is Dan's addiction to alcohol. Of course, Nora is not so fidel to her husband. She has an interest in people like Michael and Tramp. So she tells gladly: "What way would I live and I am old woman if I didn't marry a man with a bit of a farm, and cows on it, and sheep on the back hills?"

Critics say that the play is partly autobiographical. It is observed, "Even a superficial analysis of the theme of the play discloses of Synge's own life: a dark uncertainty, fear of old age and death, and the awareness that suffering is an immanent condition of human existence."[4]

The last play of Synge adapted by Naikar is *The Well of the Saints*. He calls it *Jogibhavi*. The tittle is appropriate. Here too, he has adapted the names of characters and their locales. Cultural transplantation is executed. Martin Doul is Chenamalla, his wife Mary Doul is Chenni, Timmy, a potter, Molly Byrne is Malli, Bride is Jayadevi, the Saints, Swamijis, and others. The scene is that of some Irish mountain. Naikar's scene is that of Naragund.

The theme of illusion and reality recurs in *The Well of the Saints*—although this time from a different angle. Conforming to the pattern of Synge's other works, illusion and reality are once again juxtaposed, leaving the individual free to make his choice of either. The protagonist feels that the world appears to him more beautiful in his imagination when he is physically blind than when he regains his eyesight. In fact he is deeply disappointed by the ugliness of the world including its things and beings when he is endowed with eyesight by a saint. He, therefore, wants to be blind again so that he may continue to enjoy the beauty of the world in his imagination. Although the theme is Irish in origin, it has a universal dimension and therefore enabled Basavaraj Naikar to adapt it to the Kannada culture. It has perfectly agreed with the Kannada ethos and context. That is the reason why this adaptation entitled *Jogibhavi* has been very popular in Karnataka. It was performed in Gulbarga and Hyderabad with great success. Its performance in Gulbraga won the first prize in the District level Drama Competition. It was successfully directed by G.M. Shirahatti, the Programme Executive of Gulbarga Akashwani in 1977. The lead role was played by Saraswati Chimmalagi and the other roles were played by the members of Nripatunga Sangha of Gulbarga. Later it was broadcast by Akashwani centres of Dharwad and Gulbarga in 1978. In 2001, it was produced as a Tele-play under the directorship of M.S. Gunashilan and the supervision of G.M. Shirahatti, Director of Doordarshan,

Bangalore, and telecast by Chandana and DD Television, Bangalore, and appreciated by a large number of spectators. The scenes were shot in and around the sacred complex of Patrivana Monastery at Naragund. It was also prescribed as a textbook for BA and MA classes of Karnatak University and Gulbarga University for more than nine years.

Synge's plays evince his language and style. Many people say that his style is crude. T. S. Eliot said, "Synge's plays form rather a special case, because they are based upon the idiom of a rural people whose speech is naturally poetry both in imagery and in rhythm."[5] His language is poetic. That way he reminds us of Sean O'Casey. Synge acquired such speech from his stay in Dublin, Wicklow, Galway, Aran Island and West Kerry. H.H. Anniah Gowda says, "Anglo-Irish, based upon Gaelic structure, echoing its syntax was spoken by the peasants and fishermen; Synge compressed and heightened it for drama. The rich abundant speech of the people was a delight to him. He loaded it with strong liturgical emotion as in *Riders* by making his own selection of word and phrase, choosing what would express his own personality."[6]

Basavaraj Naikar's cultural adaptation of the four plays of J.M. Synge has been very successful. In the words of Shankar Mokashi-Punekar, he has shown a model to other cultural translators of Karnataka. He has faced the problems of cultural transplantation while translating the Western texts into Indian texts and succeeded to a great extent. Many readers of these plays opine that they feel as if they are reading the original texts in Kannada, which is an evidence of the success of cultural adaptation. The North Karnataka colloquial language, which is at once rugged and poetic employed by Naikar has been wholeheartedly appreciated by the Kannada scholars like, V.K. Gokak, Mokashi-Punekar, Pachakshari Hiremath, Chandrashekhar Patil, Buddanna Hingamire, M.M.Kalburgi, Giraddi Govindaraj and Bannanje Govindacharya. Chandrashekhar Patil has frankly confessed that he experienced a sort of horripilation when he read the powerful masculine Kannada employed in translation by Naikar. He has translated the plays of the Latin dramatist, Terence, like *The Girl from Andros* and *Phormio*, the plays of the German playwright Bertolt Brecht, like *The Good woman of Setzuan* and *The Caucasian Chalk Circle* and a play by Rabindranath Tagore, *Red Oleanders*, which are yet to be published. Presently he is engaged in the Kannada translation of Dante's *The Divine Comedy,* which happens to be the most challenging task for him.

Basavaraj Naikar's translation of French short stories from English is published by Nava Karnataka Publications, Bangalore. Nava Karnataka is a leading publishing company in South India today. The famous Kannada writer, the late Niranjana, was the chief editor of the series, which brought out as many as twenty-five books of translation of world's short stories into Kannada language.

Naikar's translation of French short stories is interesting. It is entitled *Niguda Soudha,* named after the story, "The Mysterious Mansion" by Balzac. Besides, the author gives us a brief and useful glimpse of French history. This is helpful for lay readers for understanding the French life and culture through these stories. For example, France's cultural history is like this: France is a major European country with its unique culture and civilization. It is known for its novelty of ideas. Who has not heard of the French Revolution? In the pre-historical times, France was just a patch of land as Germany or Italy. The Roman general, Julius Caesar, conquered France then known as Gaul in 51 BC. During the five hundred years of Roman rule the French accepted Roman civilisation and Latin language. Later Germanic tribes overran the region until a Frankish chief Clovis (481-511) organised it under his rule. Clovis accepted Christianity. Then Pepin (741-68), Charlemagne (768-814), William, the Conqueror and others governed the country in their own ways. The Hundred Years War disturbed the growing nation. Charles VII, Louis XI, Henry IV and Louis XIV restored peace in France. The two ministers who helped the nation were Richelieu and Mazarin. But the misgovernment done by later kings led to unrest and the French Revolution in 1789. The rules of Liberty, Equality and Fraternity were ushered in. The revolution removed feudalism but failed to establish democracy. The dominance of Napoleon created ripples now and again. World War I upset France. The French cultural history is very rich. Naikar says that great personalities like Joan of Arc, Rousseau, Voltaire, the Louises, the Napoleons, Rebelose, Boccaccio, Descartes, Racine, Moliere, Stendhal, Balzac, Flaubert,

Zola, Baudelaire, Valerie, Anatole France, Jules Verne, Dumas, Proust, de Beaue, Jean Paul Sartre and many more have enriched the France heritage. Fortunately Dr. Naikar has translated the short stories of some of these great writers.

Naikar's translation of French short stories is memorable. He has translated short stories of representative French writers like Honore de Balzac, Voltaire, Stendhal, Victor Hugo, Charles Baudelaire, Anatole France, Guy de Maupassant, Henry Barbos, Albert Camus and Jean Paul Sartre. All these writers are known for their depicting the pulse of the French nation. A brief glimpse into their stories as translated by Naikar is as follows:

> The first short story is Honore de Balzac's "The Myserious Mansion". Balzac is known for his great works like *The Human Comedy*, and *Droll Stories* is his fine collection of short stories. Balzac is known for his depiction of contemporary life with diversity. He influenced realism and naturalism. He is a major European writer. What strikes us is Dr Naikar's originality in rendering the French sensibilities. For example, he translates not only the literary matter but also the literary culture. In other words, he changes the sense and sensibility to suit to the needs of the time and to the taste of Kannada readers. Of course, great writers like Goethe and Tagore advised it for translators. So Dr Naikar's translation of Balzac's story runs smooth. He has used transcreative mode of translation. Yet we do not find any omission or deletion of literature in the deal. The whole story is taken holistically and rendered into compact Kannada. Descriptions are put into descriptions as dialogues are put into dialogues. This is also true of imagery.

The "Mysterious Mansion" is about a medieval castle where certain events take place in a mysterious manner. Balzac writes of people's happenings there. What strikes us is the grandeur of the mansion that belonged to Mr. and Mrs. Meres. One day Mr. Mere notices his wife's affair with somebody. So he stops it badly. Still the lady manages to have it. There lies their life's irony too. The story hinges upon the human value of fidelity in man-woman relationship.

Francois-Marie Arouet Voltaire's story is the second one in the collection. Voltaire is known for his work *Candide* (1759), a satire.

He was a crusader against tyranny and bigotry and is noted for his wit, satire, and critical capacity. His important stories are *Contes* and *Macromegas*. Dr Naikar's translation of Voltaire's story "Jino and Koli' is interesting enough for Indians. It is about two friends going wrong over their worldly affairs.

Stendhal's story of a Jew has come up finely. As we know, Marie-Henri Beyle Stendhal was a French novelist and short story writer. *The Red and the Black* is his great novel. He is known for his depiction of human psychology. Naikar has translated Stendhal's story, "A Jew". Here a Jew as is depicted is a fine personality. But his being poor and a Jew does not bring him social honor.

Victor Hugo is another great French all round writer. His works like *Les Miserable* and *Les Chtiments* are world famous. Dr Naikar's story of Hugo, entiled "Jenny", portrays the life of a poor couple. The husband is a fisherman and he cannot fish much due to bad weather. The wife looks after the family. One day the couple adopts two children of a neighbour when the latter perishes due to poverty.

Charles Baudelaire was a famous French poet. He was a modernist poet known for his collection of poems *The Flowers of Evil*. His short story, "The Rope" is translated as "Pasha". The story is about a painter who likes a good boy. Later the boy commits suicide and the mystery of it remains a mystery.

The next story is Alpahns Dadet's. Naikar has translated it as "Last Lesson". This is about a boy called Franz.

Anatole France was a great novelist and critic. He won the Nobel Prize for literature. Naikar has translated his story "Poutvoir". This is about Barjaret and Pauslin. Guy de Mauppassant was the greatest short story writer of his times in France. He has written three hundred short stories. Dr Naikar has rendered his story, "Prisoners" under the same title. The story is about Barthin. The problems of war ring in the story from the first to last. Henry Barbos's story "Boutvoir" is translated under the same title. This story is about the theme of war.

All know the great writer Albert Camus. He was a great novelist and playwright. He has written several short stories also. Naikar has translated his story "Prostitute" under the same title.

This story is about Janin living a life of difficulties. Like Camus Sartre is a great French genius. Jean-Paul Sartre was the founder of existentialism in France. He was a noted writer of plays and fiction. Naikar has translated his short story "Wall" under the same title. The story is about Yuvan. This is the longest story in the collection.

What strikes us is Naikar's careful translation. His language is masterly. He has attained a grip over the art of telling a story in another language. This shows his bilingual scholarship. He does justice to the original by remaining faithful to it. Nowhere does he appear artificial at all. He has achieved the extreme readability, which is a hallmark of any translation.

Epic happens to be a favourite genre in Kannada. The Kannada scholars are deeply interested in the study of standard epics of Pampa, Ranna, Harihara, Raghavanka, Laxmisha and Kumaravyasa and the folk epics like *Male Madeshwara and Song of Goddess Yellamma*, etc. The Kannada scholars are interested in the comparative study of epics of different cultures of the world. Dr. Basavaraj Naikar, therefore, undertook the translation of the old English folk epic entitled *Beowulf* by an anonymous writer and translated it into Kannada in 1980, but published it in 1996. A senior Kannada scholar like B.B. Hendi advised Naikar to translate this epic in medieval Kannada in the style of Kuvempu's *Ramayana Darshanam*. But Naikar who believes in the theory that the translator has to translate a source text into the target language of the modern era to cater to the needs of the modern readers. He, therefore, has translated *Beowulf* in modern Kannada language as is spoken and understood by the modern Kannada readers. This epic deals with the extraordinary heroism of Beowulf who fights with the fierce dragon and saves the citizens of Hrothgar's kingdom. Beowulf easily resembles Bhima and Arjuna of the Sanskrit epic, the *Mahabharata*. Naikar has retained the dignity of the epic language in his translation in spite of the use of modern language and helped the Kannada comparative scholars and folklorists to undertake comparative studies in the said field. His translation has been appreciated by scholars like H.H. Anniah Gowda, L.S. Seshagiri Rao, S.L. Bhyrappa, C.R.Yaravinteiimath, Ambalike Hiriyanna, Somasekhar Imrapur, Devendra Kumar Hakari and Mallikarjuna Latthe.

In addition to *Beowulf*, Naikar has translated a Sumerian folk-epic entitled the *Epic of Gilgamesh*, which is known as the shortest epic in the world. This epic was composed earlier than the Iliad and the *Odyssey* and well known even before 2000.B.C. The story of this epic was known to Europeans long before the *Bible* was known. It is the story of Gilgamesh's quest for knowledge and immortality and belief in supernatural gods. Naikar has succeeded in retaining the dignity of the epic language of the original narrative and enabled the Kannada scholars to undertake a comparative study of folk-epics of India and the Western world. His language has been whole-hearted appreciated by Devendra kumar Hakari, H.J. Lakkappagowda and Dr. Buddanna Hingamire (himself an epic poet in Kannada).

The Indian Central Sahitya Academy is doing a pioneering work in encouraging the growth of literature in Indian languages. English is the link language for all these. The Sahitya Academy has been translating works of different languages into other languages including English. This will foster the growth of what we can call pan-Indian literature. Dr Naikar's translation of Ramanalal Joshi's monograph, *Govardhanaram* is part of such a project. Sahitya Academy published Dr Naikar's translation in 1984. This book is brought up in the series called the Makers of Indian Literature (MIL).

Naikar's translation includes as many as nine chapters of the original. The translation corresponds to the whole account of the original. The work is a comprehensive and critical compilation about Govardhanaram Tripathi's life and works.

A brief account of the monograph is as follows. Govardhanaram Madhavram Tripathi (1855-1907) was a great Gujarati poet, novelist and thinker. No Gujarati writer before Govardhanaram had perhaps such a realistic comprehension of the varied patterns of life in Gujarati, which were slowly changing under the pressures of Western learning. The Indian scholar of the nineteenth century was moved by the Indian *Vedas, Upanishads, the Gita*, epics and the works of Kalidasa as much as he was moved by the works of Shakespeare and Wordsworth from the West.

Naikar says Govardhanaram's famed novel *Saraswatichandra* vividly reflects the tensions extremely tragic in the case of the heroine Kumud and implicit in the confluence of varied cultural streams. *Saraswatichandra* depicts the socio-political life of the times. It is a realistic novel. The life of Saraswatichandra and Kumud, the central characters of the novel, is sad but glorious. It is essentially an offering of devotion unto Mother India, the spirituality she stands for. Saraswatichandra, vivid and well chiseled as a character, symbolizes the awakening released by university men marked by a sense of revivalism and reform, wonder and insight, wider identification and deeper sympathies.

Kumud stands for beauty, for love, for feminine tenderness and dedication. Spiritual experience saves both from utter misery and frustration, and lends their life a glow of self-fulfilment in pure love and service.

Basically realistic in the selection of subject and its treatment, Govardhanaram discovers within realistic pattern ideals and principles of growth. The novel's form has a multiple design, but its unity and harmony are achieved through perception of ideals to which the actualities of life inevitably point. The novel is a masterpiece, reflecting the social and ideological conflicts of the times. It is a prose epic of three generations from 1820 to 1900. It shows the writer's life. Govardhanaram was born in a Nagar brahmin's family at Nadiad and inherited the family's piety, uprightness and love of learning.

As we know from Naikar's translation Govardhanaram was born in Nadiad in 1855. His father was a banker for Kathivad princes. The young man had his education in Nadiad and Bombay. His father worked as a secretary to the Diwan of Bhavanagar for four years. The son has brought in the family experience in the novel *Saraswatichandra.*

Govardhanaram was a poet of repute. He had a command over narration whether in poetry or in prose. *Snehamudra* is an elegiac poem about the death of his first wife Hari Laxmi in 1874. Naikar says it is a bold expression of his philosophy of love. Yet its style is inadequate.

Govardhanaram's *Sakshara Jeevan* is a discursive treatise on the dharma and character of the men of letters of different grades of ability and disposition. It is a fine work of analytic social thought in Gujarati. According to the author an intellectual must be original, stimulating and relevant to his society.

Govardhanaram's other works include his critical essays and literary surveys, his notes and papers on religion, Vedanta and law, his short biographies and his scrap books. *The Scrap Books* and *The Classical Poets* are in English, the former being his diary and occasional reflections. *The Scrap Books* helps us understand Govardhanaram better, but it lacks literary charm. Govardhanaram's monographs on Navalram, Dayaram and his own daughter Lilavati are warmly appreciated.

Some of the critical works on Govardhanaram are Mansukhlal Jhaveri's *Govardhanaram*, Ramprasad Baxi's *Govardhanaram-nun-manoraiya*, Vishnuprasad Tripathi's *Govardhanaram*, Ramanalal Joshi's *Govardhanaram* in English and Naikar's translation of *Govardhanaram* in Kannada.

Naikar's translation of Ramanalal Joshi's *Govardhanaram* has come out lively. He has tried to keep to the original throughout. He does not deviate from the matter or from the style of the original. Even his Kannada language is erudite and scholarly.

Naikar's translation of M.K. Naik's *A History of Indian English Literature* into *Bharatiya English Sahitya Charitre* published by the Central Sahitya Academy, New Delhi in 2005 happens to be his magnum opus of translation. He has successfully brought out the spirit of the original critical history into Kannada by finding readable equivalents to the English critical idiom and the terse style used by M.K. Naik. This history offers a panoramic but brief view of the Indian English Literature including poetry, prose, fiction and drama from the beginning to the end of twentieth century. Naikar has done a great service to the Kannada letters by acquainting the Kannada reader with the realm of Indian English Literature.

Naikar's latest translation *Sri Kanakadasaru* happens to be a Kannada rendering of his own original critical monograph entitled *Kanakadasa: The Golden Servant of Lord Hari*. Kanakadasa happened to be a very important saint-poet coming from the subaltern strata of Indian society. He revolutionised the Kannada religious poetry with his excellent narrative poetry, *kirtanas* and *mundiges*. He was a religious reformer as well as a social critic. The corpus of his poetic output is very large, but his religious and social philosophy has been presented in a nutshell by the author.

Naikar has translated his own English version in a very readable Kannada for the benefit of the common of Karnataka as well as for the Kanakologists.

On the whole Basavaraj Naikar has shown his ability to translate drama, short fiction, epic and criticism from English and European languages into Kannada by employing the relevant registers and styles required for the purpose. Obviously he is one of the seasoned translators of Karnataka and a cultural ambassador. He happens to be translator from Kannada to English also. For example he has translated the Kannada works like *H.H.Vijaya Mahantesh* (by Pachnakshari Hiremath), *Beloved Poems* (Gavish Hiremath), *Musings of Sarvajna* (a sixteenth century saint-poet of Karnataka), *Fall of Kalyana* (by M.M. Kalburgi) and *Sangya-Balya: Betrayal* (by Rayappa Pattar) which have been nationally and internationally acclaimed. His English translation entitled *The Frolic Play of the Lord* (of Chamarasa's *Prabhulingalile*) awaits publication.

References

1. W. B. Yeats, qt by H. H. Anniah Gowda, Introduction, *The Playboy of the Western World* and *Riders to the Sea*, Macmillan, Bangalore, 2000. p. 4.
2. Synge, qt by H. H. Anniah Gowda, Introduction, Ibid., p. x.
3. All the references are from the texts *The Playboy of the Western World* and *Riders to the Sea*, Ed. by H.H. Anniah Gowda, Macmillan, Bangalore, 2000.
4. K. S. Misra, *The Plays of Synge*, The Caxton Press, New Delhi, 1977, p. 62.
5. Eliot qt by H.H. Anniah Gowda, Introduction, Ibid., p. xv.
6. H.H. Anniah Gowda, Introduction, Ibid., p. Xvi.

Works Cited

1. Basavaraj Naikar, *Paduvana Nadina Premavira*, Dharwad: Yugadwani Prakshana, 1975.
2. ————, *Kollada Neralu*, Dharwad: Yugadwani Prakashana, 1976.
3. ————, *Jogibhavi*, Dharwad: Yugadwani Prakashana, 1976.
4. ————, *Huchuchuhole*, Dharwad: *Sankramana*, 1982
5. ————, *Nigudha Saudha*, Bangalore: Navakarnataka Publications, 1982.

6. ————, *Govardhanram*, New Delhi: Central Sahitya Academy, 1984.
7. ————, *Beowulf*, Dharwad: Sivaranjani Prakashan, 1996.
8. ————, *Gilgamesh Mahakavya*, Bangalore: Kannada Pustaka Pradhikara, 2000.
9. ————, *Bharatiya English Sahitya Charitre*, New Delhi: Central Sahitya Academy, 2005.
10. ————, *Sri. Kanakadasaru*, New Delhi: National Book Trust, India, 2006.

12

Community, Gender, Tradition and Modernity in *Generations*

— Basavaraj Naikar

Neela Padmanabhan (1938—) happens to be a significant writer in Tamil. He is a poet, novelist and short story writer. An interesting thing about his life is that he is not a teacher either in a college or a university, but hails from the engineering profession. In this respect he is comparable to Yashvant Chittal in Kannada who is a scientist in a chemical factory. He worked as an Assistant Engineer in Kerala. He has published more than twelve novels in Tamil, like *Talaimuraikal, Pallikondapuram, Minulakam, Files, Vattathinveliye, Uravakal, Yathirai, Anubhavankal Samar, Udayatharakar, Ithuyame Alinthupo, Nethru Vanthaval* and so forth. A couple of these novels have been translated into English and other Indian languages. His novels are known for the depiction of complex human relationships and the regional flavour. Ka.Naa. Subramanyam's English translation of Neela Padmanabhan's *Talaimaraikal* entitled as *Generations* helps non-Tamilian readers of the world to have an intimate knowledge of Tamilian life and culture, with all its specificities. It helps even the non-Tamilian Indian reader to have a broad perspective of Indian literature in a comparative and contrastive fashion. An attempt has been made in this paper to discuss *Generations* as a typical South Indian novel.

Generations offers a broad picture of the Chettiar community as illustrated in the life of Nagaru Pillai and his network of relatives. In this sense, *Generations* may be described as a regional or provincial novel, which deals with the life of people belonging to the geographical location spread over Tamil Nadu and Kerala States. It may be described as an ethnic novel in that it deals not with the 'great tradition' of Brahmanical-Hinduism', but with the 'little tradition' of a non-Brahmanical, i.e., Chettiar community of Tamil Nadu. It is precisely for this reason that the novel assumes great importance in the contemporary literary studies in India.

It is a commonplace truth that the Indian literature abounds with works dealing with brahminical experience. Now it is high time for non-brahminical experience (like that of kshatriyas, vaishsyas and shudras) to have a legitimate place in literature. The brahminical experience should be decentred and the experiences of the marginal non-brahmins should move to the centre of literary representation. This process has started happening in India, though slowly. It helps the national and international reader to have a broader and fresher perspective of Indian literature. In this sense Neela Padmanabhan's *Generations* becomes very important as it brings the marginalized community of Chettiars to the centre of fictional depiction and offers an alternative picture of Indian life.

The members of Diravi's family like Unnamalai Aachi, Seventha Perumal, Kuttiamme, Koonangani Paatta and his wives and mistresses and other relatives represent the values of Chettiar community in general. But the community being subject to the onslaught of Time has been undergoing many changes within its fold. That is the reason why the life of this community has been changing from generation to generation thereby acquiring some qualities of modernity in it.

As the very title of the novel suggests, it deals with three generations of Chettiar community. The first and old generations is represented by Unnamalai Aachi, the second or middle generation is represented by Seventha Perumal and Kuttiamme, whereas the third and latest generation is represented by Diravi, the protagonist. The subtle changes that have been taking place within the Chettiar community through these generations hold a mirror to the gradual transition of the wider Indian society from traditionalism to modernity. Thus the novel, *Generations*, inevitably becomes a valuable record of the cultural history of South India.

On the whole, the Chettiar community is governed by patriarchal rules. The people of this community believe in the ancestry, sanctity and purity of their community, reinforced by certain myths, which are very sacred to them. The values and ideals of their community are taught by the grandparents to grandchildren and thus passed on from generation to generation. For example, Unnamalai Aachi, the sixty-year-old grandmother is a typical old woman, who is a repository of the wisdom of the community; whereas Diravi, a boy of fifteen happens to be an innocent young boy, who has to be tutored by the grandmother about the values and ideals of the Chettiar community. Grandmother Unnamalai Aachi tells the history of their community to Diravi. She tells him that they are known as Seven Towns Chettis, as they are spread over seven towns like Eraniyal, Pazhavadai, Pappanapuram, Parakkai, Midalam, Kolachal and Tiruwankode, and that their family deity is called Odupparai, Goddess of the Snake. It is because of their respect for the Snake Goddess that they name their children after the deity. As the Chettiar community believes in its own purity, the members do not want to pollute it by marrying with the people of any other community, however affluent and great the latter may be. They do not accept the so-called superiority of brahmins or kshatriyas. They do not wish to encourage the evil of miscegenation.

The ideal of the purity of Chettiar community is upheld by a mythical story, which Unnamalai Aachi narrates to Diravi. According to this myth, there was a city called Kaverppoomattinam where a king ruled. One day he received a gift of precious gems from somebody. He, therefore, wanted to get them strung into a necklace, but the gems had no holes in them. He called a well-known Chettiar and asked him to get the gems strung into a necklace. The Chettiar took the gems home and found that they had no holes at all. The gems were too tiny to be pierced with needles. He, therefore, began to worry about how to do it. But his daughters took pity on him and managed to get the gems strung into a necklace by applying jaggery water to a string and keeping them near an anti-hill. When the king learnt about the skill of the Chettiar's daughters, Thangamma and Thayamma, he wanted to marry them. "The place for such clever girls is not the house of a Chettiar, but the palace of the king. Give me your two daughters in marriage" (p.11). But the Chettiars in particular could not think of marrying off their daughters out of their caste. Even a king could not have the daughter of a self-respecting Chettiar for his bride. The Chettiar was in a dilemma, "How could the king insult me by asking for my daughters in marriage? What of my caste? What of the respect due to me? …If I refuse he will have me killed and then force them into marriage with him. My family's name will be mud"(p.12). The Chettiar was so particular about his caste-purity that he buried his daughters and himself alive in the basement of his house. The dying daughters cursed the king and the city. Consequently there were famines, fevers and earthquakes in the city. This mythical story clearly shows how the Chettiar community is very strict about the maintenance of its purity. The people of this community are so strict about this ideal of purity that they refuse to be tempted even by the money, wealth or status offered by the people of other communities. The moral ideal ingrained in this myth is internalised by all the members of the community. Grandmother Unnamalai Aachi inculcates such moral ideals in the minds of her grandchildren including Diravi.

Unnamalai Aachi, who is sixty years now, belongs to the first generation and, therefore, happens to be an embodiment of all the traditional values of the patriarchal community of Chettiars. Although she becomes a widow even before she is twenty, she never thinks of marrying anyone again. Nor does she have any secret or open love affairs with anyone. She leads a life of perfect self-control, channallises her emotions and lives for her son Nagaru Pillai. A believer in fate, she is willing to accept all the contingencies of life and brave the challenges stoically. In spite of all her marital suffering, she is never frustrated. On the contrary, she has a lot of gusto for life. She leads a life of discipline. Every day she gets up early in the morning, sweeps the street in front of her house and sprinkles the cowdung- water mixture wsrhythmically. Then she draw the design of *kolam* powder artistically. She believes that this is necessary for the prosperity of the family. After completing the morning ablutions, she massages her legs with oil – legs inflicted with elephantitis. Then she rhythmically pounds the edible leaves, betel and quicklime in a tiny mortar and prepares a paste so that can enjoy it though she has lost her teeth.

Being a highly traditional woman, Unnamalai Aachi believes in certain superstitions tacitly approved by her community. For example, when Salam says, "I am going to school" (p.16), Aachi scolds her, "You are a senseless girl. How many times am I to tell you that you should say, 'I go now and shall return,' instead of saying, 'I go to school.' It is inauspicious to say 'I go' without adding the word 'come'"(p. 16). Similarly, whenever one has to go out of the house, one has to wait for the right omen. When Diravi is about to go to school, he sees the 'head-shaking woman', which is not a good omen. Then he sees a woodchopper and Ammulu with an empty pot, which are again not good omens. He waits until he sees a fisherwoman, which is a good omen. It is only then that Aachi allows him to set out. She does not like the behaviour of the people of younger generation, which is in violation of the traditional norms. On such occasions, she cries and wants to die before seeing the worse things. For example, she does not approve of Sevantha Perumal's discarding his wife, Nagammai. "What a despicable fellow This sin will follow him and punish him"(p. 65). She does not approve of the deviant behaviour of modern men and women.

When Neelapillai aunt, after becoming a widow, elopes with Korami teacher, Unnamalai Aachi comments on it bitterly, "Nowadays widows do not behave properly; they are not modest and restrained; they don't observe our customs. As soon as the husband dies, the widow casts about for another fellow..."(p.100). Comparing her own plight and Neelapillai's, Aachi remembers her own widowhood. "He died. I was not yet twenty. I was younger than Neelapillai. I wept and wept for days and retired into the darkest corner of the house to be myself. Not one year or two, but for ten years I nursed my sorrow. Today it is difficult to distinguish between one who is a widow and one who is not. It was only the care of the family and the responsibility of bringing up my son that sustained me. This is the age of Kali; it will get worse. What can anyone say?" (p.107)

Unnamalai Aachi remains as a witness to the many changes that take place in the family. She feels sympathy for her brother in his old age as a consequence of having married two women and keeping a mistress. All these events are not up to Aachi's ideals of life, but she bears with them stoically. As years go by, Aachi grows weaker in body and spirit. One day she trips and to falls down on the floor and breaks her leg. She also becomes senile, laughs at times and cries suddenly without any reason. Then one day she dies. All the members of the family arrange for her funeral and observe the post-funeral rites at the appropriate time.

Whereas Aachi represents the first generation, her grandson Diravi represents the modern values of the third generation. Right from childhood, Diravi is an oversensitive boy, who has been observing all the events in the family very carefully. He is deeply attached to his elder sister, Nagu Akka, who is recently married to Sivananda Perumal. But one day he is shocked to learn that Nagammai is sent back to her parental house by her husband, as he is not willing to live with a person who is neither male nor female. Diravi is too young and innocent to understand the nature of the problem. When the elders go to Sevantha Perumal's house to discuss the matter, Sevantha Perumal flatly refuses to live about Nagu as his wife, as she is not a 'woman'. He does not want to divulge the secret problem with Nagu but asks the elders to get her examined by a good lady doctor. "Why talk at all? Send for a doctor and have her examined. Why should I say more? But I shall have to say this. It was wrong of them to have palmed her off as a woman and arranged her marriage as it was a sin" (p. 63). The problem is so delicate that the elders cannot settle it properly. Consequently Nagu is abandoned by Sevantha Perumal.

Now Nagu has to live in her parental house as a 'liability'. Everybody in the family, including Unnamalai Aachi, Nagaru Pillai and Kuttiamme, are deeply worried about her plight. Since all of them believe in the patriarchal values of the society, they consider it as a great insult for a wife to be abandoned by her husband, lead a life of forced widowhood and live as a secondary citizen in her parents' home. Because of their helplessness, the elders agree to the divorce between Nagammai and Sevantha Perumal. Nagu is such a docile girl that she does not know anything other than crying helplessly.

The neighbours like Annamalai Pillai suggest to Nagaru Pillai to go to court. But Nagaru Pillai hesitates to approach the court for a variety of reasons. As he confesses to Annamalai Pillai, "Our vakil will lay bare his secrets. But his vakil will lay bare our Nagu's secrets" (p. 75). Going to the court involves other risks like permanent separation between husband and wife, waste of money loss of family reputation, etc. Nagaru Pillai has thought about the different aspects of a legal fight. He explains it to Annamalai Pillai, "I asked vakil's clerk Krishnan Kutty, about this and he said that if we go to court there will be some sparks but practically no remedy for this. If either husband or wife is dissatisfied with the spouse there is no law of the land to keep them together. If a case is instituted then both would have to live apart permanently; there will then be no reconciliation possible at any time. And it will be a costly one - this business of going to court. Vakils and witnesses will demand money. And if we win the case we might get a little maintenance money from the husband – nothing more. Will it soothe my daughter's painful memories? Would we be satisfied? Our affairs will be talked about by the town a little more – that is all..." (p. 75). Obviously Nagaru Pillai has realised the futility of going to court. The problem of the daughter's marriage is too fundamental to be solved by the court of law.

All the members of the family including Unnamalai Aachi are deeply worried about Nagu's divorce. Nagu's parents-in-law send back some of the items of dowry like brass vessels, plates of coir, wood, metal, ladles of wood, boxes, brooms and other things in instalments to Nagaru Pillai's house. Now that the items of dowry are returned, Nagu's divorce seems to be irrevocably finalised. The young Diravi is very angry with Papathi (Nagu's mother-in-law) and Sevantha Perumal (Nagu's husband) for their malicious behaviour, but he is too helpless to do anything immediately.

Being a docile girl, Nagu keeps weeping about her bad luck. The sorrow and anger of all the members of Nagaru Pillai's family are further aggravated by the shocking news of the second marriage of Sevantha Perumal with the first daughter Vadivu of Ekkimatan Pillai and Bhoomu conducted secretly at Velli Malai. Diravi is so angry with Ekkimatan that he calls him a worm and a termite. For a while Nagaru Pillai is dumb with anger. "He sat like a stone" (p. 84). Then he decides to teach a lesson to Sevantha Perumal by leaving his daughter at the latter's house. He says to his daughter, "Come Nagammai. I will take you to your husband's house. Let us see what he does now.... I didn't want to make a public show of my sorrow. We should not allow things to remain as they are. Is there no justice in this town?" (p. 84) Nagaru Pillai does not take anyone with him except his daughter, goes to Sevantha Perumal's house and leaves her there. He tells his son-in-law curtly and angrily, "..this is your wife. What you do with her is your affair" (p.85). He shouts at Papathi, Nagaru Pillai has done this on account of his desperate courage. The people of the street sympathise with Nagaru Pillai and say, "Even a cow will attack you, if you tease it too much" (p. 85). Diravi is satisfied with his father's bold action. Ekkimatan Pillai and his wife Bhoomu are proud of having married off their eldest daughter into the rich family of Sevantha Perumal.

Nagu's problem is not solved so easily. The fisherwoman Vellachi (known as the newspaper in which all the secrets of all the households are published) brings the sad news that Nagu is ill treated by her husband's family by being starved and beaten cruelly. Unnamalai Aachi suggests that Nagu should be brought back from her husband's house. Nagaru Pillai's eyes are filled with tears. He does not know how to solve the problem. Before he can think of some solution, he receives another shock.

One morning Sevantha Perumal brings Nagu in a spring cart, drags a weaker and frailer Nagu from the cart into Nagaru Pillai's house and leaves her there with these words, "We don't want this person, who is neither man nor woman, to die in our house. We are not going to bear witness to her death. If she wants to commit suicide let her do it here. Don't send her back to my house. If you do we will not be responsible for what happens" (p. 88).

Nagu's desertion by Sevantha Perumal disturbs all the members of her family deeply. Sevantha Perumal has treated her so callously that she is impelled to try for suicide. The members of Nagu's family come to know it after a few days. "In a few days everything about this episode was known to everyone else. Nagu Akka, unable to bear the painful thrashings and the pangs of starvation, had tried to commit suicide by hanging herself from the crossbeam in Perumal's back veranda. Papathi, who saw her prevented Nagu from putting an end to it all. It was very upsetting and the next moment Sevantha Perumal had taken her back to her parental home" (p. 88). Nagu is, obviously, deeply disturbed and disconsolate. Unnamalai Aachi tries to console Nagu by advising her to "consider that fellow dead. Be happy" (p. 88). Nagu, somehow, continues to lead her life mechanically in the parental house. She does not have either the knowledge or courage to defy the norms of the patriarchal society and, therefore, fades into passivity like a cog in the wheel.

Meanwhile, Diravi passes his SSLC examination, but cannot afford to go to a college. He is too young to get a government job. As advised by Annamalai Pillai (his neighbour) Diravi joins a Government Basic Training School at Neyyattinkarai. There he passes his last examination. He borrows a thousand rupees from Velu Pillai by mortgaging his house, joins a private school as a teacher by bribing the authorities with a thousand rupees. But he gets a less salary than he signs for. After a few months he is lucky enough to be appointed in the Karingal Government School. He is quite pleased about the change from a private school to a government one.

In the government school, Diravi comes in contact with a senior teacher, Moses, who happens to be very generous by nature. Moses observes that Diravi is not as jovial and carefree as any young man ought to be. He, therefore, asks him for the cause of his depression. Initially Diravi hesitates to reveal the cause, but after some introspection he confides into Moses how his elder sister Nagammai's barrenness and broken marriage are the real cause of his sorrow and depression. Moses understands the delicacy of the problem, and therefore, advises him to take Nagammai to his wife, Doctor Rosammai, on a Sunday evening for a medical check-up. Moses offers a good deal of moral support and encouragement to Diravi, who, therefore, feels a new confidence in himself.

Meanwhile, the members of Diravi's family come to know certain negative aspects of Sevantha Perumal and his family. Vellachi brings the news that Sevantha Perumal's second wife

Vadivu rules the house with an iron hand; that Papathi has become old and helpless and that Vadivu has not conceived even after two years of marriage. This news makes Diravi and his family suspect the possibility of Sevantha Perumal's impotence. But the problem is so confidential and private that it cannot be tested publicly. The whole family is depressed about Nagamma's marital insecurity. Diravi's father, mother and Nagammai are so morose that they cannot sleep at all peacefully.

As days go by, Diravi's suspicion about Sevantha Perumal's manhood becomes stronger as he hears a piece of corroborating information from his friend Kuttalam. Kuttalam tells Diravi how Vadivu, the second wife of Sevantha Perumal, told him about her husband's impotence. Kuttalam draws Diravi's attention to the injustice and insult done to womanhood (i.e., Nagammai) by the hypocritical Sevantha Perumal. All these factors awaken a sense of responsibility and determination in Diravi.

Diravi has been waiting for an opportunity to take Nagu to Doctor Rosammai for gynaecological check-up, but he cannot divulge it to the members of his family, who are too traditional to allow it. One day when he returns home, he sees Nagu Akka fainting in the backyard. She has started having fainting fits these days. Diravi has a good pretext to take her to a doctor. He, therefore, asks the permission of his parents and takes Nagu in a cart to Doctor Rosammai on a Sunday evening. He does not tell Nagu the real reason for his taking her to the doctor. Doctor Rosammai examines Nagu gynaecologically and finds that there is nothing wrong with her but she is only weak. She whispers to Diravi that his brother-in-law (Sevantha Perumal) is an idiot. Diravi is really happy to learn from the doctor that there is nothing wrong with Nagu.

Now that Diravi is more than convinced about the injustice done to his sister by the cunning brother-in-law, he wants to challenge the latter, but does not know when to do so. A few days go by in indecision. One early morning he goes to Sevantha Perumal's house and asks him to take back Nagu Akka, as nothing is medically wrong with her. But Perumal angrily dismisses it as a closed case and refuses to take her back because of his status and dignity. Diravi becomes helpless once again. But after two weeks he encounters Perumal, calls him a eunuch and threatens that he would arrange Nagu's marriage with Kuttalam. Sevantha Perumal remains indifferent, though deeply insulted by Diravi. Diravi speculates about Nagu Akka for about a fortnight.

Diravi, who belongs to the third generation, is very progressive in his attitude to Nagu's second marriage and, therefore, thinks that there is nothing wrong with it. But his parents, who belong to the second generation, are partially orthodox and partially flexible. Diravi, for example, takes his father into confidence and tells him all about Nagu's medical check-up by Doctor Rosammai and Kuttalam's readiness to marry her. Though his parents do not approve of it initially because of their dissatisfaction with Kuttalam's vicious character and dire poverty, they come round when Diravi convinces them about Kuttalam's improved morals and status. He promises Nagu that he would solve her matrimonial problem. A docile lady, Nagu has no choice other than obliging her brother and parents, who have to take a decision in the interest of her future happiness. But the only person who disapproves of the second marriage of Nagu is Unnamalai Aachi, who belongs to the old generation and who, therefore, remains very rigid in her approach to life. She attributes the evils, such as Nagu's second marriage, to the nature and effect of Kaliyuga.

Diravi succeeds in persuading his parents in accepting the proposal of Nagu's marriage with Kuttalam. He wants to see that Nagu has a settled matrimonial life. All the relatives of Diravi put their heads together and decide to celebrate the marriage of Nagammai and Kuttalam at Velli Malai. In the meanwhile, the old and senile Unnamalai Aachi breaks her leg by slipping on the floor. She remains bed-ridden for about two months and finally dies. After all the post-funeral rites are completed, the relatives of Diravi resume the routine work and fix the wedding of Nagammai on a Friday. Meanwhile, Diravi is transferred from Eraniyal to Shencottah. He thinks of leaving Eraniyal for Shencottah after Nagammai's marriage. The whole family is looking forward to the celebration of Nagammai's wedding.

The news of Nagammai's wedding is widely circulated in the town. "Secrets could not be kept long in the town. Everyone minded everyone else's business. Like the rats and bandicoots that scurried from house to house in the dark, secrets too were common property. Everyone now seemed to know that Nagu's second wedding with Kuttalam had been arranged and they talked among themselves about it. The fishwife and the head-shaking old woman added fuel to the fire" (p.152). But Diravi and the members of his family are eagerly looking forward to Nagammai's wedding.

The irony of life is such that certain things happen most unexpectedly. "It was rumoured that Sevantha Perumal's shop had not been opened for two or three days. No one, not even Vadivu knew where he was. But when he returned, he behaved as if he was slightly out of gear, as if his mind was unhinged. He spoke to no one but went to the shop and returned mechanically, lost within himself. It was said that Papathi even tried to have him treated for insanity" (p. 152). The reason for the adverse change in Sevantha Perumal's behaviour cannot be accounted for. It only reflects the mystery of life itself.

One night there is a festival in the Sollamatan temple. Diravi refuses to go there though invited by Kuttalam. He sleeps at home, but cannot sleep properly. On the contrary he has a nightmare. "He was suddenly in the midst of a nightmare without being aware of when he had gone to sleep. Someone was pressing his head into a sea of sand – throttling him with demonic strength. Was it his head of hair or beard and facial hair that interfered so. His eyes had gone bloody. Someone was laughing loudly and madly..something was rattling, the noise increasing progressively... the noise was increasing" (p. 155). Diravi's nightmare forebodes the future events.

Diravi is awakened by the boy Bhoothan's knocking on the door. Bhoothan, who had been a servant in Kuttalam's shop briefly, narrates what has been happening in Sollamatan temple. "In the festival after all the dancing and singing was over Ponnappan was possessed of Sollamatan. The piper and drummer surrounded him and increased his frenzy. In the midst of all this hubbub, Sevantha Perumal, who had been listlessly wandering about as if he were senseless (as he had been all these days) shouted something horrible. But before anyone could recover, he snatched the whip and the leaves from Ponnappan's hands – (symbols of possession)—and ran away from the place and jumped into a disused well. The well was a ruined one without much water, but murderously deep though no one knew how deep it was. It was said that many bodies had been thrown into the well and never recovered. No one dared to jump into the well after Sevantha Perumal Pillai. Vadivu came beating her breast and weeping loudly. She called for someone to help her crazed husband out of the well. No one was prepared to. Vadivu was also preparing to jump in after her husband but her father and others forcibly prevented her" (pp.155-6). Ekkimatan Pillai expresses his inability to carry Sevantha Perumal from the well. Then desperately Vadivu goes to Kuttalam's house, awakens him from sleep, falls at his feet and requests him, "You will have to help me. Save my husband" (p. 156). "Whatever his bitterness about Sevantha Perumal, Kuttalam had a soft corner for Vadivu and he decided to help her. Kuttalam moved quickly, got into the well and disappeared. No one had any clue about either Sevantha Perumal or about Kuttalam for a long while. No one dared to venture after them into the well. No one knew what had happened. They stood helpless round the well. Vadivu was inconsolable" (p. 156).

Two hours elapse since this happened. The police are sent for. When Diravi reaches the temple, it is dawn. A few police constables and civilians go into the well with the help of ropes and ladders. People are tense with expectation. Finally the constables come up. "They hauled up a corpse—Kuttalam's. Diravi felt that the earth had split under his feet. He was hanging in the air. He remembered his nightmare – it was repeating itself when he was awake. He tried to rush to Kuttalam but the police prevented him – they said they would have to do a post-mortem before they could allow anyone near the body" (p. 158). Then Sevantha Perumal is also brought up, but he is alive. He is bloody, gesturing wildly and madly. He laughs loudly and maniacally. Nobody knows what exactly has happened in the well. People guess that Sevantha Perumal must have throttled Kuttalam and drowned him in the mud in the unused well. But nothing is definitely known. The deranged Sevantha Perumal is taken to Trivandrum under police escort. His hands are manacled in the van of the mental ward of Ooalamparai Mental Hospital. He laughs demoniacally.

All the plans of Diravi and his parents are upset. Their dream of arranging the marriage of Nagammai with Kuttalam is shattered. Deeply disappointed by the unexpected tragedy, Diravi and his parents leave Eraniyal for good. Fate has dealt a terrible blow to Nagammai's matrimonial prospects. They are all defeated by a force beyond their control. Nagammai is wronged both by her first husband and by her bad luck. The permanent widowhood forced upon her is indeed worse than death. The entire family has to do nothing but accept the dictates of their Destiny with a sense of resignation.

The novelist shows how a docile woman suffers in the Indian (in this case Chettiar) patriarchal society due to the male hypocrisy, double-dealing and callousness. Even when Diravi takes a lot of trouble to solve Nagammai's matrimonial problem, he and the members of his family fail in the task due to forces beyond their control. Nagammai's matrimonial tragedy, though accidentally attributable to Sevantha Perumal's callousness, is ultimately ascribable to her fate.

Nagammai's tragedy may be understood better in contrast with her elder sister Unnamalai Akka, who has no problem at all in her marital career. Her marriage had taken place a few years ago in Pazhavadai, i.e., before Nagammai's marriage. Her husband (Diravi's brother-in-law) Tapasi Pillai is very fair and looks like a white man. He is a gem of a man. He reads the *Puranas* in the Vinayaka Temple for his livelihood. He is habituated to the use of snuff. He treats Diravi very affectionately by bringing sweets for him and giving him a coin while returning from Eraniyal to Pazhavadai. Tapasi Pillai is very understanding and sympathetic by nature and easily provides a sharp contrast to the callous Sevantha Perumal. Unnamalai Akka is quite lucky when compared to Nagammai. She has been pregnant now and suffers from nausea. Diravi and his parents go to Pazhavadai and celebrate her *seemantham* ceremony and bring her back to Eraniyal in a spring axle cart. In course of time she gives birth to a baby boy.

Similarly, Visalam, Nagammai's younger sister, has no problem with her marriage. When she matures, her parents distribute sweets and fruits to relatives and friends and celebrate her mock-heroic wedding with Ammulu as the groom, according to the Chettiar social custom. After a few months, her parents arrange her marriage with a young man called Bhagavathi Appan by selling their land and house to the son-in-law to meet the wedding expenses. Thus both Unnamalai Akka and Visalam have their normal matrimonial life, perhaps because of their good luck. Their life provides a very conspicuous contrast to Nagammai's which is ruined by Sevantha Perumal and her ill-luck. Even Diravi fails in his righteous war against the injustice done to Nagammai by Sevantha Perumal.

Koonangani Paatta is another interesting character belonging to the old generation. Now he is past sixty. But he does not represent the values of the old world. Whereas Unnamalai Aachi is an embodiment of traditional values of life like virginity, chastity, monogamy, family honour etc., her brother Koonangani Paatta represents the violation of many of these values and provides a sharp contrast to his sister. As Unnamalai Aachi remembers the past glory she tells her grandson Diravi how her brother Koonangani Paatta squandered all the wealth earned by their father on cheap women. Her father had appointed a lady teacher called Eli (a Nadar woman turned Christian) to teach her the letters of the alphabet. But Koonangani, who was about sixteen years old, took unusual interest in that teacher. His father, on coming to know this, tied him to a tamarind tree and thrashed him severely. From that day Aachi's education came to an end.

Koonangani Paatta is conspicuous for his non-conformity with the traditional ideals of Chettiar community. He violates the norms of the society like the sanctity of arranged marriage, monogamy, matrimonial loyalty and sexual purity. He, therefore, provides a sharp contrast to his sister Unnamalai Aachi. As Unnamalai Aachi remembers the past and narrates it to Diravi, Koonangani's life history is revealed to the reader gradually. "The teacher was the first, it led gradually to Ammukutti..you can tell a man by what he is when young; his habits will continue till he dies" (p.54). Once when Aachi and her mother went to Velli Malai temple, they happened to see a mother of forty and a daughter of sixteen i.e. Bhavani and Ammukutti there. Aachi's eyes were dazzled by Ammukutti's extraordinary beauty. If a woman like her was so much impressed by another woman, what about a young man like Koonangani? Soon Koonangani developed a secret love affair with Ammukutti. In course of time his secret came to be known to everybody, but nobody could do anything about it. "But in course of time every one became aware of it. At long last even Father found out. But by that time Ammachi had become the mother of a boy, Krishnan Kutty, father of Sasi and not even my father could do anything about it. But Koonangani Anna stood firm; he refused to leave Ammukutti. He was a grown man; he could not be beaten like a boy. He was so firm and obstinate about it that nothing could solve the problem. Father was ashamed of his son's behaviour and at last died of shame" (p. 57).

Koonangani has violated the norm of bachelorhood and sexual purity even before his marriage. His philandering is not approved by anyone of his community. Koonangani also does not care for anyone's opinion. Because of his lascivious behaviour with the lady teacher and love affair with Ammukutti, his father has entrusted him with all the responsibility of the household, fields and gardens. Koonangani Paatta lives in sin with Ammukutti (or Ammachi) for five years, after the death of his father. Although Ammachi remains as a mistress of Koonangani, she help him to stabilise his emotional life and return to his family. He is thirty years old by that time. Then under the pressure of his mother and with the tacit approval by Ammachi, Koonangani marries Ponamu Aachi. But she did not have children even after ten years of marriage. Then Unnamalai Aachi arranges for his second marriage with Ananji Pillai Aachi. Paatta returns to Eraniyal with his two wives. But ironically enough, his first wife Ponamu Aachi has three children – Iyavu, Neelapillai and Picha Pillai. Then the second wife Ananji has twins – Thayi and Andi Pillai. Koonangani has to pay the price for his having two wives, who cannot get on well with each other and for having disobedient sons. "According to all reports all Koonangani Paatta's sons were skilled at all sorts of devious deeds, like his father in his youth. Nobody listened to what Paatta said; everyone went his or her own way in that house. Frequent quarrels would break out between the rival wives affecting everyone in the house. People were interested in taking everything he had – never giving him anything. It was a case of the son beating the father or almost near it. The son's voice was heard all over the street" (p.70). The frequent quarrels between his two wives and the disrespectful behaviour of his sons cause perpetual tension to Koonangani Paatta. The anxiety and shame that he had caused to his own father has now been caused to him by his own wives and sons. Thus there is no escape from the consequences of his own *karma*. Even the young boy Diravi feels pity for Koonangani Paatta.

Just as Koonangani Paatta violated the norms of his community by having a pre-marital and post-marital love affair with Ammukutti, he has to swallow the moral humiliation now being a witness to similar violation of norms by his first wife's (Ponamu"s) daughter, Neelapillai. Neelapillai's husband died of smallpox four years ago. Hence Ponamu Aachi brings Neelapillai and her grandson Chidambaram from Midalam to Eraniyal. Chidambaram is five year old now. The family has appointed a teacher, Kumaraswamy (also known as Korami) to give tuition to Chidambaram. But as Diravi notices accidentally, Neelapillai aunt has started a secret love affair with Korami teacher. But no member of the family, including Koonangani Paatta knows the secret. After an interval of a few months, the members of the family are shocked to learn that Neelapillai the widow has become illegally pregnant and eloped with Korami teacher, thereby blackening the family reputation and honour. The gossip circulates fast in the town. On hearing this bitter news about his daughter, Koonangani feels crushed. His wife, Ponamu is shaken beyond recovery and takes to bed. Unnamalai Aachi comments bitterly about the promiscuous behaviour of modern widows like Neelapillai. She remembers how she became a widow before she was twenty and how she lived for her son. Ponamu Aachi is still bed-ridden, but yet she wants to see her son Iya Pillai married. But Iya Pillai has kept a mistress in some Pandarathi's house in eastern Mandapam – much in the manner of his own grandfather Koonangani Paatta. At last Iya Pillai is married to a poor spinster, Velammai, granddaughter of a big *lathi* Pothi. Koonangani Paatta, who has led a sexually lax life, does not have the moral courage to advise others when they commit sins similar to his.

Koonangani Paatta has maintained his keep Ammukutti separately though he has two legal wives. He has a son by Ammukutti named Krishnakutty. Sasidharan Kutty happens to be the son of Krishnakutty. Thus Koonangani Paatta has maintained two families, one illegal and the other legal. He has defied the traditional norms of Chettiar community because of his lascivious nature. His wives do not like his being intimate with his mistress. Once when the innocent boy Diravi conveys Ammukutti's secret message to Koonangani Paatta openly in the presence of his wives, the latter begin to quarrel with Paatta and abuse Ammachi severely. His three legal sons, i.e., Malu Pillai, Picha Pillai and Andi Pillai go to Ammachi's house and abuse her roundly. Thus Koonangani Paatta becomes helpless because of his divided loyalty to three women. Frequent quarrels between his two wives disturb his mind deeply and make him bitter.

Bhargavi,· Koonangani Paatta's illegal daughter by Ammukutti, has eloped with a coconut tree climber of Nadar community, thereby tarnishing the reputation of the family. She has a son and a daughter by him. Her husband is a self-respected man, who does not want any help from his parents-in-law. Now that he has broken his leg by falling down from a coconut tree, he has been unable to earn his living and hard pressed for money. Bhargavi has not contacted her parents for the last ten years. But now she has become so helpless that she has secretly written to her mother, Ammukutti, for some financial help. Consequently Ammachi consults Koonangani Paatta secretly about what to do. Koonangani Paatta offers some money to Ammachi and asks her to help their daughter out of the difficulty. Koonangani Paatta has become too helpless to change the course of his life. He, therefore, believes in the view that things happen as fated. Though the Chettiar community upholds the ideals of blood purity, family honour and sanctity of marriage, some members of the community violate the norms as they are compelled by their biological urges and emotional attractions to go astray. Whether the Chettiar community approves of it or not, life has to go on. People have to tolerate the violation of norms if not approve of them wholeheartedly

As Koonangani Paatta grows old as years go by, he has to face many unpredictable emotional problems. The legal and the illegal issues happen to be intertwined. For example, his first wife Ponamu Aachi has been suffering from diabetes and developed an abscess in her back and dies rather unexpectedly. Now the property is partitioned over the dead body of Ponamu Aachi as per the court order. Koonangani Paatta succeeds in getting a share of his property to his keep, Ammachi, also. This act of his exasperates his legal sons, who, therefore, declare vengeance on him. Thus Koonangani Paatta has to suffer deep mental anguish because of his dilemma between his legal wives and illegal mistress.

Now a new chapter of suffering begins in Koonangani Paatta's old age. Any man in old age needs the help and cooperation of his sons and daughters-in-law. But ironically enough, he is deserted by all of his relatives when he needs their help most. For example, his son Ivayu Pillai (and his wife) and Picha Pillai leave for Trivandrum. Similarly his second wife Ananji Pillai goes to Nagarcoil along with her daughter Thayi and son, Andi Pillai, because Andi Pillai is appointed as an electrician there. Ananji Pillai is remorseless and leaves Koonangani Paatta to his fate. He has allowed them to go to Nagarcoil to lead a better life. He accepts his loneliness boldly and wants to live in peace. The bitter experiences of his life seem to have brought in an inner change in him and given him a desperate courage. He decides to lead a lonely life. What is admirable about him is that he develops a stoic courage to face the exigency of life with a sense of resignation. He refuses to take his food even from his sister, Unnamalai Aachi. He is self-respected and adamant. He is in a passion of bitterness. One may easily see some sort of growth in his personality from juvenile truancy to yogic detachment. He starts reading the *Mahabharata, Tiruvilayadal* and *Garuda Purana.* He has learnt not to expect anything from his children and therefore not disappointed. This kind of spiritual *vairagya* is born out of his disillusionment with the worldly life and testifies to his maturity.

Papathi, the mother of Sivananda Perumal, is one of the key characters in the novel. She easily represents a type of character in Indian literature, i.e., that of an aggressive and arrogant mother-in-law. She is notorious for her lashing tongue and selfish nature. As her husband, Kannu Pillai, has been suffering from some disease, she has mercilessly driven him out of her house thereby falsifying the high ideal of a Hindu wife. "Kannu Pillai, the father was a sick man. His face was swollen with some disease. His fingers were contracted, wrinkled and always dirty. Saying it was contagious, his wife, Papathi had driven him away from home. That house, that shop and all that they had, had been his property. He was living with the Krishna woman, his mistress. She cooked and cared for him in his ill-health while his wife and his son had driven out of his own house...at least the Krishna woman was kind" (p. 20). Papathi, thus, happens to be a very selfish, arrogant and inhuman wife, who does not bother to look after her own legal husband.

Papathi's greed and possessiveness are exhibited at the time of negotiation of marriage between her son Sivananda Perumal and Nagammai. She demands a variety of things from the bride's father. For example, she demands some land, gold, cash and vessels. "Why do I haggle like this, crying till my voice is hoarse? Whatever you do, it is going to be for your daughter. Tomorrow she is going to be for your daughter. Tomorrow she is going to be the lady of this house, lording over it all. Give her a dowry, some old lands which will yield five *kottais* of paddy to feed the family. Make thirty sovereigns worth of gold jewels; and give some two thousand rupees in cash. That is all. But you should foot the expenses of the wedding. Vessels for domestic use, enough sweets to distribute among the townsfolk, milk, fruits and other things – you know all the usual things. You should do enough so that no one might have cause to feel that things were not sufficiently well done nor given – that is all I ask. I have no other son you see; he is the only one. If I miss this chance I cannot celebrate a second wedding" (p. 33). Papathi's demands are too high to be fulfilled by Nagaru Pillai. At last the elderly Koonangani Paatta arbitrates and fixes the total cost of the wedding at eight thousand rupees.

After six months of marriage, Nagammai is unfortunately divorced by Sevantha Perumal on the pretext of her so-called barrenness. When the divorce is decided by the Community Trust, Papathi, the miserly lady refuses to return the cash, gold, jewellery and vessels to the bride's home because she argues, that they have fed Nagu for more than six months. It is quite obvious that none can be meaner than Papathi.

Papathi has to pay for her evil nature. In her old age she has become too weak and helpless. She and her son, Sevantha Perumal, are overlorded by her second daughter-in-law, Vadivu. As the fisherwoman Vellachi describes, "The old lady has become skin and bones. It is the young lady who rules the house with an iron hand. There is no appeal beyond her word. She sends most of the household goods and groceries to her mother's house. The old lady does not question her...Papathi and her son were now reaping the results of their wrong doing" (p.109). Now the erstwhile domineering mother-in-law has become helpless at the hands of her own daughter-in-law, thereby proving the veracity of the Indian proverb, "If a mother-in-law has power at some time, the daughter-in-law enjoys power at some other time." Thus Time has taught Papathi the lesson of her life. As the Hindus believe that one has to face the consequences of one's *karma* in the present life itself, Papathi has to suffer at the hands of her daughter-in-law for the wrong that she has done to her own husband directly and to her first daughter-in-law indirectly. Thus there is poetic justice done to her thereby satisfying the moral expectations of the reader.

Generations happens to be a powerful ethnic novel recreating the culture specific atmosphere of the Chettiar community in South India. The novelist offers a detailed picture of the myths, legends, folksongs, customs and rituals of the people thereby evoking the distinct ethos of the South Indian community, which easily assumes the beauty of unfamiliarity for the non-Tamilian and non-Indian readers. The novel offers a rich mine of cultural information to anthropologists in addition to lovers of literature. There is a preponderance of rites, rituals and ceremonies in the novel. As Vasantha Surya rightly points out, "Chettis throw themselves into the observation of rites and ceremony, abandoning all caution and frugal instinct, in fact all their other anxieties and concerns, as soon as any festive opportunity presents itself. It is believed that to hang back when auspicious moment is at hand is to spurn Laxmi, the Goddess of Fortune" (*Introduction*, P.xii). Rites strengthen bonds, establish hierarchies of power and give expression to creative as well as destructive energies. Likewise ceremonies weld the community together in the face of their special Goddess, Nagammai, after whom the luckless Nagu has been named. The wedding rituals (of Nagu and Visalam) preceded by *nichyatambulam*, singing of *kolava* songs, *seemantham* ceremony (of Unnamalai Akka) 'touching the pots' ceremony, maturation ceremony and mock-wedding ceremony (of Visalam), birth ceremony, funeral and post-funeral rites –all these ceremonies have been described by the novelist as elaborately as picturesquely.

Similarly the religious fairs and festivals like the Odupparai Festival, the Sollamatan Fair, the regular holy service at Velli Malai Temple, the possession dance of Ponnappan – all these are depicted very vividly. Likewise, the Chettis' belief in horoscopes, good and bad omens, superstitions (like sighting the coconut trees in the morning, not crossing a cow's tail,) use of local proverbs, dress codes, ornaments, eating habits, blessings and curses and songs are all described meticulously, patiently and picturesquely. Such an ethnic presentation of the Chetti community by Neela Padmanabhan may be easily compared and contrasted with the ethnic picture of the Yoruba community in the novels of Chinua Achebe and other African novelists. The use of Tamil culture-specific words like *kabaddi, karpaga, kolam, kottai, kolava, kumkum, thali, Pillayar, muhurtham kandangi, murukkus, alengo, mundu, atha, rasam, Onam, seemantham, chakram, payasam, singhi, kozhukkotai, padaiyal, ponkal, prasadasm, symbalan, adi, aavani, purattasi, aaipasi, margazhi, thai* and *villuppattu*, etc., contributes a lot to the creation of local colour and ethnic beauty of atmosphere.

The novel depicts not only the contradictions of the Chettiar community like adherence to and violation of the cultural norms, but also the gradual creeping in of modernity in the otherwise traditional life of the community. The effect of modernity on the people of Chettiar community is rather slow. Whereas the first generation represented by Unnamalai Aachi is very rigid in its adherence to the community ideals, the second generation represented by Nagaru Pillai, Kuttalam and others is less rigid in its adherence to the old ideals and willing to adapt at least partially to the modern situations of life. The third generation represented by Diravi is readily willing to absorb modernity as much as it can. Behind all the events in the novel, one may easily perceive the transition of values from the old to the new due to the effect of Time. In this sense *Generations* may be described as a transition-narrative.

Apart from the temporal change, there is also a spatial change depicted in the novel in terms of the internal migration of South Indians from one place to the other thereby testifying to the imperceptible social mobility. When Diravi and his parents' efforts to arrange the remarriage of Nagammai with Kuttalam fail due to the unexpected tragic death of Kuttalam, the entire family leaves Eraniyal and goes to some other town. As Vasantha Surya rightly points out, "The novel describes the immiseration of a family and a caste, leading to migration. Family legends preserve the experience of uprootings and migrations within the southern country. These 'little' migrations over relatively smaller distances than those across the seas disprove the stereotype of 'unchanging India'. Many families, even in the relatively more stable South, have a history of having come from 'somewhere else', carrying with them an irreducible minimum of cultural baggage, which will affirm their distinct identity. Young Diravi, descendant of a clan of small trader-farmers of the Chetti caste, who had migrated from Tamil Nadu to the princely state of Travancore centuries earlier has imbibed throughout his childhood certain socialising values along with his grandmother's stories of vanished glory" (p.x). One may easily see how the earlier migration is recaptured by Unnamalai Aachi through her community-legend and the present migration is suggested at the end of the novel. As Vasantha Surya says, "A work of great imaginative power, this is also a readable story of how social change has sometimes taken place in India" (p.xiii).

The novel offers a picture of the Chettiar community with all its cultural texture. Ethnologists have a rich treasure here for analysis and comparison with other ethnic groups. The novel is written is a realistic style. The inter-personal and inter-familial relationships within the Chettiar community have been depicted very authentically and convincingly. In spite of the rich regional flavour, the novel has a universal human appeal. Neela Padmanabhan "does not squander his narrative resources and every word, image and anecdote has a bearing on Diravi's development" (p. xiii). The novel begins in the present, goes back to the past again and again through the memories of Unnamalai

Aachi and connects the past and the present to convince the young Diravi. *Generations* is indubitably a significant novel, which captures the quintessential spirit of Tamil culture of South India.

Cited Work

Neela Padmanabhan, *Generations*, tr. Ka. Na. Subramanyam, Chennai: Macmillan, 1997. All the page references are to this edition.

13

The Spider's Web : A Short Story

— Basavaraj Naikar

I had spent a lot of money on my election and succeeded in getting elected as an MLA. Later I was lucky enough to become a Minister on the strength of my caste and popular support. After assuming charge as the cabinet level Minister, I had to visit the different districts in Karnataka to streamline everything in the State administration. I had decided to plug the loopholes in my department and bring law and order in the bureaucratic set-up. That day I had fixed the date of my visit to Dharwad and inspected the various offices of my department. My car zoomed along the road from Bangalore to Dharwad. I had to stay in the Circuit House on the elevated hill of Dharwad commanding a beautiful view of the surrounding landscape. My car was followed and preceded by the security officers' cars with flickering lamps on them.

As I reached Dharwad via Hubli, the police constables and PSIs and the SP had grown alert and were following my car diligently. Later on I had to meet the members of my party and then participate in the public function in the Collector's Compound.

As my car entered the Circuit House, the police officers saluted me with style and welcomed me with great respect and awe. The double room was decorated with new furniture, cushions and curtains. Everything was spic and span. A cup of hot steaming coffee was served to me as I relaxed on the decorated chair. The benzamin tree outside the Circuit House displayed a splurge of bright red blooms. From the western window of the room I could see the imposing clock tower of the Karnatak University building in white granite rock. I remembered the educationist, Dr. D.C.Pawate who struggled to build the Great University in Dharwad and named it as Karnatak University much against the will of the south Karnataka politicians. After my completion of morning ablutions, the cook brought me hot *idlis, masala dosa* and hot coffee for my breakfast. The officers appeared to have taken very keen interest in the inauguration programme and neglect their office work. I realised that they had taken so much trouble over the function only to reduce the time available for my inspection of their offices.

As I had become a Minister recently, I had a good reputation of being a man of discipline. People saw in me, a man who would not tolerate any official delay or corruption and the officers, therefore, were very apprehensive. I was secretly proud of my reputation.

A large gathering of people was there at Kadapa Maidan in the morning. I went there about 10.30 a.m. The police officers made way for my car. All the local politicians received me with joined plams and smile of recognition. Everything was kept ready and everybody was waiting for me to inaugurate the Mallikarjun Mansur Kalabhavan. I went straight to the main gate of the Kalabhavan and cut the ribbon and entered the corridor. The members of the Reception Committee led me to the large portrait of the late Pundit Mallikarjun Mansur fixed on the wall of the corridor. I put a large jasmine garland on the portrait and lit the two lamps beside it. The entire gathering of people clapped their hands in appreciation. Then I rushed to the Open Air Theatre to participate in the party meeting. We discussed with the party members how to retain a good name for us as well as for our party and how to win the hearts of voters to our side. By that time, I realised that I had very little time for the inspection of my departmental offices. As I was rushing through the inspection, a few people approached me and submitted a petition. I asked the Deputy Commissioner to look into their grievance, which was against the local Circle Inspector.

Then we returned to the Circuit House for lunch. When the lunch was served to me and other dignitaries, I found that the fried fish was very tasty. When I reached for the plate for another helping, someone hurried forward to serve me. "The fish is very good," I said. "Where do you get it from?"

"The fish is from Karwar beach sir. I got it from there, because I know you like it," said the man.

"Oh, you got it from such a long distance?" I said, and he smiled with a sense of satisfaction.

After the sumptuous lunch I chewed the delicious Kashmiri *panabida* with real gusto and belched with a sense of satisfaction. I moved to the lounge and sat chatting with the Deputy Commissioner. I asked him casually about the poor folk's complaint, "About whom are they complaining?"

The Deputy Commissioner looked at the man who served me the fish. The man sped out of the door. I understood the situation. The Deputy Commissioner said, "He is the local Circle Inspector. The hut-dwellers of Attikolla have complained against him for bribery."

The Muncipal President added, "They have complained to us also against him."

"Then it is a serious problem," I said, "we have to do something about it."

While chatting in the drawing room later, the Deputy Commissioner sat gazing at a spider's web at one corner of the ceiling.

In the evening I went in my car to the Collector's Compound to make my public speech to the local audience. Thousands of people had gathered in the large pandal. Loudspeakers were blaring. There was a big din. As I climbed the platform, the din subsided. There was pin-drop silence. The function began with a welcome song by some high school girls to the accompaniment of harmonium and tabla. The song was very serene and enthusing. Then the local MLA introduced me as a man of action and concern for poor people and justice. The flattery pleased me. I felt secretly elated. After his introduction, I stood up to speak. There was great silence of expectation everywhere in the audience. I began to speak in my clear and stentorian voice. I told them how we Indians should be proud of our country and our State and how we have to build a new nation and compete with other advanced nations of the world. This we could achieve only with hard and sincere work and by being free from corruption. The MLA had described me as a man of action and not of mere words. I, therefore, declared my resolve to put down corruption. I felt encouraged by the thunderous clapping in the audience and wanted to demonstrate my action-orientation. I, therefore, declared, "Today I have received a complaint against an officer about corruption. I learnt that there is some truth in it. I am, therefore, going to order the Deputy Commissioner to suspend that officer right now."

The dignitaries on the dais began to clap loudly. The audience also joined in the clapping. Before the applause could subside, someone at the back of the gathering collapsed and people surrounded him. My gunman rushed to the spot, returned and told me, "Sir, he is said to be one Mr. Durgadas, the Circle Inspector of this town. He is unconscious."

I felt deeply disturbed. I asked the Police Inspector sitting near me to take the man in his jeep to the hospital. Within half an hour of my return to the Circuit House, the Deputy Commissioner brought the news that the Circle Inspector had died before he could reach the hospital. The Municipal President remarked, "Who knows what diseases he had harboured?"

But I was deeply agitated. "He case is closed now. Why discuss it then?" said I, and averted my face.

The visitors left the Circuit House one by one. At last, only the Deputy Commissioner and I remained in the room. I looked at him, but he was gazing at the spider's web. An insect was flying around it. It used to touch the strands of the web and fly way. But the spider waited patiently. How long can the game of death continue? As last the insect was trapped. The harder it struggled to extricate itself, the tighter grew the bond of the web. At last the insect's struggle ceased.

We looked at each other and I asked the Deputy Commissioner, "I am sorry, was Durgadas so very sensitive?"

"I know, sir. Poor fellow. He must have been shocked when he heard you declare his suspension. He must have felt forlorn. He probably wished to make the same request to you as he had to me," said the Deputy Commissioner.

"Tell me what his request was!"

"I do not know if I should talk about it. If we hide it, we will have to undergo Durgadas's condition. I do not say that Durgadas was a very honest man. Nor do I deny that we received a share. Everything is like a spider's web and everybody is sure to be trapped because of some attraction or inevitability."

I did not like his circumlocution. "Come to the point," I snapped.

Then the Deputy Commissioner cleared his throat and said in a gentle voice, "Six years ago, Durgadas was a Circle Inspector already and I was working as an Assistant Commissioner here. The then Deputy Commissioner used to be very enthusiastic about arranging grand dinners for visiting VIPs. He was himself a good eater. He used to arrange vegetarian and non-vegetarian food as well as drinks. The man who would arrange all that was Mr. Durgadas. Nobody bothered to consider how a low–salaried officer like Durgadas could meet the high expenditure of such parties. Nobody bothers about it even now. On rare occasions a high officer would ask for the bill and thank the hosts. Would the money offered by one or two officers suffice to meet the total expenditure?

"Durgadas was not a fool either. He thought that it would be a sign of incompetence if he were to spurn that work. He, therefore, found an easy way out. He knew there were a few huts on the government land near the Attikolla. Some huts wee erected there with Municipal permission and some others without that. Thus, a slum came into existence on the Attikolla. Whenever the huts were ordered to be demolished, the hut-dwellers appealed to the leaders. How would the leaders allow the demolition? Durgadas knew that it was impossible for him to demolish them. But at the same time, he knew that he could extract some money from the hut-dwellers by threatening them of demolition. The money raised thus would be sufficient both for the arrangement of a couple of dinner parties during that month and for his own livelihood. Durgadas would repeat the trick the subsequent month also. The poor people's complaints against Durgadas were sent to the Government, but all of them were referred to the Deputy Commissioner, who was also implicated.

"Eventually, I was appointed to inquire into the matter. As usual, I sent a notice to him and asked for an explanation. His answer confounded me. He said it was true that he had extracted money from the hut-dwellers to arrange dinners for VIPs and added, 'Is there anything not known to you?' How could I answer that question?

"I suggested to the Deputy Commissioner to transfer the Circle Inspector to some other place. But he wanted to punish him. I suggested, 'You may transfer him to a place where there is no scope for such corruption. Why tarnish your image unnecessarily?' Luckily, he agreed and transferred Durgadas to some other place.

"But Durgadas was back here when I came here on transfer after six years. I was surprised to see him again. I came to know that there was nobody to look after the Circuit House satisfactorily. Some people advised the Deputy Commissioner to replace him with a better man. Hence, Durgadas returned to this place again.

"I do not know whether Durgadas was happy or not this time. Now his family is not small unlike in the past. He has four children. His eldest daughter and son are studying in the high school. Besides, he has to maintain his elder brother also. He seemed to have been dragged into a whirlpool. In spite of all that, he would continue to squander many on feeding the officers. Besides, there were many who would encourage him. When I went to his home, his wife said tearfully that he had squandered the entire amount of festival advance of this month for the same purpose. I wonder if there is any beginning or end to this vicious circle."

I know I had not paid the bill for the food I had had here the last time. Today, the fish that was offered by Durgadas was not yet digested. I felt very uneasy.

The Deputy Commissioner was staring at me. "We are all lovers of tradition, sir, especially when it is convenient. We can see people like Durgadas in every department. But it is unfortunate that there are many leaders who deem it to be a sign of able administration to kill the serpent and feed it to the eagle. We should have thought about the evil consequence of this system long back. Excuse me sir I had to tell you this only because you asked."

Much later, I lay in bed staring at the light overhead. Hospitality, obligation, festival advance, squandered money... complaint..a family of eight members. Durgadas would not have bothered about any of these. His sole intention was to please the higher officers.

What about me? Am I a man of principles?...I too have a wife and four children. Haven't I done so many illegal things for their sake? My inner voice asked me, "Can a man be like this?" My head began to reel...the light began to grow dim...Did I kill him? I grew nervous and felt my heart with my palm. My heart had begun to pound incessantly. I rubbed my eyes, got up and walked a few steps. The wind flew against my head...I asked myself if it was right for one in my position to be so sensitive.

My gunman announced that dinner was ready. I instantly remembered Durgadas. I said, "I am not hungry. Some fruit juice is enough." I paced up and down in the room. The attenders seated on the stairs disappeared into the darkness. Once again, I felt lonely. I wanted to forget the whole thing by rationalising.

The breeze whipped me in the face. As its intensity increased, the curtains in the room began to flutter. The gunman came and said he had placed the fruit juice on the teapoy. I turned back slowly. I thought that probably worries bother only those who worry and fear harasses only those who fear. I came back to the drawing room and sat on the sofa. The plastic cover on the glass of fruit juice was blown to the ground. I took up the glass to empty it, but I saw in it an insect of the size of a bean struggling and dying. My whole body shivered but I began to sweat. I kept the glass back on the teapoy and stared at the spider's web in the corner and the insect caught in it. I saw the dead insect floating in the fruit juice. "We can see people like Durgadas in every department, sir." These words of the Deputy Commissioner pierced my heart again and again.

I got up from the sofa, tottered to the bed clutching my head in both hands and lay down. It was dawn when I woke up.

14

The Tale as Useful Artefact: Basavaraj Naikar's *The Thief of Nagarahalli and Other Stories*

— Christopher Rollason

This article was published in *IJOWLAC* (*Indian Journal of World Literature and Culture*) (Bhubaneswar, India), Vol. 2 (July-December 2006), 79-90. The present version corrects a small number of errata from the print edition, and is the one that should be quoted by any scholars wishing to cite the article.

***

I

"Every real story," Walter Benjamin declared in "The Storyteller", his famous essay of 1936, "...contains, openly or covertly, something useful." The great Jewish-German critic goes on to specify: "The usefulness may, in one case, consist in a moral; in another, in some practical advice; in a third, in a proverb or maxim. In every case the storyteller is a man who has counsel for his readers."[1] Benjamin was of course writing about the tradition of storytelling that may be variously called oral, folk, artisan or traditional - the tradition which, he believed, lay behind the tales of the ostensible subject of his essay, the nineteenth-century Russian writer Nikolai Leskov, and which he carefully distinguished from the fictional mode of the novel: "What differentiates the novel from all other forms of prose literature— the fairy-tale, the legend, even the novella - is that it neither comes from oral tradition nor goes into it. This distinguishes it from storytelling in particular. The storyteller takes what he tells from experience—his own or that reported by others. And he in turn makes it the experience of those who are listening to his tale."[2]

The novel is commonly seen as a "Western form"—a judgment which may not be totally accurate, but none the less serves to differentiate that narrative mode from other, older modes which exist both in Western oral and rural traditions and in the various storytelling traditions that persist outside the Western world. European and American literature provide examples of "authored" short stories with a marked traditional patina: the short stories of Thomas Hardy, with their plots resembling folk ballads (as in "The Three Strangers" or "The Withered Arm"), point back to a tale-telling tradition that precedes the novel, while Mark Twain's mining-camp anecdotes such as "The Celebrated Jumping Frog of Calaveras County" or "Dick Baker's Cat" are built around the simulacrum of a demotic speaking voice.[3] In the evidently different context of modern Indian writing, whether in English or in Indian languages, it is likely to be part of the reader's expectation that a short story will be ventriloquised through the mouth of a narrator resembling the traditional storyteller, or, at least, that something of the feel of such a figure will be communicated through a more "modern" or "sophisticated" narrative voice. A canonic example here would be Rabindranath Tagore's famous story "The Cabuliwallah" (originally written in Bengali), which communicates a clear moral message of shared humanity through an almost didactic first-person voice that gives the illusion of a storyteller haranguing his rapt audience.[4] At the same time, that usefulness—moral, practical or proverbial—which Benjamin identifies as central to the artisan tale may also be expected to be present at the story's kernel.

The short story as it has evolved over the last two centuries is, of course, a form that exhibits remarkable diversity, and not all critical and creative perspectives on it propose an affinity with the folk-tale. Twain, certainly, in his essay "How To Tell A Story", advocates, for the "humorous story", a deadpan, poker-faced approach that in some ways recalls the traditional tale-teller ("I only claim to know how a story ought to be told, for I have been almost daily in the company of the most expert story-tellers for many years").[5] There is surely, too, an echo of that same figure in Edgar Allan Poe's model of the short story as a narrative constructed around "a certain *single effect* to be wrought," that aims to spellbind the reader for the time required to take in the tale ("And by such means, with such care and skill, a picture is at length painted which leaves in the mind of him who contemplates it with a kindred art, a sense of the fullest satisfaction"):[6] behind the more sophisticated painterly image, the concepts of "skill" and the "wrought" object suggest the traditional story-craftsman at work. Other modern approaches, however, diverge radically from the artisan model; one need only think of Franz Kafka's allegories of an alienating social universe, Jorge Luis Borges's deliberate transgression of the borderline between story and essay, or the "poetic", impressionistic short story as practised by Anton Chekhov or Katharine Mansfield.

The "traditional" folk-oriented approach will, at all events, serve as the best way into *The Thief of Nagarahalli and Other Stories*, the collection published in 1999 by Basavaraj Naikar of Karnataka state (India) and shortlisted in 2000 for the Commonwealth Writers' Fiction Prize (Best First Book, Eurasia section). This volume consists of ten stories which, the author explains in his preface, he has selected from twenty years' production in the genre. Though all written in English, they are intended as specifically Indian, in both subject-matter and expression: "I believe in the view that we Indians must write in our native branch of English and should not ape the British 'masters'. Our imagery and style should be redolent of our cultural ethos." They are also clearly intended as useful, in something like Benjamin's sense: "The ten stories ... represent various aspects of human relationships in our life. They range from the elemental to the social to the mythical dimensions of life" (5).[7] That which is typical and representative, that which signifies one or other of the "dimensions of life", may be considered to offer some tangible use-value to the Indian reader.

II

Before considering the potential usefulness of Basavaraj Naikar's stories in greater detail, it is first desirable to examine the coherence of the volume as such, considered as a collection of interrelated texts whose signification as a whole should prove greater than that of the sum of its parts. It is here useful to fine-tune our expectations of such coherence by looking at the internal organisation of a number of other contemporary short-story collections by English-medium Indian writers, both resident and non-resident. For this purpose, a total of seven examples in the genre (stretching the definition of "Indian" slightly to include V.S. Naipaul) will now be summarily compared and contrasted.

The seven volumes of stories in question are: V.S. Naipaul's *Miguel Street* (1959), Rohinton Mistry's *Tales From Firozsha Baag* (1987), Nisha da Cunha's *Old Cypress* (1991), Salman Rushdie's *East, West* (1994), Vikram Chandra's *Love and Longing in Bombay* (1997), Jhumpa Lahiri's *Interpreter of Maladies* (1999), and Anita Desai's *Diamond Dust* (2000). Of the seven authors, da Cunha is India-resident, Naipaul is a Trinidad-born British citizen of Indian origin, and the remaining five may be identified as non-resident Indians. Three of the collections employ a linking or framing device, i.e., the stories are interrelated by common locations and recurring characters: *Miguel Street* is about the inhabitants of a single street in Port of Spain, Trinidad; *Tales From Firozsha Baag* comparably focuses on the dwellers of a single Bombay apartment block (the final story sending its first-person narrator to Canada); while the stories of *Love and Longing in Bombay*, though about diverse lives and narrated in the third person, are linked by being placed in the mouth of a single Bombayite storyteller. Naipaul employs the same first-person narrator throughout, while Mistry alternates first- and third-person modes. Those three volumes, as well as those by Lahiri, da Cunha and Desai, are examples of what might be called the "purpose-built" type of short story collection, i.e., most or all were first published in the volume in which they appear and the collection therefore gives the impression of an organic whole; Rushdie's *East, West*, by contrast, is conceptually more of a rag-bag, made up for the most part of stories first published at different times and in different contexts, though the author attempts to give his volume some degree of retrospective coherence by arranging his nine tales into three themed sections. Nonetheless, despite their purpose-built appearance, Lahiri's *Interpreter of Maladies* and Desai's *Diamond Dust* are not necessarily much more coherent, taken as books, than Rushdie's collection: Lahiri's stories variously concern Indians in America, expatriate Indians vacationing "back home" and "real Indians in Bengal"; Desai's subjects and locations range from "pure Delhi", through

"Indians in Canada", to totally non-Indian encounters set in Britain or Mexico. Da Cunha's collection, by contrast, enjoys the coherence that comes from her setting every story in Goa. If the collections vary in the nature of their spatial locations and — Naipaul's apart — deploy multiple narrative voices, almost all observe a certain unity of time (setting all their stories in what, for their initial readers, will be the present or near-past), the one exception here being Rushdie, who sets certain of his tales either in the historical past or in a nowhere-land.

If we now apply the criteria emerging from his fellow-writers' collections to Basavaraj Naikar's volume, it first has to be said that *The Thief of Nagarahalli* lacks any kind of overarching frame-narrative (of the type employed by Naipaul, Chandra and Mistry). There is no single first-person narrator to confer coherence on the volume: eight of the stories are narrated in the third person and two by (different) first-person narrators. Equally, unity of time as practised by most of Naikar's compeers is absent: two of the stories are set in the Raj era, one in a non-specific mythical past, and the rest, either explicitly or implicitly, in or near the present day; in other words, there is a temporal heterogeneity comparable to that found in the Rushdie collection. By contrast, there is a visible coherence in the matter of place: all the stories are set within in a restricted geographical compass, namely, in various locations in today's Karnataka state, and, especially, the vicinity of Dharwad city. We thus find that concentrated sense of place which is absent from the Lahiri, Desai and Rushdie volumes, but conversely does characterise the collections by Naipaul (Trinidad), Chandra and Mistry (Bombay) and da Cunha (Goa). This suggests that if we are to seek interconnection in Naikar's story collection, it should be through that sense of place; and that, accordingly, what binds his ten stories is in some sense an essential Indianness, or, at least, a distinctively Indian approach to the tale-teller's art.

Basavaraj Naikar has himself, in his critical essays and in relation to his translations from the Kannada, stressed his companionship with what might be called a humanist or exemplary tradition of autochthonous Indian writing. Writing on Nirad C. Chaudhuri, he has praised the Bengali writer for his social realism ("Chaudhuri has been able to give a clear and convincing picture of the Indian society in his works")[8] and his "concreteness of diction,"[9] while endorsing Chaudhuri's view that the Indian writer in English should, despite the possible pitfalls of the alien language, "be native both in theme and in style,"[10] preferring the style of "an Indian who ...has not de-Indianised and Anglicised himself."[11] Similarly, commenting on the fiction of another classic English-medium writer, Mulk Raj Anand, Naikar observes: "He must be congratulated for the creation of a number of character types which are indigenous to Indian society."[12] As a critic of Indian writing in English, then, Naikar clearly admires what is realist in scope and reference and is rooted in local tradition; and, indeed, similar criteria emerge from his comments on older vernacular literature, as in his praise of the classic Kannada poet Sarvajna (a selection of whose aphoristic three-line poems he has translated):[13] "The very name of "Sarvajna", which means "the omniscient", testifies to his comprehensive knowledge and vision of life."[14] Naikar expresses a certain humanist perspective which, though rooted in India, does not exclude more universal reference. Thus, in an essay on Raja Rao he evokes Shakespeare, declaring that "*The Serpent and the Rope* can be designated as the tragedy of philosophy of an Indian Hamlet"[15] (and we may here recall that in 1971 Raja Rao published *The Cat and Shakespeare*, an eminently South Indian novel which none the less reaches out in its title to a wider literary universe).

The critic Naikar defends an inclusive model of social realism and of the useful text which the reader may expect to find carried over into his creative writing. The ten stories that make up *The Thief of Nagarahalli* are nothing if not diverse, but all reflect the time-honoured tradition of the tale-teller's art. The title story, set "in a village called Nagarahalli situated thirty-five miles away from Dharwad," (9) in the days of the Raj, centres on a thief whose skill is such that he may, paradoxically, be considered an artist in dishonesty. "All For Gold", the collection's other Raj-era story, tells of an extramarital affair followed by a bloody revenge. "Mother's Husband", the most archaic narrative in the collection, re-enacts archetypal passions in a mythical setting which is, nonetheless, still recognisably Karnatic. Among the stories located in the contemporary world, "The Invisible Face" and "Coffin In The House" both investigate the deceptiveness of social appearances, as respectable individuals are revealed to have dark secrets; "Her Husband Went to America" broadens out the frame of reference to take in India's relations with the wider world, though far from happily as an émigré spouse employs a cruel trick to desert his wife for an American bride; while "The Anonymous Letter" strikes perhaps the lightest note in the collection, offering up a vignette of South Indian university life in a tale of minor intrigues around an atmospherically evoked provincial campus.

In their diversity (multiplicity of themes) framed in a certain continuity (the Karnataka setting), Naikar's stories may be read, for the most part in a classical realist sense, as typical and representative of a certain Indian cultural, social and psychological reality. In addition, the collection acquires a deeper coherence from the presence of a recurring theme, namely, that of human identity. Through their diverse narrative strategies, these stories examine such crucial questions as how an individual can create and maintain an identity within society, how far that identity is malleable to our will or mutable at the hands of outside forces, and whether people's social masks correspond to their hidden drives and desires.

The specifically Indian typicality of Naikar's writing has been finely brought out in an essay published in 2002 by Asha Choubey, "*The Thief of Nagarahalli and Other Stories*: Essentially Indian Stories." Taking an authenticist approach, Choubey argues that Naikar's ten stories may be interpreted in terms of a psychological model. This is not that of Freud or Lacan, but the eminently Indian model of the nine *rasas* (emotions or states of spirit), as first adumbrated in the classical Sanskrit treatise on the theatre, the *Natyasastra* of Bharata[16] - *sringara* (eroticism), *karuna* (compassion), *bhaya* (fear), *santa* (tranquillity), etc. Thus, "the title story evokes hasya or comic along with vira or heroic in the daring exploits of the protagonist, it ends admirably in santa with the bold thief having reconciled himself to his defeat at the hands of one of his rivals"; while "'Her Husband Went to America' works through sringara and karuna or compassion but ends in santa," and "'Mother's Husband' has elements of sringara ... as well as adbhuta or marvellous." Choubey concludes: "Naikar's stories are closer to Indian sensibility as after all the upheavals, there comes reconciliation with the prevailing situation. And Indian optimism is evident in the fact that this final reconciliation comes not from passive submission to fate but from recognition of human courage and fortitude despite fate-imposed limitations."[17]

Within this context, as identified by Choubey, of Naikar's "essentially Indian sensibility,"[18] it may now be useful to broaden out the analysis, returning to Benjamin's more general conception of traditional storytelling while striving not to lose sight of the subcontinental perspective. Accordingly, I now propose a more detailed examination, with particular reference to Benjamin's notion of the tale as a useful object and repository of "counsel", of the three stories not mentioned so far, namely: "She Wanted a Child", "When the News Came", and the book's closing story, "Fulfilment".

III

Like several other stories in Naikar's volume, "She Wanted a Child" might superficially be considered a somewhat journalistic production. It is a tale that, certainly, reads as if it were based on a *fait divers* from a local newspaper. The story runs thus: Manjula, a young woman two years married in the Kannada town of Chitradurga, is still childless. She is offered and accepts a job at the post office in Dharwad. Desperate to conceive, she takes a lover, only to have it confirmed that she is infertile. Finally she uses a stratagem to steal a newborn baby from the hospital, but is caught and arrested. The tale ends with the baby restored to its rightful parents.

Material like this may seem the stuff of provincial scribes, and, indeed, we are told that "the news of a theft of the child by a stranger had appeared in headlines in all the leading newspapers" (124). However, it is Walter Benjamin himself who warns that the storyteller's art is, inherently, something totally different from the methods of the journalist: "Every morning brings us the news of the globe, and yet we are poor in noteworthy stories. This is because no event any longer comes to us without already being shot through with explanation. In other words, by now almost nothing that happens benefits storytelling; almost everything benefits information. Actually, it is half the art of storytelling to keep a story free from explanation as one reproduces it."[19] It will here be interesting to consider how Naikar's art of storytelling manages to raise his narrative above the level of the mere "information" criticised by Benjamin.

"She Wanted A Child" opens on a highly traditionalist note, manifested in a sharp reprimand cast at Manjula by her unpitying mother-in-law: "'You have not even a single child to keep the lamp of our family burning. I don't know what is wrong with you. At your age, I was a mother of three,' complained the mother-in-law in the kitchen." (112) This opening, in both its directness and its traditionalism, may be compared to the celebrated first sentence of Vikram Seth's novel *A Suitable Boy*, in which a mother declares to her younger daughter, on the occasion of the elder one's wedding: "'You too will marry a boy I choose', said Mrs Rupa Mehra firmly to her younger daughter."[20] Naikar, following in the wake of Seth, immediately establishes his characters as typical and representative members of a society in which traditional values are the norm.

This is of course a classically realist narrative strategy, and social and descriptive realism are very much to the fore throughout this story. Quintessentially South Indian details are present as the characters eat idlis and dosas or sip "sweet hot coffee." (116) Typical elements of subcontinental urban life appear in, for instance, the din of the traffic in the town of Hubli ("Auto-rickshaws were honking and hooting and trucks and buses were roaring past the Lodge" - 117), while Indian bureaucracy is gently satirised in passages whose detail might recall similar scenes in Raja Rao's *The Cat and Shakespeare* ("The constable asked the typist to type out the First Information Report. When the FIR was ready, the constable pressed two rubber stamps on it and got it signed by the sub-Inspector" - 123). The reader is constantly reminded of the events' location in a specific place and time, and it is also noteworthy that on two occasions it is stated that the (literate) characters are conducting their business in Kannada - not, therefore, in English, the language in which the tale is nonetheless being narrated.

It is, then, within a specifically Indian (South Indian and Kannada) context that Manjula's human drama unfolds. Within this context, it is no doubt legitimate to seek in it the kind of useful message that Benjamin finds in the traditional story. From a conservative point of view, Manjula would be viewed as a disturber of the cultural order: appropriating a child who is not her own by deceptive means, she separates it from its biological parents and thus creates a rent in the fabric of society. That rent is made good at the end, with the miscreant locked away in jail and the natural parents reunited with their offspring. Indeed, it is with those parents' joy that the narrative ends: "The Sub-Inspector narrated in brief the whole story of the theft of the child and how the thief was under arrest now. Fatima and her husband thanked the PSI and his staff profusely and returned home with a great sense of satisfaction." (130) It so happens that Fatima and her husband are Muslims (121), and although the dimension of faith does not receive major emphasis in the text, the theft by a Hindu of a Muslim couple's child could none the less be read as metonymically symbolising the disruption not only of the social order as such but also of that element of it which concerns harmonious intercommunal relations. At all events, on a metanarrative level the "great sense of satisfaction" which the relieved parents feel after being narrated "the whole story" by the policeman could be taken as reproducing, in the form proposed by Edgar Allan Poe, the "sense of the fullest satisfaction" felt by the reader at the end of a successfully negotiated short story. That satisfaction would here also, for both characters and reader, reflect the feelings of gratification produced as the social equilibrium is safely restored.

However, the narrative may be read somewhat differently if it is considered from the point of view of the disturber, Manjula. From this vantage point, the question of personal identity would come to the fore. Manjula feels deprived of her "normal" or "natural" identity as a woman by being childless, and clearly believes that, despite being married and employed, she can effectively have no identity in society unless and until she has borne a child — or, at least, appears to have borne one. Her solution to this dilemma is to concoct strategies. The first — her extramarital affair with her work colleague, Sekhar — is presumably posited on the possibility that her husband, not she, might be infertile. This strategy fails when, showing no signs of pregnancy after three months of intimate relations with Sekhar, Manjula consults a doctor only to be told she is infertile. The next day, she does not report for work; Sekhar, significantly, is from that point never mentioned again in the text. This detail of omission suggests that he has all along been merely a pawn in Manjula's strategy, and she now tries a second one. She enters the maternity ward at the local hospital, where she impersonates a newly arrived doctor, drugs all the women in the ward with specially prepared sweetmeats, and finally walks off with Fatima's baby. Unfortunately, her ingenuity is far from complete, and ultimately fails her: she does not notice what a policewoman at the bus station immediately does, namely that the child looks nothing like her ("she is quite fair in colour, but the child is dark" - 127). Nor does she manage to create any kind of rapport with the child, which she is clearly using as she used Sekhar: "Manjula ...sat there trying to breast-feed the child. But the child used to cry continuously" (126).

Her best-laid plans were doomed to failure, and finally, instead of gaining a socially-approved identity as a mother, she loses all trace of such identity, reduced to the condition of a felon. Despite this fate, however, Manjula's actions could be read as the trajectory of a protest — blind and self-defeating no doubt, but still a protest — against the whole notion of a socially imposed identity. If Manjula is infertile, then she cannot assume the one identity that her society considers acceptable for her, and the ultimate blame for the whole episode may be shifted on to a society that fails to offer its female members a sufficiently diverse set of approved identities. Yet again, though, from a more traditionalist point of view it might be said that Manjula was rebelling against her karma: if it was her destiny, because of events in her previous life, to have to live as a childless woman, then her error was to rebel against her destiny instead of accepting it. On this reading, her true identity in this life would be identical with her *karma*. Naikar's text thus presents the question of a woman's identity in society and the world, through a narrative that permits more than one reading of the problem, while finally leaving it to the reader to judge. The storyteller's tale thus reveals itself as, in the traditional sense, a useful artefact, leaving the reader to reflect creatively on the whole unsolved question of the individual's true place in the world.

IV

In the next story that I shall examine, "When the News Came", Naikar uses a number of strategies similar to those of "She Wanted a Child". This narrative too reads as if it had sprung from a newspaper *fait divers*. Chennappa, a truck driver from the Kannada village of Navilur, bids farewell one morning to his wife Rudravva and their young son Chandru, and departs on a routine mission. A week later, the police summon his wife and confront her with the corpse, identified by due process as her husband's, of a truck driver killed in a road accident. The face is so mangled as to be unrecognisable. Rudravva officially becomes a widow. However, after another week has passed, Chennappa, whose mission had been unilaterally extended by his boss, returns to Navilur, only to find his home deserted and himself ostracised as a ghost. Accompanied by a friend from an adjoining village, he asks the police to clear up the mystery. It transpires that the cadaver was in reality that of a different truck driver, also called Chennappa, from the locality of Kavalur. The body had been misidentified by clerical error. Chennappa is reunited with his wife and son and all return to their home village.

Here as with the tale of the infertile Manjula's baby-snatching, the story's journalistic origins appear likely enough. Indeed, the title itself contains the word "news" — and that "news" could variously be interpreted as referring to the news of the highway death, the village rumours of Chennappa's ghost, or the final revelation of his return. Another element that links this story to "She Wanted a Child" is the prevalence of local colour and typically Indian detail ("She lit the lamp before the framed picture of Lord Siva and waved the burning joss sticks before the deity"- 132; "The driver of the jeep had to struggle hard to manoeuvre his vehicle through the narrow and crooked lanes of Navilur" - 133); also present, as before, is the satiric presentation of bureaucracy. Furthermore, this tale too ends with the restoration of the order that had been disturbed. Chennappa returns to society, his wife ceases to be a widow and their son regains his father: "'Both of you have a sort of rebirth now,' said an elderly woman in the gathering. The next day Chennappa, Rudravva and Chandru went back to Navilur in a bullock cart"(147). However, the disturbance of order is of a rather different order here than in "She Wanted a Child"; and if here too the usefulness of Naikar's story may be found to reside in its exploration of the problem of identity, the context diverges substantially from that of the preceding story.

Chennappa's identity as a member of society is structured, above all, around house and family. This is clear from the first page, when, just before he sets off on his fateful journey, "Rudravva served him hot steaming *rotis, dal* and fragrant rice" (131). Returning to the village in all innocence, he discovers he no longer has a home: "He found that his house and the neighbouring houses were all locked ...He did not know where to spend the night. So he went back to the temple of Virabhadra and lay down in the open hall there" (139). He sleeps the next night at a bus station. Bereft of his home, become a waif or stray, he has effectively lost his identity. Such a theme is not uniquely Indian: in nineteenth-century French fiction, Honoré de Balzac explored something similar in *Le Colonel Chabert*, his novella about a soldier long believed dead who makes an unexpected return. Naikar nonetheless gives the motif a specifically Indian twist by also focusing on the predicament of Chennappa's beleaguered wife Rudravva. The news of her husband's apparent death catapults her from the accepted social status of wife to what is, in traditional Hindu society, the highly problematic position of widow. Widowhood descends on her, as an elderly neighbour "took a small chunk of stone and broke the bangles of Rudravva and wiped the vermilion dot from her forehead" (136). She is obliged to give up the signs of her married woman's identity and see her son become an orphan. It is thus, for her, an enormous triumph when, at the story's end, her married status is restituted through the restoration of the all-important symbols: "The womenfolk assembled in the kitchen and helped Rudravva put on her nose-ring, sacred *tali* and *kumkum*" (147). This collective gesture serves to welcome her back into the community of socially legitimated females.

The vicissitudes in the life of this couple — from homelessness to the return home, from widowhood back to wifehood — appear as the outcome of chance compounded by human error. In other words, the cultural order is disturbed, not by a deliberate act of revolt like Manjula's in "She Wanted a Child", but by a pile-up of circumstances beyond any individual's control. It is, at least on one level, chance that dictates that Chennappa is absent longer than expected, and chance too that not only kills a man on the highway who bears the same name, but also mangles that stranger's face so as to make the cadaver unrecognisable and therefore misattributable. It is human error— clerical error, bureaucratic error — that has the body officially misidentified, thus temporarily exiling the living Chennappa from society: "The Sub-Inspector now realised the possibility of a wrong entry in the register. He called Constable Patil and asked, 'Patil, are you sure that you have made the right entry in the register? This gentleman tells me that there is a man called Chennappa in Kavalur also'" (143). Finally, the same Sub-Inspector apologises to the object of the confusion: "'Because our constable wrongly mentioned Navilur instead of Kavalur, all this mix-up has happened'" (144). It could of course be argued that, rather than attribute the events to pure chance, a socially and politically aware reading should take account of the labour relations that allowed Chennappa's boss to extend his mission time unilaterally, of the infrastructural conditions that led to the other Chennappa's death at the wheel, and the political system that may arguably leave undue scope for bureaucratic error. However, such interpretations are for the reader to supply. If this story leaves a useful message, or counsel, in visible and accessible form, it appears to be the notion that the identity in society of ordinary men and women is not a fixed or stable given: rather, identity is subject to the winds of change and chance, and can be blown apart and fragmented — and also reconstituted — in the most unexpected ways.

V

The story which closes the collection is, significantly, entitled "Fulfilment", as if once more to confirm Edgar Allan Poe's notion of the well-told tale that rewards its readers with "a sense of the fullest satisfaction." Here, Naikar's writing, though remaining essentially within a realist frame, takes on additional connotations, drawing on the riches of India's literary tradition, that may be considered symbolic or even mythical. The narrative, set in modern times in an unnamed town in Karnataka, unfolds as follows. One evening, Bharati, only daughter of the widower Kasinath, a devout and conservative retired judge, goes with her father to the theatre to see a performance of a classical Kannada drama. She falls in love with the lead actor, Chandrasekhar, and, even though he is an untouchable and she a Brahmin, elopes with him. They consummate their love-marriage, set up home in his village and raise a son. Her father reacts to the shock by giving up his worldly position and becoming a sadhu. After several years of marital bliss, Bharati's husband, falsely accused of a crime, is obliged to disappear for twelve years, after which time he returns home and the couple are united.

The realist mode evidenced in the stories discussed earlier at first predominates in "Fulfilment". Typical details of Indian urban life are once more foregrounded: "Bharati was gazing at the posters which were decorated with colourful lights thus providing a sharp contrast to the dull effect of the corrugated iron walls and roof of the theatre. The loudspeaker was blaring a popular Kannada song" (180); "They waited for their driver who was puffing at a *bidi* near a *paṇ*-shop. It was only when Kasinath sounded the horn that the driver Hussainsab grew alert and rushed towards the car" (182-183). Despite this realist atmosphere, however, the theatre performance itself introduces a different dimension, connecting the latter-day events to a much older symbolic tradition: "From inside the stage the smoke of incense rose in gyres and the bell was rung ...The harmonium-master played the benedictory tune and all the actors together sung it from behind the main curtain" (180). The play itself, by the twelfth-century Kannada dramatist Basaveswara, centres on a social and cultural scandal of its day, "a marriage between the so-called untouchable bridegroom and a Brahmin bride" (181). The ancient drama sets the scene and provides a precedent for what will then happen outside it, the apparently improbable love-match and elopement between the untouchable actor Chandrasekhar and the Brahmin girl Bharati.

Bharati's very name suggests an older tradition, recalling Bharata, the theoretician of the *rasas* whom we have evoked earlier in this essay. As the narrative advances, its archetypal Indian connotations become deeper and more evident. The lovers get married in a Hanuman temple (188), in a reference harking back to the beneficent monkey-god of the *Ramayana*. Bharati's father replicates a time-old tradition by metamorphosing from judge into sadhu: "Kasinath collected a few clothes and a couple of silver bowls, gave the key of his home to a neighbour and set out on his pilgrimage to the Himalayas" (192). The sudden unexpected turn in Chandrasekhar's life — exile from home and separation from wife and child — takes on connotations of the *Ramayana* and

Mahabharata (Rama and Sita exiled in the forest and then separated; the Pandavas banished from their kingdom). The theme of lovers separated by chance — for chance alone can explain the false and arbitrary pinning of a crime on Bharati's upright husband — also (if we recall the story's theatre theme) points back to another great work of the Indian tradition, Kalidasa's drama *Shakuntala*, with its passionate lovers, king and woodland girl, who come together across a social gulf, are separated by a fatal bout of amnesia, and are finally reunited in the play's closing consummation. Basavaraj Naikar's characters are thus made protagonists in a love-drama that is eminently and anciently subcontinental, right up to the tale's closing moment when "both of them remained in a paradise of silent sweetness" (193).

The counsel or use-value that may be drawn from this story of Naikar's can, once again, be said to centre on the question of identity. For all three protagonists — Bharati, her father and her husband — identity proves to be something that is not fixed or static but can, rather, evolve and mutate in unexpécted ways, affected by both choice and chance. Bharati chooses a love-match, and thus a life totally outside the traditional limits that would otherwise have determined her existence. Her father has denied her a college education, and her expected future would have been an arranged marriage. It is meanwhile clear — and here Naikar shows considerable artistry via discreet understatement — that if there is a precedent for Bharati's act of revolt, it lies not in the alien influence of "Western liberalism," but in the Indian and Kannada tradition itself — in Basaveswara's play from the twelfth century, which long ago dramatised the possibility of a love-match crossing caste boundaries. Chandrasekhar, as much as Bharati, chooses to give his life an unexpected direction by surrendering to the unexpected love-relationship and taking it all the way to marriage; later, when he is pushed into exile and disguise ("he went to Bombay in the guise of a beggar" - 189), his life is once again reshaped, but this time by forces totally outside his control. Kasinath, for his part, finds himself a prey too to the unexpected, to the shock of his daughter's elopement, but manages finally to transcend it through an act of conscious choice: the decision to become a sadhu and centre the rest of his life on the spiritual. He thus creates a new identity for the final years of his life. This choice is, at the same time, an option available to him within Indian tradition (the life of a sadhu is even recommended to men of advanced years whose offspring have grown up), and he takes the decision after consulting a high religious authority, in fact being "advised by H.H. Sankaracharya" (192). Kasinath, then, makes a life-choice that is legitimated by mainstream Hindu tradition, whereas his daughter's life-choice may be said to stem from a dissident or critical strand within that same tradition. The intertwining of chance and choice in human lives may be said to form the kernel of the counsel that this story offers the reader. Here the reader may wish to think back to the ancient literary tradition, and to the arguably parallel teaching that emerges from *Shakuntala,* where choice and chance combine to generate the characters' complex vicissitudes.[21]

Naikar's tale is, in fact, both traditional and contemporary, sketching an emancipatory possibility for India's womenfolk while rooting that very emancipation in an alternative reading of the tradition. From the contemporary angle, an interesting analogy exists with the closing tale in another story collection published almost at the same time as Naikar's, namely "The Rooftop Dwellers," the concluding narrative of *Diamond Dust,* Anita Desai's volume (as mentioned above) of 2000. Desai's story tells the fortunes of Moyna, an independent-minded young girl from the provinces who arrives in Delhi seeking work, and manages to survive triumphantly as a single woman in the capital, keeping herself afloat in the difficult environment of the publishing world, with the help of a cat and an emancipated female friend and despite substandard rooftop accommodation and an unsympathetic landlady. Moyna, unlike Naikar's Bharati, seeks her freedom not through a love-match but through the world of work — "such was her determination," says Desai's third-person narrator, "to make her new life as a working woman in the metropolis succeed," even though "her mother did not understand ...the attraction of living alone, in Delhi and could think of it as only a poor substitute for living at home."[22] Anita Desai's approach is, certainly, more ideological than Naikar's, with an evident feminist undercurrent; it remains worth remarking, however, that two virtually contemporaneous collections should conclude on the same theme, a young woman's creation of a new identity for herself through a successful defiance of cultural norms.

VI

The three stories by Basavaraj Naikar that we have examined in detail all fall clearly within the terrain of the traditional story, focusing from different angles on the subject of human identity and thus offering the reader counsel, or useful material for reflection. Further analysis would no doubt find similar features in the other stories in the volume. Naikar has, while remaining faithful to the Indian tradition, succeeded in endowing his narratives with a broader universality that pays tribute to the age-old human faculty of storytelling. Closing his volume, the reader, satisfied yet also stimulated to thought, may legitimately recall the celebrated words with which Benjamin ended his study of traditional narrative: "The storyteller is the figure in which the righteous man encounters himself."[23]

***

Notes and References

1. Benjamin, "The Storyteller", 86.
2. Ibid., 87.
3. See Hardy, *Selected Short Stories*; Twain, *Short Stories*.
4. See Tagore, *Collected Short Stories*.
5. Twain, "How To Tell A Story", 266.
6. Poe, "Tale Writing. Nathaniel Hawthorne", 446.
7. Naikar, "Preface" to *The Thief of Nagarahalli and Other Stories*. All subsequent running-text references in this essay will be to that book, as its main subject.
8. Naikar, *Critical Articles on Nirad C. Chaudhuri*, 6.
9. Naikar, *Critical Articles*, 106.
10. Ibid., 103.
11. Ibid., 114.
12. Naikar, "The Image of New Woman in Anand's *Gauri*", 1.
13. See Naikar, trans., *Musings of Sarvajna*.
14. Naikar, *Sarvajna: The Omniscient Poet of Karnataka* 4.
15. Naikar, "Coming Together: the Central Problem in *The Serpent and the Rope*", 52.

16. The *Natyasastra* is thought to have been composed at some point between 500 and 700 CE. There is some dispute as to the number of the *rasas*, with some commentators arguing that there are eight rather than nine, with the ninth, *santa*, best characterised as the absence of emotion and therefore not a *rasa* proper. Useful on-line accounts of *rasa* psychology may be found at: <http://www.nadanam.com/general/g_navarasa.htm> and: <http://www.saigan.com/heritage/dance/rasa.htm>. For a general discussion of Bharata's treatise, see Rajan, "Introduction" to Kalidasa, *The Loom of Time* 28-33.
17. Choubey, "*The Thief of Nagarahalli and Other Stories*: Essentially Indian Stories", *passim*.
18. Choubey, *loc. cit.*
19. Benjamin, 89.
20. Seth, *A Suitable Boy*, 3.
21. For the role of chance in *Shakuntala*, cf. Rajan, "Introduction" to *The Loom of Time* 50-52.
22. Desai, *Diamond Dust*, 161, 207.
23. Benjamin, 109.

***

Works Cited

Benjamin, Walter. "The Storyteller: Reflections on the Works of Nikolai Leskov" [1936]. Trans. Harry Zohn in: *Illuminations* (1970). London: Collins/Fontana, 1973, 83-109.

Chandra, Vikram. *Love and Longing in Bombay*. London: Faber and Faber, 1997.

Choubey, Asha. "*The Thief of Nagarahalli and Other Stories*: Essentially Indian Stories", 2002. <http://www.scholars.nus.edu.sg/landow/post/india/literature/choubey4.html>

Da Cunha, Nisha. *Old Cypress*. New Delhi: Penguin India, 1991.

Desai, Anita. *Diamond Dust* [2000]. London: Vintage, 2001.

Hardy, Thomas. *Selected Stories* [1879-1897]. London: Macmillan, 1966.

Kalidasa. *The Loom of Time: A Selection of His Plays and Poems* [*The Cloud-Messenger; The Gathering of the Seasons; Shakuntala*] [1st millennium BCE?]. Trans. and ed. Chandra Rajan. New Delhi: Penguin India, 1989.

Lahiri, Jhumpa. *Interpreter of Maladies* [1999]. London: HarperCollins, 2000.

Mistry, Rohinton. *Tales from Firozsha Baag* [1987]. London: Faber and Faber, 1992.

Naikar, Basavaraj. "The Image of New Woman in Anand's *Gauri*". In *Studies in Indian Writing in English, vol. I.* Ed. Rajeshwar Mittapalli and Pier Paolo Piciucco. New Delhi: Atlantic Publishers and Distributors, 2000, 1-12.

_______________, "Coming Together: the Central Problem in *The Serpent and the Rope*". In *Studies in Indian Writing in English, vol. II.* Ed. Rajeshwar Mittapalli and Pier Paolo Piciucco. New Delhi: Atlantic Publishers and Distributors, 2001, 43-52.

_______________, *Critical Articles on Nirad C. Chaudhuri.* Dharwad: Sivararanjani Publications, 1984.

_______________, *Sarvajna: The Omniscient Poet of Karnataka.* Dharwad: Sivararanjani Publications, 1984.

_______________, *The Thief of Nagarahalli and Other Stories.* Calcutta [Kolkata]: Writers Workshop, 1999.

_______________, (trans. from Kannada). *Musings of Sarvajna.* Dharwad: Sivararanjani Publications, 1990.

Naipaul, V.S. *Miguel Street* [1959]. Harmondsworth: Penguin, 1971.

Poe, Edgar Allan. "Tale-Writing. Nathaniel Hawthorne" [1847]. In *The Fall of the House of Usher and Other Writings.* Harmondsworth: Penguin, 1967, new edn. 1986, 437-447.

Rao, Raja. *The Cat and Shakespeare* [1971]. New Delhi: Orient Paperbacks, 1996.

Rushdie, Salman. *East, West* [1994]. London: Vintage, 1995.

Seth, Vikram. *A Suitable Boy* [1993]. London: Phoenix, 1994.

Tagore, Rabindranath. *Collected Stories.* Madras [Chennai]: Macmillan India, 1974.

Twain, Mark. "How To Tell A Story" [1894]. In *Short Stories* (q.v.), 666-670.

_______________, *Short Stories* [1865-1909]. Harmondsworth: Penguin, 1993.

15

Sangya-Balya: Betrayal: A Folk Tragedy

— *S. John Peter Joseph*

> Suit the action to the word, the word to the action, with this special observance, that you o'erstep not the modesty of nature. For anything so overdone is from the purpose of playing, whose end, both at the first and now, was and is, to hold as 't were the mirror up to nature, to show virtue her own feature, scorn her own image, and the very age and body of the time his form and pressure.
>
> (*Hamlet*, Act III. Sc ii. Lines: 15-21)

Drama constitutes an integral part of any civilised society. It is true that the dramatic instinct is quite universal. The theatre whether in the sacred or the secular form has never failed to hold its powerful appeal to man. Undeniably every nation and every race has its own dramatic history. Drama as the best form of literary composition mirrors the social, political and cultural history of a people and the characteristic nature of the genius of any nation cannot be fully comprehended and appreciated without its study. Since 'a nation is known by its theatre' the impact of dramas and theatres over the masses cannot be easily ignored. One can learn about the character of a particular nation more from its immortal plays than from the pages of a formal historical treatise or the records of the nation. Drama, which is the outcome of human nature and human character "is an imitation of people, their environment, emotions, feelings, situations they are found in, mental and physical states and actions" (M.L. Varadpande 273).

In the words of G.B. Tennyson, "Drama is a story that people act out on a stage before spectators" (3). Eric Bentley observes: "The theatrical situation, reduced to a minimum, is that A impersonates B while C looks on" (150). Marjorie Boulton remarks: "Drama, at its best, is an exercise of the imagination not only for writer, producer and actors but also for the audience. The writer of plays creates characters and places them in situations that are interesting and in some way relevant to general human experience" (196). The rich variety of the drama as an art form and its indispensable human nature have been remarkably highlighted and summed up by the great theatrical producer, Max Reinhardt as follows:

> It is to the actor and to no one else that the theatre belongs. This does not mean, of course, the professional actor alone, but the actor as poet, as director, stage-manager, musician, scene-designer, painter and certainly not least of all, the actor as spectator, for the contribution of the spectators is almost as important as that of the cast. The audience must take its part in the play if we are ever to see a true art of the theatre — the oldest, most powerful, and most immediate of the arts, combining the many in one.
>
> (Qtd in Hemendra Nath Das Gupta, ii)

According to Professor H.H. Wilson, the primary object of dramatic representations is "to convey instructions through the means of amusement and with this view, they must affect the minds of the spectators with the statements which they express" (ii). From the artistic point of view drama and the stage indubitably possess an ethical and a historical value of their own.

The art of drama, considered to be the fifth 'Veda' in India, is quite ancient. Undoubtedly India possesses a rich and glorious dramatic tradition going back more than two thousand years. The phenomenal growth and development of drama in India had its origin in Sanskrit dramas. A.B. Keith is of the view that "Indian tradition, preserved in the *Natyasastra*, the oldest of the texts of the theory of the drama, claims for the drama divine origin, and a close connection with the sacred Vedas themselves" (12). A.L. Basham, a well-known historian, observes: "The origin of the Indian theatre is still obscure. It is certain, however, that even in the Vedic period dramatic performances of some kind were given, and passing references in early sources point to the enaction at festivals of religious legends, perhaps only in dance and mime" (434-435). Indian drama is absolutely and precisely of Indian origin. It evidently grew and developed quite independent of any occidental influence. Affirming the unique and the independent nature of Indian dramas and the outstanding quality of the Sanskrit language Sir William Jones remarks that Sanskrit which is "more perfect than Greek, more copious than Latin and more exquisite than either" (qtd in Hemendra Nath Das Gupta, 2) could easily produce dramas quite independent of the Greeks or the Yavanas.

Bharata, considered to be the father of Indian dramaturgy, inscribes in *Natyashastra* that the primary aim of a drama is that it should give knowledge to the ignorant. Moreover, it should both be a source of entertainment and enlightenment. The major constituents of a drama, according to *Natyashastra*, are plot, actors and aesthetic taste. Though world-renowned dramatists like Kalidasa, Bhasa, Bhavabhuti, Shudraka, Ashvaghosha, Shri Harsha and Vishakhadatta mostly affirmed the views expressed in the ancient treatise on drama they started writing dramas in Sanskrit with a few modifications regarding the nature of drama as an art. The dramas of these great and outstanding artistic personalities are remarkably known for their elegance, rich and graceful poetry, proper execution and delicacy of subtle dramatic art. They not only depicted wonderfully the human sentiments but they also revealed "a deep acquaintance with the mechanism of the human heart as well as with nature" (Hemendra Nath Das Gupta, 54).

Though India is known for its heterogeneous culture, customs, languages, habit and outlook, the traditional theatre of India got ample inspiration from great epics: the *Ramayana* and the *Mahabharata* and the *Puranic* literature. The playwrights drew stories and characters for their plays from these renowned sources. The stories found in these ever-cherished epics and puranas have been orally passed on from generation to generation and also through the artistic medium of puppetry and other performing arts and ultimately through the written texts. These stories have not lost their enduring and everlasting charm and even now serve as essential and generative source for creative expression in literature and art.

Drama as an extensive and a comprehensive art delineating the variegated saga of human life in all its complexity includes the performing arts of dancing, singing and playing on musical instruments. Obviously India is one of the great storehouses of performing arts especially the traditional or classical, folk and devotional dramas. Though folk theatre in India follows the widely accepted dramaturgical traditions of *Natyashastra* it has emerged as a powerful medium of social communication in traditional societies or communities. As it is spirited, dynamic and ingenious in form and rich in variety and colour it expresses the cultural heritage of a region very effectively. While stressing the fact that folk theatre happens to be a very powerful medium of communication in folk cultures J.C. Mathur observes:

> Folk theatre freely uses songs, dances and instrumental music, blends dialogue and acting. This multiple approach results in a form that is self-contained and a complete entertainment. It is more than entertainment, it is a complete emotional experience and aims at creating an environment of receptivity in which communication of ideas is an effortless process (3).

As an indigenous form, the folk theatre makes cultural explorations and influences the psyche and strengthens the time-honoured value systems of the folk people. Dissanayake makes a relevant comment in this context. According to him, folk theatres "provide entertainment, disseminate information, include socially accepted norms and values and perform a general socializing function" (12). Folk theatre represents a combination of singing, dancing, prose-dialogue and music with elements of social criticism. What Eapen says of folk media in general can easily be applied to folk theatre:

> There is a commonality about them. Acceptability, cultural relevance, entertainment value, localized language; legitimacy, flexibility, message repetition ability, instant two-way communication, etc are among their virtues (18-19).

Every State in India has its own distinctive forms of folk theatre. Folk performance generally forms a part of a community or social celebration. The various elements found in folk performances invariably appeal to the educated and the uneducated, the rich and the poor, the young and the old and children with their exciting themes, melodious music and songs. Unlike the classical theatre, which has rigid rules, the folk theatre allows spontaneity. Among the several types of folk plays religious plays; social plays and historical plays are significant ones. Religious plays depict stories and characters from the puranas and epics. Social plays portray social evils, which affect people in their day-to-day life. Historical plays deal with historical characters and themes.

The folk theatre of North Karnataka has a rich and glorious tradition. The folk tradition in North Karnataka is known by different names like *Doddata, Hire Ata* (Grand play) or *Bayalata* (open-air play) etc. *Doddata* can be differentiated from *Sannata* (small play) or *Dappinata* (Dappu = little flat drum, ata = play). "Whereas *Doddata* is characterized by grand themes, grand stage properties, grand costumes, grand songs and dances, *Sannata* is marked by simple themes, simple stage costumes, simple songs and dances" (Naikar, *The Folk Theatre of North Karnataka,* 14). *Dappinata* is a play (*Bayalata*), which contains songs sung to the accompaniment of a *dappu* or small drum. The label *Sannata* is used to differentiate *Dappinata* from *Mudalapaya* (or *Doddata*).

Indian Drama in English certainly depends very much upon the translation of regional plays into English. The translation of Indian drama into English unlike the translation of novels and poems written in regional languages into English is quite scanty and inadequate. Some of the well-known and established dramatists who have translated their dramas from their regional languages into English are Rabindranath Tagore, Badal Sircar, Mohan Rakesh, Girish Karnad, R.S. Badal, C.C. Mehta, Mahasweta Devi, Vijay Tendulkar and Gurujada Apparao. Many dramas written in Bengali, Hindi, Kannada, and Marathi have been translated into English. These translations have undeniably embellished the corpus of Indian Drama in English. The exemplary nature and illustriousness of Indian Drama in English is essentially based more on translation than on original plays written in English. Basavaraj Naikar's *Sangya-Balya: Betrayal,* an English translation of Rayappa Pattar's folk play in Kannada, is unquestionably a welcome addition to the realm of Indian Drama in English Translation.

Basavaraj Naikar's translation of Rayappa Pattar's Kannada folk play into English marks the fame and reputation of the

Sannata form as a part of the glorious tradition of the folk theatre of North Karnataka. According to Naikar, "*Sangya-Balya: Betrayal is a dappinata,* in which songs . . . play an important part" (*Sangya-Balya* ix). Moreover, the element of music, which is an integral part of the folk theatre, is an impressive characteristic of this folk play. Dance also happens to be an indispensable component of the play. The oral text of the play is said to have been composed by Rayappa Pattar, a native of Bailawada village of Basavanagouda taluk of Belgaum district in North Karnataka. While acknowledging the sources of the play Naikar observes: "The text of the present play is taken from the oral version recited by Sri Basavanagouda Patil, Gangappa Mulimani and Fakirappa Madiwalar of Mutanala village (in Belgaum district) and published by Dr. Malikarjuna Latthe, retired Professor of Kannada at Gulbarga University, Gulbarga in 1991" (xii).

Sangya-Balya: Betrayal (2004) is a folk drama, which "deals with the elemental passions of love and betrayal as they interweave with the destinies of ordinary mortals" (Ravi Shankar Rao, 75). The action of the play is set in North Karnataka, as it is very popular there. The central thematic concerns of the play are love, immoral sex, poverty, betrayal and revenge. Though the playwright has taken the theme of the play from a real event, which took place during his lifetime, he has made it a memorable one by providing "an artistic image of his vision about human relationship and values" (*Sangya-Balya,* x). The author's fine blending of fact and fiction is quite remarkable in the play.

Sangya-Balya: Betrayal is a folk tragedy. The tragedy in the play occurs due to the serious violation of long-cherished social and moral norms relating to chastity, trustworthiness and loyalty. Like a typical Elizabethan tragedy this folk drama depicts common human weaknesses and the play excellently shows how these vulnerable tendencies such as love, lust and revenge finally end in a cruel tragedy and the loss of precious lives. The protagonist of this play Sangya is murdered ruthlessly and the lives of Ganga and Virabhadra get ruined irretrievably. The point of ruination starts when Sangappa (fondly called Sangya), a handsome and rich young man, is enthralled by the bewitching beauty of Ganga, the young wife of a rich landlord, cum-businessman named Virabhadra (fondly called Iranna or Irya). Knowing that her husband is on a long business tour Sangya persuades his friend,

Balya, a poor man in the same village, "to brainwash Ganga so that he can have her in his bed" (*Sangya-Balya* 53). Balya, though he happens to be a childhood friend of Sangya, expresses his unwillingness to act as a go-between. He even advises his friend:

> *Balya*: Listen to me, dear friend, Sanganna,
> Ravana lost his heart to another's wife
> And consequently lost everything,
> Lest you should suffer like him,
> Remove the idea from your mind . . .. (49)

Owing to his utter poverty and keeping in mind the generous nature of Sangya, Balya finally meets Ganga and reveals the intention of his friend to her. But as a chaste wife of a respectable man in society Ganga rejects the whole idea at once and sends him away. Sangya's malicious plan of buying her with money and costly gifts also miserably fails. Being obsessed with the bewitching attractions of Ganga, Sangya himself directly goes and meets her and expresses his uncontrollable desire to possess her. Ganga censures Sangya for his evil and unethical desires and tires to reason out with him:

> *Ganga*: Why do you pester me, Sangya?
> How shall I bear the public charge?
> This affair cannot last long,
> You may receive a dangerous jolt.
> Don't you remember the story of Kama?
> How Kama lusted after the woman
> And was burnt to ashes by Lord Siva
> Who was angry beyond measure?
> Remember the evil *angrezi* government,
> I advise you to be very careful,
> Lest you should suffer like a monkey
> Which has eaten lime paste by mistake.
> You better go back to your wife,
> And live with her happily,
> I am sorry, man; I cannot oblige you (63).

Yet Sangya is highly adamant and without any scruples. Once again Ganga tries to point out the evil nature of his intention.

> *Ganga*: This is not the right thing
> For you to do, man

Be not subject to *maya*,
Lest you should ruin yourself.
Don't you know the story
Of the ten-headed Ravana?
He abducted chaste Sita,
And suffered a lot of trouble.
. . . .
Don't you know the story
Of Dushyasana the evil one,
And what happened to him finally?
Try to understand everything, fool
I am doing my best to convince you (65).

Unable to convince Sangya about the impending danger awaiting him Ganga furthermore adds:

Ganga: Why are you mad after my form?
Like a firefly you enter the lamp.
Don't you know my terrific husband,
Virabhadra feared even by tigers?
He may hack you to pieces,
In broad daylight, fool,
Unnecessarily, nincompoop? (66)

Still unconvinced, Sangya seeks advice from a Koravanji, and based on her advice he approaches Paramma who is willing to take up the evil mission of arranging a clandestine meeting between Sangya and Ganga for a pair of saris, a pair of blouses, a pair of golden bangles and a pair of buffaloes. When she tries to persuade Ganga to yield to Sangya, Ganga tells her:

Ganga: I join my palms in reverence to you
Paramma, speak not of such a thing lest,
It should ruin my happy marriage.
Don't burden my head with ill fame.
. . . . I don't want it at all (73).

Like one of the three witches who ensnare Macbeth into the eternal world of curse and tribulation Paramma, with her artful and crafty words, ultimately pulls Ganga into an irredeemable trap. As if conforming to the words of Hamlet, "Frailty, Thy name is woman! (*Hamlet* Act I., Sc. ii., line 146) Ganga is unable to be firm in her moral stand and eventually falls a prey to the lustful wishes of

Sangya. One can be sure that Ganga's fall from her long-cherished traditional moral code in life will certainly end in a terrible tragedy. The following words of Ganga reveal her innate weakness and turpitude:

Ganga: I have invited you, young man,
Out of my deep love for you.
Let us put aside the fear of Irya
And unite like milk and fruit.
I have full sympathy for my husband.
I fear the ruination of my marriage,
. . . . (77).
Come on, my dear young man
Let's ascend the bed
And have a great deal of pleasure.
Let's enjoy ourselves as sweetly
As milk fermented into curd, and
As the sweet siesta in the afternoon.
. . . . O dear,
God has brought us together like
A combination of pearl and amber (78).

When the whole village begins to gossip about the affair between Sangya and Ganga, Balya realises the inevitable doom of both. He fears that "Sangya will have to face the blade of a sickle" (79). The illegal love affair between Sangya and Ganga continues undisturbed till Virabhadra, Ganga's husband, returns home from his business trip before his scheduled time. He becomes furious after hearing about this illicit relationship between his wife and Sangya. He rushes home and finds the two indulging in the immoral act. Ganga's total degeneration and moral debasement is revealed when she tells Sangya the following words even after knowing that her husband has come home and is knocking at the door:

Ganga: I have fallen deeply in love with you,
Our union has been sweet like milk and ghee.
Fie on my bad luck, I don't like my husband,
I shall sunder my relation with him
Tomorrow itself. I don't care for what
The people of the village might say (82).

Virabhadra charges his wife with adultery and accuses her of bringing disreputation and dishonour to his honourable family. He, therefore, sends his wife away from home after confiscating all the gold ornaments and other valuables from her. Moreover, he conspires to murder Sangya and in order to succeed in his effort he wants to wean away Balya from Sangya. He tells Balya:

> *Virabhadra:* You must get Sangya for me,
> I shall give you hundreds of rupees,
> Sixteen oxen and a sturdy cart.
> I shall even give you my house,
> And landed property for the favour (90).

Balya tells him that since he and Sangya happen to be childhood friends and trust each other deeply he cannot betray his bosom friend. But he finally agrees to betray him when Irya threatens to cut him into pieces. Fearing for life and being avaricious for money Balya finally makes up his mind to join hands with Virabhadra and hasten the tragic death of Sangya. He even stoops to the level of forging the letter of Ganga in which she reveals the conspiracy of her husband to kill Sangya and asks Sangya not to come to her place at any cost. But Balya impersonates himself for Sangya and changes the content of the letter to suit his treacherous plan. Sangya believes the content of the letter and goes to the village of Ganga. Ganga tells Sangya about the conspiracy hatched by Virabhadra in connivance with Balya. Sangya understands the wicked nature of Balya when he is left alone in darkness in a strange place after Balya takes leave of him on some pretext. The pathetic condition and the mental agony of Sangya is revealed in the following speech:

> *Sangya:* I trusted Balya far too much,
> Did you betray me at last, Balya?
> Did you talk sweetly with me
> For the sake of gold?
> And leave me at the hands of hooligans?
> Did you forsake my company
> For the sake of a pair of buffaloes
> And kick me out?
> You took thousands of rupees from me
> And sneaked away from me, Balya.
> You left me alone in the jaws of death (97).

Sangya is cruelly murdered with sickles and axes by Virabhadra and his brothers. They murder him to regain their honour and prestige, which they had enjoyed in society. Then Virabhadra begins to be afraid of the consequences of the murder. He reveals his fear to his brothers:

> *Virabhadra*: My dear younger brothers,
> We could not simply guess
> The consequences of this murder.
> Why did we murder Sangya?
> . . . .
> We were bold until killing him,
> But now are scared of the government.
> My dear brothers,
> I cannot foresee the future (99).

Then they surrender to the *mamledar* (magistrate) and confess their crime. On the whole, the story ends in a tragedy. Sangya loses his life. The illicit affair ruins Ganga's married life. The lives of Virabhadra and his brothers are ruined irrecoverably because of their hasty, emotional and unbalanced decision of doing away with the paramour of Ganga. Though Paramma is asked by Virabhadra before he leaves for his business trip to 'guard' Ganga she easily betrays him for money without any qualms. Ganga also believes that her husband gives more importance to money than to her. She tells Paramma:

> Ganga: The wealth of the
> family is called goddess Laxmi
> My husband must have asked
> you to guard this goddess and not me (33).

When Virabhadra tells his wife that he is going on a business trip to seek fortune Ganga tries to dissuade him by saying:

> Ganga: My dear husband, please tell me how I should live alone in this three-storied mansion. Being a young wife, I cannot live away from you. Please take me along with you (30).

But Virabhadra does not accept her idea and proceeds on his business tour after telling her:

Virabhadra: The purchase of pearls and jewels will yield me a profit (31).

The irony is that though he has purchased pearls and jewels for profit to be got in future he has lost his wife. Thus the play deals with the themes of illicit love, lust, and avarice for money, betrayal and revenge. It also depicts very clearly man's moral infirmity and decrepitude excellently.

Obviously the folk audience enjoys the romance that takes place between Sangya and Ganga and at the same time learns the moral lesson from the play that loose morals and the violation of established social and moral codes will certainly lead to one's downfall and ruination. Extramarital affair, illicit love and sex are considered to be immoral in a traditional folk society. The moral codes of society call for appropriate justice and punishment. That is the reason why Sangya has to meet with a cruel murder and Ganga loses her happy married life. Commenting on the relevance of the play, Ravi Shankar Rao observes: "The *Sannata* is an operative performance that, unlike the other types of *Bayalata*, brings folk theatre to the social plane. It is essentially a social play which takes up for dramatic representation issues and concerns that are central to the society of its time" (77). The playwright points out that one should not give too much importance to money through the characters of Virabhadra, Paramma and Balya. They become corrupt and morally debased due to their avarice for money. Sangya and Ganga become morally corrupt and weak because they give too much importance to bodily pleasures. Though both know very well that their illicit relationship can only be a temporary one they still continue their immoral relationship without any fear for society and its moral values. Though both are married people and, in fact, Sangya has children they do not care for the voice of their consciences and become mindless of the future consequences. While commenting on the play Naikar observes:

> It [the play] is also a comment on the fallibility of man in general. Sangya's improper attraction for Ganga, her yielding to sexual temptation and Balya's treachery towards Sangya caused by his poverty and helplessness are several instances of the fallibility of man. The tragic end of Sangya is affected by the inexorability of the moral law of life.

> Sangya who tries to negate the moral principles of life, (like the sanctity of matrimony) gets himself liquidated by the moral law of life manifested in Virabhadra's vindictive act (*Sangya–Balya*, xii).

Structurally the play comprises five acts, and like any Shakespearean drama it contains dramatic elements like exposition, crisis and denouement or resolution. The plot of the play is simple, plain and straightforward. The action is lenient and every event takes the story forward and events from the first scene in Act I to the last scene in Act V are coherently and logically linked with one another. As a *Sannata* the play gives importance to music and songs. Throughout the play songs are followed by prose dialogues containing summaries of the songs. In his introduction, Naikar, the translator, points out: "Almost every song is followed by a prose dialogue containing the summary of the song which may look like unnecessary repetition to Western readers. But this would be very effective on the stage in the presence of a live audience" (xiii). The themes dealt with in the play are quite popular and are appealing to the folk audience.

The play is quite popular among both village and urban audiences because of its style, language, diction, images and metaphors. Like in a Greek tragedy, the Chorus plays a vital role indicating the impending serious action in the play. The playwright does not fail to use irony and satire. The scene, which takes place in the Marwari shop, and the scene of conversation between Paramma and her old husband are deliberately introduced by the playwright to satisfy the aesthetic sense of the groundlings of the folk audience. Moreover, like in Shakespearean tragedies, these scenes act as comic interludes followed by serious actions, which ultimately lead to the tragic end of the play. When one reads these scenes one is reminded of the Porter Scene in *Macbeth* and the Gravedigger Scene in *Hamlet* to some extent. The songs and the music in the play never fail to appeal to the spectators. The images, which reflect the day-to-day activities of the folk people, have freshness and originality. The play has several memorable passages, which abound with splendid images. Describing the beauty of Ganga, Paramma says:

Paramma: See how the young lady walks
Fast and straight like a mail carriage.

Look at her beautiful body
Her legs are like plantain trunks,
She moves about with such grace
Like a stringed puppet, like a puppet.
Her nose stud sparkles like a splint
Struck on another splint
And like a star in the sky,
She is clad in a shining silken sari.
Her neck is decked with golden garlands.
Behold this pretty young lady.
Behold her bewitching beauty (40).

Appreciating the beauty of Ganga the priest in the temple of Lord Basavanna says:

Priest: Who is the pretty lady
Standing behind you?
She has the complexion of a lemon,
. . . .
Whose wife is the pretty lady
Who has a big chest like a hefty bull,
And who has a narrow waist,
Whose eyes are lined with collyrium
And whose complexion is like that of a cobra? (42)

The moment Sangya sees Ganga in the temple fair he is very much impressed by the beauty of Ganga and he reveals his heart to his friend Balya later.

Sangya: Balanna, my dear friend,
I saw a young lady beautiful
Like the veritable goddess Rati,
Her waist slender like a snake
And decked with a silver girdle,
Her breasts were covered with
A blouse with a floral pattern,
Her teeth immaculate, like
The tiny seeds of pomegranate,
Her cheeks as clear as a mirror.
I saw a young lady in the fair
Who looked like a royal parrot.
She carried a platter on her head (48).

While expressing his deep love to Ganga Sangya tells her:

Sangya: Ganga, my dear Ganga,
Your face is like the moon
Exuding bewitching light on the earth.
The lustre of your pretty face
Is like a lamp lighting the world (61).

Painting a verbal picture of the beauty of Ganga, Sangya tells Koravanji:

Sangya: What a beautiful figure she has!
It is like the curls of incense smoke.
Getting Gangi into my arms
Would be like tasting pancake and ghee (69).

The playwright has succeeded in creating characters with great mastery and unfailing touch. His characters are, no doubt, strongly humanised. They happen to be neither gods nor people with extraordinary powers but real human beings with common human vulnerabilities and susceptibilities. Undeniably they have the solid reality of life itself. Sangya, Balya, Ganga, Virabhadra and Paramma are real and authentic human beings whom one comes across in one's every day life. They have nothing artificial about them. Unlike the characters of Ben Jonson the characters in the play are not types representing particular virtues and vices. They are unquestionably rounded, whole and capable because they live, move and by way of singing rapturous songs and uttering thoughtful dialogues they enthrall the folk audience. They have universal characteristics, which elicit our sympathy for them. This is quite evident because characters such as Sangya, Ganga, Balya and Virabhadra are moved by elemental passions and instincts such as love, lust, greediness and revenge. Even minor characters like Paramma; her husband; Marwari and Koravanji have become highly memorable. They also reflect the folk consciousness of society.

In the words of Naikar: "The character of Gangi which is central to the play is a memorable one in the history of the folk-literature of North-Karnataka" (*The Folk Theatre of North Karnataka*, 84). On the whole, the characters undeniably bear witness to the fecundity of the dramatist's imagination and his animating powers. What Hudson remarks about Shakespeare's characters is applicable to Naikar's characters in the play: "Shakespeare has endowed them with the reality and the mystery of life" (187).

Basavaraj Naikar's translation of Rayappa Pattar's *Sangya-Balya: Betrayal,* originally composed in Kannada, is certainly a great milestone in the realm of Indian Drama in English Translation. Being a novelist, well-known short story writer and renowned critic, Basavaraj Naikar with his true artistic ability and genuine craftsmanship introduces the play to the English knowing audience. Himself "a product of North Karnataka" and "rooted in its soil, its culture and customs" (Thirumeni, 11) Naikar shows his remarkable ability in transmuting the essence and the central ethos of the North Karnataka people from the oral text in Kannada to English translation with verisimilitude. As a translator he is able to bring out the moral vision of the original text of the play in his translation. He himself admits: "I undertook the translation of this play into English as I feel that the elemental theme ingrained in it has universal appeal and therefore deserves international publicity" (*Sangya-Balya,* xii). Commenting on the universal appeal of the play Thirumeni remarks:

> The play will be a success in any language and in any country, because it plays with the basic instincts of common people; adultery is an absorbing theme in any theatre and the audience will be eager to see through the adulterous affairs of the protagonist to the end. It is Claudius' adultery that killed his own brother and paved the way for his own death at Hamlet's hands (Thirumeni, 11).

Though Naikar feels that "the melody and rhythm of the original Kannada poetry cannot ever be dreamt of being expressed" (*Sangya-Balya,* xiii) he not only has succeeded in making the translation clear but also in employing apt words for dramatic situations which certainly appeal to both the vast reading population and the theatre goers. With his incisive and thought-provoking dialogues in English Naikar is able to communicate the central vision of the play. His effective use of the spoken language of the folk people and images shows his proficiency in dramatizing a situation suitably. He does not introduce rhetoric juggleries and grandiosity. His words and images are natural, genuine and straightforward. He seems to write the play with ease and confidence, and without any artificiality. As a true artist he paints pictures quite vividly and effectively. His perception of thought and the scope of imagination are reflected in his style. His felicity of expression reflects his mature style, which shows his mastery over the English language.

Naikar's ability to create convincing dramatic dialogues in English shows the genuine dramatic capability and the theatrical craftsmanship of the translator. As a writer who understands the fundamental tenets of translation as a branch of literature he does not fail to provide a detailed glossary to enable the English speaking readers to understand the meaning of certain technical terms found in the Kannada language and used by the people of the North Karnataka region. As a writer with true insight into language skills and translation techniques Naikar makes the play a real *tour-de-force.* Obviously one reads or watches the play not only for the poetic beauty and excellence but also for the moral truth and the practical guidance to be practised in one's day-to-day life. Unlike the classical and the 'closet' dramas of certain other writers Basavaraj Naikar's *Sangya-Balya: Betrayal,* a folk play in translation with its eternally appealing themes and powerful dramatic dialogues, melodious music and enrapturing dance, can be effectively staged. No doubt, the play with its universal themes dealing with the universality of life becomes relevant to all times and all countries. On the whole, Basavaraj Naikar's *Sangya-Balya: Betrayal* is certainly a welcome addition to the corpus of Indian Drama in English Translation.

WORKS CITED

Basham, A.L. *The Wonder That was India.* New Delhi: Rupa Co, 1987.

Bently, E. *The Life of the Drama.* London: Methuen, 1965.

Boulton, Marjorie. *The Anatomy of Drama.* London: Routledge & Kegan Paul, 1960.

Dissanayake, Wimal. "New Wine in Old Bottles: Can Folk Media Convey Modern Messages?" *Journal of Communication,* Spring 1977.

Eapen, K.E. "Specific Problems of Research and Research Training in Asian/African Countries", *Communication Research in the Third World: The Need for Training.* Geneva: Lutheran World Federation, 1976.

Gupta, Hemendra Nath Das. *The Indian Theatre.* Delhi: Gian Publishing House, 1988.

Hudson, William Henry. *An Introduction to the Study of Literature*. New Delhi: Kalyani Publishers, 1978.

Keith, A.B. *The Sanskrit Drama*. Delhi: Motilal Banarsidass, 1992.

Mathur, J.C. *Drama in Rural India*. London: Asia Publishing House, 1982.

Naikar, Basavaraj. *Sangya-Balya: Betrayal*. New Delhi: Minerva, 2004.

_______________ , *The Folk Theatre of North Karnataka*. Dharwad: Karnataka University, 1996.

Rao, Ravi Shankar. "Rayappa Pattar. *Sangya–Balya, or Betrayal*, trans. Basavaraj Naikar" – A Review. *The Literary Criterion*, Vol. XXXX, No. 2, 2005.

Shakespeare, William. *Hamlet*. New Delhi: S. Chand & Company Ltd, 1979.

Tennyson, G.B. *An Introduction to Drama*. New York: Holt, Rinehart & Winston, 1967.

Thirumeni, M. "A Karnataka Folk-Play in English Translation" (Book Review). *Indian Book Chronicle*. Vol. XXIX, No. 9, September 2004.

Varapande, M.L. *History of Indian Theatre*. New Delhi: Abhinav Publications, 1987.

16

Success Despite Inadequacy : Analysis of Basavaraj Naikar's Translation of Sangya-Balya

— *M.C. Prakash*

The theatrical success of a play, perhaps, depends on various aspects as a play is obviously a complex art involving a wide array of paraphernalia. Though costumes and stage props may contribute severally to the effectiveness of a play, even when they are too simple to expect any contribution from them or when they are too trite to be impressive, there are other factors like the talent of actors, the emotionally packed dialogues that are delivered well, the songs, if any, that are sung to the taste of the audience etc., that may contribute to the theatrical success of a play. Even as a 'box office hit film' raises a series of thoughts in us as to what various aspects might have appealed to the spectators, a play of legendary success like Sangya-Balya sends ripples of conjectures through us about the secret of its success. Such a question has to be raised as the play appears to enjoy the excitement of retaining its mysteriousness without easily lending itself to the reader.

Sangya-Balya is a folk play popularly staged in the Northern parts of Karnataka, a state in which Kannada, a language of the Dravidian family is prominently spoken. Sangya-Balya is in a dialect of Kannada. It belongs to *Sannata*, a variety of folk theatre which generally has simple stage arrangements, plain costumes and properties. *Sannatas* generally deal with devotional theme either to Shiva or Vishnu. But there are a few plays of the *Sannata* tradition that have social themes of which our present play Sangya-Balya is one. The authorship of play is attributed to one Pattar Masthar. The term "Masthar" is a provincial corruption and dialectization of the English word Master, used here to mean a teacher. Though the word is generally used for a school teacher and may imply that the above mentioned Pattar was a teacher, as the word is used even in the case of a coach or a trainer or a director of plays, he might have been a trainer of actors for staging plays. Nevertheless he has kept his identity obscure. It is said that he had written a few other plays too. Let it be as it may, *Sangya-Balya* is one of the most popular folk plays in Kannada. Chandrashekhara Kambara's statement that 'Perhaps there is not even a single village in North Karnataka which has not staged this play', is a testimony to the popularity that the play has enjoyed. (Introduction to *Sangya-Balya*, 1980, p. v)

The credentials of *Sangya-Balya* for being branded as a folk play have to be perused. In its typical structure a *Sannata* begins with a 'gannapada', that is an invocation to the local deity for the successful performance of the play and an appeal to the audience for their co-operation to make the performance successful. It is an opera and the play develops rather through songs to the tune of which the characters dance than well constructed dialogues. An introduction in prose form before every scene sums up the action that follows and this cannot be conveyed to the audience unless it is read out aloud. Or, it may serve as a clue to the actors to evolve the dialogues offhand. Several versions of *Sangya-Balya* perhaps exist of which, two are metioned here. One of them has been edited by Keertinatha Kurtakoti and Chandrashekhara Kambar and this has the above said structure. The other version which Basavaraj Naikar has translated into English has dialogues between characters, songs, introductions in prose and even the role of chorus. One wonders whether the original text prepared by Pattar Masthar was merely a pretext. In addition, many of these versions are variants in terms of the use of the local dialect, allusions to the local deities and such other superficial details keeping the text, if there was one, in essence intact.

Sangya-Balya is a play based on an event that took place about 100 – 120 years ago at Bailawada, a village in Belgaum district in Karnataka. Eyewitnesses to the event were, it is said, alive till recently. The incident was around an illicit relationship between

Ganga, the wife of a merchant and Sangya, a wealthy villager. Balya, a bosom friend of Sangya, does the dual job of helping his friend under the force of circumstances on the one hand and helping Veeranna, Ganga's husband, murder Sangya, on the other. Ganga is an austere wife and is loyal to her husband. Her husband Veeranna has to be away from home for some time on his business and though reluctant to do so, he does it to earn money leaving her under the care of Paramma, an old woman next door. Sangya and Balya are bosom friends though the former is very well to do and the latter is equally poor. Sangya accidentally comes across Ganga and has instantaneous infatuation for her. Balya tries to win her for his friend but fails. Finally Paramma does the job of trapping Ganga. When the lovers unite the news spreads all over and Sangya is discovered by Ganga's husband who murders him with the help of his brothers. Eventually the brothers surrender to the police hoping for justice. The story, thus, is betrayal in more than one away. The murderers, in the real episode, were afraid of capital punishment. Two of them escaped it by becoming Christians. Veeranna, the husband and main culprit, however, could not escape it and was hanged to death. The event was too colorful not to attract people's attention and this, perhaps, accounts for its instantaneous popularity on stage at the time when the incident was yet green, and the persons involved were still alive. They moved the court and succeeded in effecting a ban on staging the play. The ban, for official purposes still exists on paper. But, as already mentioned, the play has not lost the freshness of appeal to people and its popularity has not suffered any decline.

But does this alone account for its success on stage? It is pretty evident that the play deals with primordial and elemental emotions which have the animosity generally present in folk literature. Pattar Masthar, the playwright, realised the dramatic potential of the event and made a play out of it. The legal complication involved and, more than that, the persons involved still being alive must have prompted him to keep himself obscure.

What did the fear of the police and court induce in the playwright, whoever he was? What did the betrayal of Balya, a poor man and apparently a parasite on Sangya suggest to the writer? Is the play a veritable folk play, albeit it a *Sannata,* telling a story with a few details of modern life making its appearance in society and is that the basis of its unprecedented popularity? These questions have been raised by critics and for our understanding two schools may be verified, one by Keerthinatha Kurtakoti, a fellow-editor of one of the text versions and K.V. Akshara, a theatre activist as well as thinker and critic.

Admitting that the play is essentially about the primordial passions Keerthinatha Kurtakoti maintains that it is set in a typical folk play structure. It has received modern influence but only in the form of superficial details like – playing cards, a marwari merchant, police, court, etc. In essence, according to him, it is a folk play in modern robes. Praising it for its poetic force, he says that the union of Ganga and Sangya and Sangya's murder which are the zenith of climactic action in the play are performed ritualistically. But he does not allow any more significance to the conversation, characters, action and the modern details of the play than yielding aesthetic joy and thus equates it with any folk play.

K.V. Akshara's is a distinct stand though it takes a curious turn at the end. The play, in essence, according to him, is a modern play in folk robes. It has retained the traditional folk-play structure but within it introduces not merely details of modern life but essentially modernity itself. Drawing profusely from the folk tradition, its form and, its typical characters, it ushers several modern issues both in details and values. Besides such details as play of cards, courts and policemen, the play documents the radical changes society was undergoing in its value system of money, wealth, friendship, wife's austerity and so on. For, Sangya and Balya are thick friends but the difference in their social and monetary status causes the discriminatory treatment meted out to them by society; Sangya is shown respect by the cloth merchant whereas Balya is not considered even trustworthy. They play cards instead of any other games generally observed in folk literature. Ganga's husband leaves her in the care of his brothers for making money as against the old couple of neighborhood who do not want to be separate from each other even for a while. Eventually after committing murder the brothers surrender to the police and court and not the village authorities. To crown it all the play keeps the question of the possibility of obtaining fair justice from the court open without concluding it with any finality. Through these explanations he arrives at the conclusion that the play is not only apparently modern in its superficial details but is so in its core. So he takes the position that instead of considering *Sangya-Balya* as the last link in the tradition of folk plays in Kannada as it has been hitherto done, its place is due to be determined as the first modern play through a proper revaluation.

The compound of modernity and the folk element in the play, according to Akshara's assessment, is more profound than this. The folk structure and folk characteristics and the modern outlook are more inseparably woven than one is likely to observe. Paramma, for instance, who emotionally blackmails Ganga and holds her on ransom to agree to the illicit relationship, is contrarily passionately attached to her husband and vice versa and, this is an anti thesis of her own role. Still she is also a typically cunning woman, a ready made character assigned with mean contrivances, and a character commonly found in folk plays in Kannada. It may be recalled here that Hamlet, despite his uniqueness, philosophical profundity and magnificence, was also a character typically labeled as 'melancholic' during the Elizabethan times. It requires great artistry to weave both the characteristics – the typically traditional with the uniquely novel.

This instance is only one example and the fusion runs deeper. The play presents a dramatic tension between the traditional and the modern – in its structure, in details, in the values, in loyalty and betrayal – of multiple facets like Ganga's to her husband, Paramma's to the assignment given her by Veeranna to take care of Ganga, Balya's dual faced betrayal and so on. The play, metaphorically, is in itself a betrayal, in the sense that it eludes the reader who tries to determine its inclination with any final judgment.

Akshara narrates another curious and meaningful experience he had while staging the play. It was his intention to present the play as an antithesis of Kurtakoti's interpretation and to show it as a modern play and not as a mere folk play. But he experienced that the play was drawing in the other direction through its details and repeated reminders. When he was inclined towards presenting it as a folk play it began to make him conscious of its underlying modern ingredients! This proved to him the inseparable presence of the two, a proof of the elusive mysteriousness of the play and the cause of its popularity till date.

While considering such an explanation, however, we should not lose sight of factors that might have impressed people and resulted in its legendary success. How far the play might have been comprehended from the point of view propounded by the above analysis is a questionable issue. Elemental passions are prominent in the play and have been expressed through potent and raw syntax. It would be nearer the truth that they have enjoyed the passionate song - conversation accompanied by dance and that the raw and rustic robustness has appealed to them, an appeal further intensified by the realistic event based on which it was written. Under such circumstances the language, action, poetic beauty, the music of words turn out to be significant factors in the success of a play.

The play, as mentioned earlier, is written in a local dialect of Kannada of North Karnataka and is in the form of folk poetry. Though not poetically rich in every bit, it is occasionally rich, forceful and uses a variety of imagery. Its musical quality is dissolved in its words and the sound of their music. The dialect used cannot be easily understood by people who are from other provinces. Then the difficulty of translating a play like this into English which is alien to the culture and idiom of the original language should be anyone's guess. It is indeed a formidable challenge. Translation, it should be accepted, is ever far from perfect leaving the reader wondering about the original text.

Naikar has ventured this formidable task and it is commendable. Choosing the version that includes chorus, songs and conversation in prose, he has attempted its rendering in English. He states in his introduction: "The text of the present play is taken from the oral text recited by Sri. Basavangowda Patil, Gangappa Hulimani and Fakirappa Madiwalar of Mutanala Village and published by Dr.Mallikarjuna Latthe, retired Professor of Kannada at Gulbarga University, Gulbarga in 1991". [Introduction to *Sangya-Balya*: Betrayal' p.xii) The chorus, songs and the conversation in prose being available the translator has ample room to exercise his imagination, linguistic skills and discreet liberty. From this point of view one wonders whether the translation has exploited the potential to the extent possible.

First of all coinage of a dialectical form in English to impress a feel of the original would have been a desirable but tough target to set as well as reach. The translator, instead, has chosen simple, standard English, perhaps considering the other type beyond the realm of probability. He has been fairly successful in his deliberately chosen path. But the success is at the expense of the original force and robustness. It is a limitation any translation is prone to and of this the translator is very much aware: "The texture of the play, a mixture of prose and poetry, has been brought out in the present translation quite clearly, though alas, the melody and rhythm of the original Kannada poetry cannot even be dreamt of being expressed even partially." (Ibid. p. xiii). An instance of his simple translation may be examined here.

Ganga : (Sings)
Come on, my dear young man
Let's ascend the bed
And have great deal of pleasure
Let's enjoy ourselves as sweetly
As milk fermented into curd, and
As sweet siesta in the afternoon.

(Ibid., Act IV, p. 78)

Other than the murder scene this is the zenith of action in the play; it is also ecstatic and very intense and in Kurtakoti's words, resembles a ritualistic performance on stage. One does not have to probe further to see how the simple rendering into English, though intentional, pales in the process thus robbing it of the original intensity. Recollecting the constraints in such an effort, Naikar says, "But, as a translator, I believe that the language of theatre transcends all linguistic barriers to communicate its vision. The non-Kannada or the western spectator will be sure to grasp the essential vision of this play in spite of the deficiencies in the translational work". (Ibid., p. xiii). Theoretically it is hard to contest the opinion. But if emotional aspect is so inseparably integrated in the linguistic component how can the experience reach a spectator or reader alien to the language and culture? It may be recalled here that in his experiment with Yakshagana presentations before non-Kannada speaking audience in Delhi, Shivarama Karanth had edited a lot of dialogues – elaborated and expanded extempore by actors on stage according to their own competence and according to the instantaneous response of the audience — and used the dance more prominently to convey the ideas and emotions. Though dance may convey a gross emotion or a vague sense, it cannot be as precise as words. This has to be admitted in spite of the fact that the yakshagana artists are many times censured for their over-loquaciousness, detouring from the essential issue, swayed by the immediate temptations of the applause of the audience. Considering the circumstances Karanth's effort can be called more a strategy in experimentation than performing the true art.

Naikar's translation has to be examined in the same light. But one cannot help wondering that the use of rhyme scheme and similar poetic techniques might have served as a better strategy to convey to the reader a glimpse into the original. Owing to this the poetry and the prose in the translation do not show a striking distinction. The following lines may be observed as an example. Balya, expressing his inability to go to Ganga's house as a convoy says.

> I cannot do it, friend,
> I cannot do it at all.
> The members of that family
> Are known for their arrogance. (Ibid. Act iii, p. 53)

And he continues :

> Sanganna, I am a poor fellow. Please, don't force me to do such a thing. I cannot do it at all.
>
> Sings. How shall I go to her house ?
> Friend, I cannot locate it.
> You give me some clue
> And make things easy for me.
>
> (Ibid., Act iii, p. 54)

Notwithstanding the fact that the original force and flavor of folk literature cannot be brought into another language a poetic syntax along with rhyme scheme would perhaps have been more effective. The elaborate introductory explanation conveys the tension within the play and its potential for multifarious interpretations. The translation could have been oriented towards this possibility had it been the translator's choice.

A translator has certain options before him. If being loyal and faithful to the original is one, taking liberties with it so that the translation can convey the original intention is another. Even here the extent of loyalty or the self permitted liberty varies based on the translator's choice. Those who opt the former assume that the original is potent enough to retain its strength in translation too. Naikar takes this stand. One is likely to feel that in the present case the strategy of taking liberty with the original would have been a more effective strategy to convey the original force. In its loyalty to the original the translation succeeds, nevertheless, in bringing the thematic aspects out. The loss of one is the gain of another. This is the inescapable plight of all translations. Dr. Naikar's translation succeeds even amidst its inadequacy.

Cited Works

Sangya-Balya, Ed. by Chandrashekhara Kambara & Keerthinatha Kurtakoti Manohara Granthamala, Dharwad, 1980.

Mavina Maradalli, K.V.Akshara, Akshara Prakashana, Baleya Hannu Heggodu, 1998.

Adhunika Kannada, Dr.K.Marulasiddappa, Lipi, Nataka, Prakashana, Bangalore, 1993.

Sangya-Balya, Dr.Basavaraj Naikar, Minerva Press India (Pvt) Ltd.: Betrayal, New Delhi, 2004.

17

An Interview with Basavaraj Naikar

— Jaydeep Sarangi

Basavaraj Naikar was born on August 1, 1949 at Naragund in he then Dharwad district (present Gadag district) of Karnataka. He has a younger brother, Chandramowli. He also has two stepbrothers, Somasekhara and Manohara and a stepsister, Girija. His mother Nilaganga was the second wife of my father Sivasankarappa, who was a Sisrastedar and sometime Mamledar in different places of Dharwad district and retired from Navalagund. His great grandfather Sri. Virabhadranayaka was a *Dandanayaka* (or Administrator) in Naragund Samsthan during the lifetime of Bhaskararao Bhave, who was defeated by the East India Company. His great-grandfather, Virabhadranayaka, laid down his life in protecting the palace of Bhaskararao Bhave in Naragund during the 1857-8 war with the British (i.e., East India Company rulers.) Their family name became Nayakaru and finally Naikar now. According to historians, my ancestors belong to the family of Shivappa Nayaka of Keladi Kingdom in southern part of Karnataka and after the fall of Shivappa Nayaka they migrated from Keladi towards the northern part of Karnataka and were shelter by the grandfather of Bhaskararao Bhave in his Samsthan about four hundred years ago.

Basavaraj Naikar's father was known in the entire district for his non-corruption in spite of being right in the midst of corrupt atmosphere of the Revenue Department. He was very pious by nature and never took his food without offering it to the family deity, Lord Sankaralinga, whose temple was just in front of our house. He was deeply influenced by his moral uprightness and pious nature.

He spent the first four years of my primary school in the Government Training College for Men at Dharwad under the care and protection of my grandmother, Lingamma. During that period he initiated into the religious poetry of Nijaguna Sivayogi by my maternal great grandfather, Sankanagowda Patil.

After his primary education at Dharwad, he returned to Naragund to continue his education in the Municipal High school. His father sent me to the local music school run by the famous musician Dattubuwa Thakurdas. He was trained in Hindustani classical music. Even as a boy of eleven or twelve he used to give public recitals along with my guru. Because of his keen interest in music his father wanted him to be a great musician like Basavaraj Rajaguru.

But fate was very cruel to his family andhim. His father expired very unexpectedly when he was hardly thirteen years. Although his father was a Government Servant they did not get the family pension simply because none in the family knew how to file the pension papers and whom to approach. Consequently they underwent a hell of economic tragedy.

Then his maternal grandfather (mother's uncle) came to their rescue and provided for their education.

After his S.S.L.C, he shifted his home from Naragund to Dharwad where he completed B.A. and M.A. in English from Karnatak University in 1972.

Please say something about your childhood

Naikar : My childhood spent in the Government Training College for Men at Dharwad was paradisal one, retrospectively speaking. But when I returned to Naragund for High School education, paradise continued until my father was alive. After his death, we had the experience of hell until I was able to get a job in the University. Although my primary interest was in music, I could not continue it further. For some time I learnt and practised sitar, but soon gave it up because of the exigencies of my life.

Your education

I passed my B.A. (with English as major and Kannada and Sanskrit as minor subjects) from Karnatak Arts College, Dharwad in 1970. During my college days I was deeply influenced and inspired by Professor K.S.Narayanacharya.

Then I passed my M.A. in English (with American and Indian Writing in English as optional subjects) from Karnatak University, Dharwad in 1972. During my University days I was deeply influenced and inspired by my learned teachers like Dr. S.T.Kallapur, Dr. M.K. Naik, Professor T.R. Rajasekharaiah, Dr. Shankar Mokashi-Punekar and Dr. R.A. Malagi among others.

I earned my Ph.D. on Shakespeare's Last Plays under the guidance of Professor T.R.Rajasekharaiah from Gulbarga University in 1986.

I was awarded D.Litt degree from the International University at Los Altos, California (USA) for my over all contribution to Literature in general and for my book, *Shakespeare's Last Plays: A Study in Epic Affirmation.*

Teaching experience

I had completed thirty-five years of postgraduate teaching experience in Gulbarga University and Karnatak University, Dharwad. I have taught British, American, Indian English, Commonwealth Literatures and Indian Literature in English Translation.

I have guided Ph.D. students in American, Comparative and Anglo-Indian Literature.

I have guided M. Phil Students in Indian English Literature.

How did you start writing short story?

During my postgraduate education, I happened to study Indian Writing in English, which was something new to me. I had a faint idea and hope of becoming a writer of Indian English then. At that time I happened to bring Mulk Raj Anand from Belgaum aerodrome to our University campus. I had an animated discussion with him about his writing, Marxism, propagandist literature etc. I was deeply influenced and inspired by his humanism, affection for youngsters and concern for the nation. He advised my friends and me not to confine our attention to only British literature but to read European and especially Russian literature extensively. He patted on my back and encouraged me to become a writer in future if I liked. I said I wanted to be one. Then he advised me to start my writing career with my autobiography. But I have yet to write my autobiography. However, I began my writing career with a short story, "Fulfilment" during my M.A. Final days. Then I went on writing stories at irregular intervals. I was deeply influenced by the writings of Mulk Raj Anand, Raja Rao, Tagore and Sri Aurobindo. I liked them for different reasons. But I did not like R.K. Narayan's novels or stories because I was not sufficiently enlightened by them. I was rather irritated by the hollowness of his vision of life, which was perhaps good for high school students. I felt reading R.K. Narayan was a criminal waste of my time. Then I decided never to waste my time on reading Narayan.

Who is your mentor?

My mentors or models are Mulk Raj Anand, Raja Rao, and Chaman Nahal and Khushwant Singh.

Who are the Indian short story writers you rate high?

Raja Rao, Mulk Raj Anand, Bhabani Bhattacharya are important short story writers according to me. Among the younger writers, Rohinton Mistry is an important short story writer. I have great admiration for them.

Do you consider your bilingualism as a virtue?

Definitely yes. All the Indian English writers should be bilingual so that they may give an authentic picture of Indian life and culture. The anglicised writers of India cannot give an authentic picture of native Indian culture although they may write good English. A bilingual writer of India is able to absorb the essence of Indian culture available in Sanskrit or his regional language like Kannada and Marathi and so on and express it in his English writings. But an anglicised writer or a writer who has had his education in English medium from his childhood or the one, who is educated in foreign universities, cannot write authentically about India, although some of them may be lucky to enjoy the media-hype.

What made you translate *Fall of Kalyana*, a play by M.M. Kalburgi dealing with the legend of Basava?

Basaveswara was one of the greatest social reformers and mystics of the world. Many of his ideas, especially the concept of *'kayaka'* are easily comparable to Karl Marx's concept of labour. But he is not presented properly and effectively by any creative writer in English so far. When Girish Karnad wrote his *Tale-Danda* and showed it to Dr. Kalburgi, the latter did not like it because of its partial and simplified presentation of Basava's life. But Karnad could not make any changes in his preconceived plot and published it as it was. As an answer and corrective to Girish Karnad's unsatisfactory play, Kalburgi wrote his *Kettittu Kalyana*, which succeeds in giving a comprehensive picture of Basava's life and mission. I translated it into English to give it international publicity.

How important is the Basava's 'third eye' in the modern context?

Basava fought against meaningless rituals in the twelfth century. The he preached alternative ideals and values like *kayaka* (i.e. physical or mental labour done with a sense of dedication to God), gender-equality and social equality and social mobility from the lower caste to higher caste purely on the basic of purity of mind and moral conduct. His ideas easily foreshadow Karl Marx's ideas of labour and Dr. Ambedkar's ideas of social equality and the modern feminists' ideas of gender-equality. Hence Basava's philosophy is ever relevant to the Indian context. He envisioned a classless and casteless society, which is almost utopian and practised it in his life by establishing a mystic Academy called *Anubhava Mantapa*, which resembles Plato's Academy. Under his charismatic influence several female saints coming from all the sections, especially downtrodden sections of society composed *vacanas* or prose poems about their socio-mystic experiences. Nowhere in the world have so many women saints composed so many *vacanas*. That shows the perennial relevance of Basava's third eye or vision of life in the modern context.

***The Thief of Nagarahalli* was short listed for Commonwealth Fiction Prize from Eurasia region in 2000. How did that influence you as a writer?**

I was very happy to know that my *The Thief of Nagarahalli and Other*

Stories was short listed for the Commonwealth Fiction Prize from Eurasia in 2000. I missed the prize very narrowly. But this event gave me sufficient confidence to continue my creative writing.

Most of the stories in *The Thief of Nagarahalli* deal with dehumanisation of man/woman. Do you have any specific reason behind this?

You have put it rightly. In modern days man has unfortunately been becoming more and more selfish, lecherous, inhuman and corrupt. My depiction of such characters is based on real people that I have seen or heard about. I am really unhappy about this moral degeneration in India, which is otherwise known as a religious country with several wonderful philosophies to boast of.

'Mother's Husband', a story in *Thief of Nagarahalli*, reminds me the incest of Oedipus and Jocasta culminating in shame, guilt, and so on. Why did you make the story read like this?

"Mother's Husband" is a folk-mythical story very popular in Karnataka. It is known as Setavi story. It shows the Oedipus complex in the Indian context and also the inevitability of Fate in human life. This story is told by village men and women in North Karnataka. It is very sketchy and vague. I have tried to give some allegorical and symbolic names to characters and make the story acceptable on a mythical level as it easily corresponds to the story of Oedipus so common in the West.

Do you think that your education in Freud has helped you to deal the complex man-woman relationship?

It is true that I have read Freud and Jung extensively and admire them. But Freudian thought is not totally acceptable to me as an Indian. I don't want to borrow his ideas for my writing although I admire him. Man-woman relationship in the Indian context has to be depicted according to the local cultural values of life.

Some of your short stories deal with falsification as the subject. Is there any definite reason behind this?

The specific reason is my righteous indignation against the falsification.

Why do you think there is a great boom of diasporic short story writers?

That is because the diasporic writers are lucky to get good international publishers and huge royalties. The same writers cannot be published in India because our publishers are a shameless lot, who do not wish to take risk and encourage new writers. They are interested in publishing only established writers, textbooks and annotated editions, which is another name for guides. Also, the diasporic writers have something new to say, which is different from the native experience of Indian writers.

How do you rate them?

The diasporic writers give us a picture of their Trisanku experience, which has to be taken note of by all the Indians. These writers are interesting because of the their depiction of the cultural clash and existential dilemmas. They extend the frontiers of Indian experience in a way. I, therefore, respect them.

Who is your desired reader?

I write for non-Kannada Indians and non-Indians in general. I do not wish to forget my Kannada roots. But I want my depiction of Karnataka life and culture to be read and appreciated by the non-Kannada readers. Just as I enjoy a Punjabi novel in English, the Punjabi or a Marathi reader should try to understand and appreciate my depiction of Karnataka life.

How would your rate yourself internationally?

I do not know how the international readers like me. But I am happy to know that some British, Canadian and European critics have appreciated my writings and compared and contrasted me with Rohinton Mistry and Amitav Ghosh among others.

Do you write in Indian English?

Yes. I write in Indian English. By this I mean, we Indians should not try to imitate the British and American writers in parroting their style. Although we use the English words and grammar, our sensibility should be Indian and it should be redolent of our culture, especially ethnic culture. It should not be colourless convent English, which is neutral without the flavour of specific culture in which it is born.

Indian writing is moving away from the pure British English that first marked colonial and postcolonial literature and is widening to include an Indianness that we've been seeing more and more of late. What do you think of this shift. What is now your "natural" way of writing?

To repeat what I have already said, the Indian writers should consciously aim at being Indian in the expression of their sensibility, by using Indian phrases, idioms and imagery and symbolism. They should fertilise the English language with local colour, myth, legend, swear words, etc., just as the African writers like Chinua Achebe, Ngugi and Wole Soyinka have done in their writings. My intention is to write like an Indian in this manner.

What do you think of postcolonial writer? Do you deliberately infuse postcolonial constructs in your writings?

To go back to native culture is to be postcolonial. I want to write like an Indian without following or imitating the Western writers. I wish to go back to my Kannada writers and Sanskrit writers for my models. This I want to do with vengeance.

Are you satisfied with critics on you?

Yes. Most of my Indian and Western critics have satisfied me by their sharp analysis and appreciation of my writings. That has given me a sense of satisfaction and confidence. Some of them have shown me my weaknesses also. That will definitely help me in future to improve my writing.

Name a few significant critics on you

Dr. Christopher Rollason, Dr. Stephen Gill, Dr. O.P. Mathur, Dr. Pashupati Jha, Dr. M.A. Jeyaraju, Dr. Usha Bande and Dr. Asha Chaubey, Dr. Alka Singh, Dr. Bhagabat Nayak, Dr. Nagendra Kumar, Dr. Jaydeep Sarangi and Dr. P.D. Deshpande are some important critics who have written very perceptive articles on my stories and novels.

Why is Indian short story not so popular among the academics?

That is because short story happens to be a minor form and the theory of short story has to be developed from the Western as well as Eastern models, which is rather difficult for the Indian academicians. They would be very enthusiastic to study the short story if the Western books are made available to them.

Do you figure in any university in India or abroad?

The University of Chicago (USA), and the Nagoya University of Japan refer to my translations and dramaturgical books.

Are you satisfied with the so-called accepted canon of Indian Writing in English in Indian Universities?

Not completely.

How about your novels?

So far I have written two novels. One is historical, *The Sun Behind the Cloud* and the other one is philosophical one, *Light in the House.* More than thirty Indian and foreign scholars have reviewed and written research articles on the first novel. Several scholars are busy writing articles on the second novel now.

What are your major themes in novels?

Colonial encounter between the a Peshwa King of Naragund kingdom and the authorities of the East India Company during 1857-58 War of Independence (wrongly described as Mutiny by the British), betrayal of faith, loss of kith and kin and kingdom and quest for freedom at any cost are the major themes in *The Sun Behind the Cloud.*

Disillusionment with the worldly life, tragic suffering, ephemerality of life, search for a guru, success in finding a guru, social reformation and communal harmony, final salvation and merger with God, are the major themes of *Light in the House.*

You seem to champion Indian social issues as major concern in novels. Do you subscribe to the idea, art is the criticism of life?

Definitely yes. Literature should be a reflection as well as a critique of life and culture.

You make a lot of authorial comments in your works. Do you want to propagate any particular idea?

I do not propagate any particular idea. But I must show some pointers in my works to help the reader understand the characters, events and the philosophy behind them.

Any immediate wish?

Right now I am giving finishing touches to a novel on the heroic Rani Chennamma of Kittur Kingdom, who fought with the East India Company around 1826, long before Rani Laxmibai of Jhansi fought with the British.

Index